Irfan Orga

Portrait

of a

Turkish

Family

PORTRAIT OF A TURKISH FAMILY

To Margarete, my wife, with love

I. O.

Contents

1	Introducing the Family	1
2	An Autocrat at the Hamam	11
3	A Purely Masculine Subject	26
4	Sariyer	37
5	The New House and Other Things	52
6	The Changing Scene	64
7	Week-End Leave and the New Bride	78
8	Muazzez Makes Her Debut	93
9	A Long Farewell	101
10	Trying to Build Again	113
11	The End of Sariyer	127
12	Disillusionment of an Autocrat	140
13	Ninety-nine Kuruş in Exchange for a Hero	150
14	Poverty Makes a Bargain	163
15	Charity School in Kadıköy	176
16	Ending with the Barber's Apprentice	191
17	Kuleli	209
18	The New Republic	222
19	A Bayram Morning and a Journey into Bleakness	231
20	Return to İstanbul	242
21	My Batman Averts a Crisis and Muazzez Finds a Beau	253
22	Feminine Affairs	259
23	The Wise Woman of Eskişehir	264
24	The Beginning of the End	272
25	Disintegrating Family	281
26	Goodbye Şevkıye	286
27	The End of the Story	302

1

Introducing the Family

I WAS BORN IN İSTANBUL ON THE 31ST OF October, 1908. I was the eldest son of my parents, my mother being fifteen at the time of my birth and my father twenty. Our house was behind the Blue Mosque, overlooking the Sea of Marmara. It stood at the corner of a small cul-de-sac, with only a low stone wall between it and the sea. It was a quiet, green place and a very little mosque stood near it, and among my earliest recollections is the soft, unceasing sound of the Marmara and the singing of the birds in the gardens. Our house was a big wooden house, painted white, with green shutters and trellised balconies front and rear. It belonged to my grandfather and my grandmother, and we lived there with them. Looking back, it seems to me that the whole of my early childhood was linked with the sound of the sea and with the voices of my parents and grandparents as they sat eating break-fast on the terrace overlooking the gardens. Still can I feel the contentment of awakening in the low, sunny room filled with the reflected white light from the sea, still hear faintly the domestic sounds from the kitchen and the high-pitched, smothered laughter of our black cook. I would creep out of bed, absurd in my old-fashioned nightshirt, and lean my head against the protective iron bars on the windows and call down to the family group below me.

This was the signal for my father to toss aside his napkin and shout up to me that he was coming. I would hastily scuttle back to my bed, laughing a bit with anticipation, for I had already learned that I was an important member of the household. Each day began for me with the throwing aside of my father's breakfast napkin, the sound of his footsteps running up the stairs, and his repeated tossing of me into the air to the accompaniment of my excited, terrified screams. But it was a terror I could not resist, and my day would not have been properly begun if my father had omitted this thrilling game. Attracted by my laughter, İnci would appear, her black eyes rolling in her small dark face and her mouth screwed up with laughter. İnci was my nursemaid, coal-black and only thirteen years old, yet she had full charge of me.

She was the daughter of Feride, the upstairs maid, and she had been born in İstanbul while her father was a servant in the palace of the sultan. After the death of İnci's father, my grandmother had taken her and her mother to our house, where, after my birth, İnci had been given to me. I loved her very much and could not have imagined life without her. She was always good-humored and used to make me shout with laughter when she rolled her eyes at me or pulled funny faces. Even when I was more than usually fractious, screaming at her or stamping my feet with temper, she would remain good-humored, merely administering a good sharp slap where it hurt most; then she would leave me to kick out my tantrums alone.

With the arrival of İnci each morning, my father would stand me on my feet, telling me to be a good boy, pat İnci's crinkly hair, and then leave us. İnci and I would stare at each other solemnly for a moment or two; then she would start to make her funny faces and waggle her flat hips, and the pair of us would burst into laughter and I would run to her, flinging my arms about her. She would commence to wash and dress me. Firmly grasping me under one arm and holding me over the shallow china basin, she would lather my face and neck with soap, most of which used to get in my eyes. And all the while I kicked the air, struggling futilely to get free. The combing of my hair was the next torture to be endured. I had thick curls that were my mother's pride and joy; they were İnci's pride, too, when they were arranged, but the arranging of them was pierced by my cries of temper and distress and İnci's commands to keep still and let her finish. My hair finally combed to her satisfaction, we would glare at each other, my scalp still smarting from the tugging of the comb and my eyes still red-rimmed from the soap. It was a daily battle and as much a part of existence as the sound of the sea or my father's kiss, but in five minutes it was all forgotten and I would go dancing down the stairs, ahead of İnci, to see my mother and my grandparents. My mother's kiss set the seal of perfection on the day. All the things that preceded it: my waking to a light-filled room, my father's tossing me into the air, my battle with İnci, were only the sweet high prelude to my mother's kiss—the kiss that was cool and light and held the perfume of roses in it.

She was very beautiful. Her hair was black and shining and coiled into smooth curls on top of her head. Her face was pale and oval, with a small, uptilted humorous mouth and great melancholy eyes that lightened like jewels when she smiled. She was always very slender and liked to dress in pastel colors, in soft shimmering silks that smelled of lavender water or eau de Cologne, and she wore long gold necklaces, twisted two or three times around her throat. She was a gentle, silent person, her hands delicate and useless-looking and weighted down with the number of flashing rings that she invariably wore. She did the most lovely embroidery and petit point, and she would take each ring off very carefully before she started, dropping them with a little chink into a small satin-lined box kept solely for that purpose. She was very elegant and might have been a noted beauty had she been born in Europe; but because she was a Turkish lady and had to wear a veil to cover her face whenever she went out, she was unknown except to the members of her family. She married my father at the age of thirteen, having been promised to him at the age of three. She rarely went out, and never alone, but spent the most of her time on the terrace

or sitting under a fig tree in the garden, much as the women of her
family had done for generations before her. She appeared perfectly
happy, content to be solely an ornament in her husband's home.
My grandparents were a devoted couple and spoiled me very much,
perhaps because I was the eldest grandchild. They seemed very old
to me, although looking back to the time of which I write, the
spring of 1914, my grandmother must have been only in her early
forties, since she too had married very young. But to the eyes of a
child a bit over five, she seemed incredibly old. It is strange now to
sit here and look back to the past and see them so clearly before me,
the people who made me and molded me and were, in part, responsible for whatever I am today; the people who are now dead and
forgotten by all who knew them, forgotten by me too, until I began
to look backward to my far-off childhood. I did not know I was
capable of remembering so much, but now that I have begun, the
subconscious yields its secrets and the memories come crowding
thick from the buried years. I cannot describe my grandfather, yet
I remember dimly the tall old man who used to give me sweetmeats
and fruit fresh from the garden, with the dew still on it. He used
to take me for walks while İnci attended to my small brother or
helped Feride with the upstairs work. It was the custom after breakfast for my grandfather to go to a coffeehouse and smoke the
narghile, or hookah pipe, and after my fifth birthday I used to be
taken with him. He would sit in front of an open window in the
coffeehouse, leaving me to play in the gardens, ever under his
watchful eye. But sometimes he would engage in earnest conversation with his friends, and his eye became not quite so observant;
and then I used to play with the dirt, making mud castles for myself, a lost, rapt little boy, absorbed with the feel of the wet mud
running through my fingers. I would be oblivious to the stones
cutting into my knees, but presently a sharp slap on the arm would
recall me to the present. Letting the remaining mud trickle dreamily
through my fingers, I would look up to find my grandfather staring
down at me with eyes that pretended to be fierce. All the way home
he would make me walk a little behind him, like a puppy with its

tail between its legs, crestfallen and very conscious of the old man's displeasure. Upon arrival at home I would be delivered into the hands of İnci, who looked severely at the dirt on my person and on my clothes, then whisked me off to be washed in time for luncheon.

I remember that one day when I was in the coffeehouse gardens, I wandered over to the large, ornamental pool in the center, intent upon playing "boats," a game that was as thrilling to me then as it is today to my small son at the Round Pond in Kensington Gardens. My game, however, was not played with boats but with various pieces of sticks. On this particular day, in my absorption, I leaned too far over and fell in up to my neck with a terrible splash. The water was icy cold. My clothes held me down and I thought I was going to drown. My piercing screams brought my grandfather and a couple of waiters running at the double, and I was unceremoniously fished out, blue in the face and coughing up what seemed to be gallons of water. And oh! the safety of my grandfather's arms. I was taken into the coffeehouse, stripped of all my clothes, and wrapped in a blanket while a messenger was dispatched to my home for dry clothing. Hot milk was forced through my chattering teeth, and my grandfather, looking white and shaken, scolded me without ceasing. I was finally taken home in dry clothes, still trembling with fear and cold. My grandfather refused to speak to me. After that episode I was left to kick my heels at home for days on end. My grandfather's morning kiss became fraught with ice, and he would pay no attention to me when I timidly inquired after his health. He would stalk off to the coffeehouse, leaving me on the terrace with my mother and my grandmother. I used to play in the garden under an apple tree that was my retreat when the burdens of the world became too much. When I grew tired of being alone, I would wander back to the house in search of İnci. Hacer, the cook, would perhaps softly call me into the kitchen, giving me *lokum* (Turkish delight) to eat, then shooing me off quickly lest my grandmother discover me there. Hacer, like İnci, was my friend. She was enormously, grotesquely fat, and when she laughed her whole body rippled and her eyes were lost in rolls of flesh. She had been with my grandmother for many years and was intensely jealous of Feride, whom she suspected of receiving more favors than herself. She used to make secretly for me little *pastas* with funny faces or give me cloves to eat, a forbidden luxury. Sometimes, when I knew my grandmother to be safely out of the way, I would steal in to Hacer and she would give me cakes. If she were in an especially good humor, she would dance for me and sing quaint old Turkish songs that made the heart ache with melancholy. Her dancing was a joy to me. Her gigantic old stomach performed lewd posturings, her unconfined breasts shook merrily, and her backside did a little dance all its own. Attracted by my shouts of laughter, İnci would come in search of me, pulling me sharply by the ear out of the kitchen; or, worse still, my grandmother would hear me and come in like the silent wind, her face a stony threat, and poor Hacer's breasts would give a final leap into the air, her performance coming to an abrupt end.

My mother was most likely to be found in the salon, that is, if she were not sitting out in the garden or paying calls with my grandmother. But my grandmother only occasionally liked to ride behind the cream-colored horses in the phaeton; and as my mother was not permitted to go driving alone, she rarely left home. If this arrangement bored her, she gave no sign. Mother displayed no temper, being invariably tranquil. If I were to wander into the salon to find her sitting there, she would lay down her embroidery, pat the seat beside her, and invite me to tell her what I had been doing with myself. More often than not I would refuse the invitation, feeling constrained in the face of such perfect tranquillity and preferring the more robust ordinariness of İnci. But İnci in the mornings was usually helping Feride or doing something for Mehmet, my baby brother, and the upper regions of the house were forbidden territory for me. Bored and lonely, I would seek the garden again, climbing the little apple tree to watch the passing boats on the Marmara. Many long childish hours I dreamed away in that tree, listening to the soft crying of the sea gulls and only being recalled to the present by İnci's voice ordering me to come into the house.

One morning my father awakened me early and, after tossing me two or three times into the air, told me that my grandfather wanted to see me in his room. I rushed to him, peering cautiously through the door, and saw him sitting up in his bed, his eyes twinkling under the white nightcap pulled low over his forehead. He looked comical and called to me to come in. I leaped into his bed joyfully, for I had smarted under his displeasure and was wildly happy to be here in this great, adventurous bed again. It was a bed that was exciting to explore and held possibilities of delicious terrors for a small boy who ventured too far beneath the clothes, delving deeper and deeper into the blackness while Grandfather pretended to be a fierce old lion, emitting the most awful roars. When my screams became too hysterical, he would pull back all the clothes and I would creep out again, my heart still pounding. He would instruct me to ring for Feride, and when she appeared he would ask for my breakfast to be served with his. The morning of which I write was ho exception to the general rule. We played and romped and growled fearfully at each other, and when I was taken away to be dressed my grandfather called after me that I could accompany him to the coffeehouse later on. Then I really knew that we were friends again.

Yet we did not go to the coffeehouse after all, for he suddenly changed his mind as we were setting out. And it is perhaps this one thing that makes that day, with all its events, still remarkably clear in my memory. For we walked that day by the Marmara, the first and last time I ever walked and talked with my grandfather, for never before had I been any farther with him than the local coffeehouse. We walked that brilliant young day like old comrades. Nowadays, whenever I walk beside the Marmara on just such a soft young day, I am again a child of five, skipping along beside the lost figure of the kindly old man. And that morning, for all his talk, he seemed to lean more heavily on his stick; presently he sat down on a rock, saying he was tired. He told me I could play in the sand if

I did not go too near the sea. I started to hunt for shells, and whenever I found a particularly nice one I would shout to him, telling him of my find. But once when I shouted he did not reply, and when I turned to look at him he was gesturing to me with his hands.. I ran to him, feeling, as children instinctively feel, with that little extra sense of perception that is in them, that something had gone wrong with the morning. Yet equally instinctively I refused to recognize the perception, so that even though I ran to him I was rebelliously shouting that I wanted to play, I wanted to play. . . .

He said: "Grandfather is not well, my darling. Let us go home quickly."

And I gathered my shells mutinously, but with a very little icy thread of fear touching my heart.

It is odd how intuitive children and animals are. Today if any danger threatened I doubt if I would have the clear warning I had as a child. Sophistry and the years have combined to stifle, to overlay that quick animal sense, and I believe I could actually walk into danger without so much as a flicker of the heart. But that day I felt it surrounding my grandfather like an aura.

I held his hand tightly, my heart almost suffocating me with the premonition I had. Halfway home we met the imam from the little mosque, and he came up to us, looking concerned and speaking softly to my grandfather. I felt a great, overwhelming relief that another person was here to share my fear. The imam took my grandfather's arm and slowly, painfully slowly, we ascended the last long hill that led to home.

Once at the house I was delivered to İnci, who was in the garden with Mehmet. Mehmet was eighteen months old at that time, and just starting to walk. He was supposed to be delicate and I resented him, for whenever I wanted to shout and run, I was inevitably hushed by İnci or my mother and warned that he was sleeping. It seemed to me that he never did anything else but sleep, and I despaired of the day ever coming when he would be considered big enough for me to play with. But I also sometimes loved him and liked to stroke his soft cheek and feel the down on his head. Now and then he would call me to him, curling his fingers over my hand and chattering. The day we brought my grandfather home, I was unable to respond to the laughter in his eyes, for I was consumed with uneasiness and curiosity.

İnci's dark eyes were big with question, and she asked what it was that had happened on the walk.

We stayed out in the hot garden all through the morning, and when we went into the dining room for luncheon my mother looked odd and lonely seated alone at the great table. We children and İnci used to eat at a smaller table in a little recess, and all through that meal I was conscious of my mother as she toyed with her food and poured many glasses of water for herself from a crystal carafe. In the middle of luncheon Feride came hurriedly in, announcing that the doctor had arrived; without any ceremony, and leaving her meal half-touched, my mother left the room. İnci called to Feride and asked what was the matter, but Feride, with a quick warning look at me, said she did not know.

During the afternoon my father was sent for; and I remember his thin worried face as he passed me, without being aware of me, where I stood in the hall.

İnci took us to the playroom, for it was too hot to play any more in the garden. I vaguely recall playing with bricks, with Mehmet crawling over a large mat on the floor and İnci sitting in a rocker by the window, a pile of mending at her side. We were all listless with the heat. After a little while my father came for me and, picking me up in his arms, said: "Grandfather is very ill but he wants to see you. Will you be a good brave man and come with me?"

I nodded dumbly and we left the room together, the tall young man and the solemn little boy who was once again overcome by the events of the morning.

In my grandfather's room it was twilight. The windows stood open, but the cool green shutters had been fastened against the glare of the afternoon sun.

My mother was seated on one side of the bed, holding a silver pitcher which I knew to be filled with water from the grave of

Mohammed. I knew also that this precious water was only to be used in times of extreme emergency. My grandfather had once made the pilgrimage to Mecca and brought this water back with him; afterward he was always known by the title of Haci, signifying that he had been to Mecca.

My grandmother stood by one of the windows, staring through the little spaces in the shutters. The fierce white glare from the gardens must have hurt her eyes, yet she seemed oblivious to it. She stood perfectly still, like a statue, and the tears poured unchecked down her cheeks. It was a shock to see my usually composed grandmother crying so unrestrainedly, and it tightened the feeling of fright that already half-paralyzed my heart.

A doctor was washing his hands in a corner quietly, quietly, making scarcely any sound.

As we came in, my mother put the silver jug on a side table and took me from my father. He went to the other side of the bed and took up the Koran, beginning to read aloud from it in his soft, musical Arabic. I stood looking at my grandfather, awed by the unaccustomed sight of so much solemnity surrounding him. He moved his fingers and my mother lifted me up to him, saying, "Father, this is İrfan."

He laid his heavy old hand on my head as though giving me his blessing, then his fingers moved feebly through my curls and down, down, slowly down over my face. I kissed his hand and ached with unshed tears. He tried to say something and the doctor came quickly over, motioning to me with his head, and my mother took me out. She told me to go back to İnci, then left me and returned to my grandfather's room, the door closing gently behind her. I started to cry suddenly, there on the quiet landing, and still I remember, as if it were yesterday, how a big fat wood pigeon flew past the window, coo-cooing in his soft throaty voice.

It is still the best remembered sound from that day.

2

An Autocrat at the Hamam

NOW AND THEN, USUALLY ABOUT ONCE IN a week, my grandmother had a sociable turn of mind, and when these moods came upon her she invariably went to the *hamam*. Hamams, or the Turkish baths, were hotbeds of gossip and scandal-mongering, snobbery in its most inverted form, and the excuse for every woman in the district to have a day out. Nobody ever dreamed of taking a bath in anything under seven or eight hours. The young girls went to show off their pink and white bodies to the older women; usually the mothers of eligible sons were in their minds for this purpose, for these would, it was hoped, take the first opportunity of detailing to their sons the finer points of so-and-so's naked body. Marriages based on such hearsay quite frequently took place, but whether or no they were successful few of us had any means of knowing.

In the hot rooms of the hamams little jealousies and rivalries were fanned into strong fires, and very often fights took place between the mothers of attractive daughters vying for the favors of the same young man.

As against the mothers of daughters, the mothers of sons took pride of place. There was a sort of sharp dividing line drawn between them, and it was quite easy for a stranger to tell which of the

plump, matronly ladies had the best wares for sale. For whereas the
mothers of daughters were inclined to laugh much, to draw attention to their family groups, the mothers of sons lay aloof on their
divans, too conscious of their own superiority to contribute to the
general noise and scandalizing. They would lazily nibble fruit, eye
the simpering, posturing young girls critically, and sometimes accept
the offer of having their backs washed by some ravishing young
creature. However, this was granted with such condescension that
immediately the wildest speculations were engendered in the other
female breasts as to why such an obvious favor had been shown at
all. The back washing concluded, the ravishing young creature
would be dismissed; then one by one the mothers of the ignored
daughters would sidle up to the devilish old autocrat who had just
had her back washed and whisper the most damning things about
the character of the recent elated but now vanished back washer.

My grandmother had no eligible sons for sale, but this did not
prevent her from making her presence felt.

Sociability would develop in her, over a period of days, until one
morning she would grandly announce to my mother that on such
and such a day she would go to the hamam. My mother, having no
social conscience or the nature maliciously to enjoy intrigues or
broken or pending romances, rarely accompanied her to the baths.
Generally she sighed at the thought of all the extra work my grandmother's decision was going to make for the servants.

Quite frequently I was taken by my grandmother, although after
my fifth birthday the seemliness of taking such a grown-up young
man to a place full of naked women was strongly doubted by the
other members of the family. My grandmother, however, who
would be the first to object to this in other people, always set aside
the idea that five was a great age and would insist on taking me
with her.

She always engaged private rooms for herself at the hamam:
a room for disrobing and another for washing herself, feeling that
decidedly she could not be expected to mix entirely with the common herd. Sociability could only go so far. I well remember the

flutter she caused in the household when she announced one day that on the morrow she would go to take her bath. It practically paralyzed the administration, so to speak, for it could not be lightly decided that one was going to the hamam less than twenty-four hours hence. Preparation was necessary. Special foods had to be bought and cooked and packed. The private rooms had to be booked. My mother vainly tried to dissuade her to wait a day longer, but this interference unfortunately only had the result of making my grandmother's determination stronger.

Feride was sent to the hamam to warn them of our arrival on the morrow, for it already had been decided that I should go too. Looking back, I have a suspicion that Feride rather enjoyed this sort of mission; she had lived so long with my grandmother that she quite enjoyed creating sensations and bullying the servants of others by right of her exalted position as personal factotum to my grandmother, whose social position was undoubtedly the greatest in the neighborhood. The owners of the hamam were, of course, well acquainted with the various foibles and idiosyncrasies of my grandmother and thought nothing of giving her private rooms whenever she wished—even on occasion dispossessing women who had previously engaged them. My grandmother was a great force; but, because she knew this very well, she shamelessly took advantage of it and altogether behaved like royalty.

The rooms having been reserved for her, the next thing of importance was to have long and futile discussions with Hacer as to the sort of food she wished to have prepared for eating in the hamam. Murat, the coachman, was dispatched posthaste to the market, just when my mother wanted him for something else, with a basket almost as big as himself, for he was a small man. He invariably returned with enormous quantities of food, most of which would undoubtedly be wasted. But my grandmother, at her most gracious now that she had gained her own way, and with hospitality simply dripping from her, explained this extravagance away by saying she liked a large selection of food from which to choose and that in any case she liked to feel that the unfortunate ones left at home would enjoy the same delicacies that she would be enjoying at the hamam. Food was good at all times in the house, for she always ordered everything herself, never allowing my tranquil mother to express any preference, completely disbelieving that any-body's ideas could be better or more original than her own. Further-more, she did not encourage originality of thought, cherishing the belief that this, when related to food, ruined the digestion, injured the lining of the stomach, tore the nervous system to little pieces, and was the cause of every known disease.

All that memorable day Hacer was kept busy over the cooking stove. *Dolmas* were made from vine leaves stuffed full of savory rice and currants and nuts and olive oil. Every few minutes my grand-mother would dart into the kitchen to interfere and offer her un-wanted advice to the more experienced, phlegmatic Hacer. My grandmother tasted everything. This was an awful business for Hacer, and on these nerve-racking occasions I would wait for her to burst into wild tears of rage or swipe all the crockery off the tables and have a fine display of hysterics. Poor Hacer was always the luckless one. She would stare apprehensively as my grandmother critically poked and sniffed at her cooling dolmas, and nine times out of ten she was ordered to prepare and cook fresh ones as those already made were only fit for the Christians to eat.

Feride was called in to superintend the making of *kadin-gobegi*, heavy, syrupy doughnuts which when properly made are light as air and heaven to eat. I was very fond of kadin-gobegi and purposely delayed in the kitchen, looking for a chance to steal one of them as they were cooling in the rich syrup. The advent of the supercilious Feride caused sulkiness to mount in the breast of Hacer, and she muttered many unmentionable things beneath her breath.

With her beloved Feride safely installed in the kitchen and noth-ing likely to go wrong—or so she fondly hoped—my grandmother next went upstairs to her bedroom, taking İnci with her, to my mother's annoyance, since this left Mehmet and me with no super-vision. İnci was instructed to sort out the clean linen and bathrobes and innumerable towels that would be required at the hamam. Bars of soap, a large bottle of eau de Cologne, and all the other appurtenances needed for the correct toilette of a lady about to take her bath were brought from their hiding places. İnci was told to pack all these things in little embroidered cloths that were kept especially for this purpose, and I was several times called upstairs and warned of all the things I must not do at the hamam. By the time my grandmother had herself uselessly run up and down the stairs several more times, she suddenly came panting into the salon and threw herself, without the least semblance of elegance, into a large chair. She fanned herself vigorously, complaining to my mother that she was very tired and that she could not understand why it was that whenever she wished to take a bath it was she who had to do all the work about the place. Hacer, she said, was more than ever useless and she did not know why she continued to keep her, unless it was because she felt pity for her, knowing that no other household in the world would keep her for more than a day. My mother, who had a soft spot for the maligned Hacer, here interrupted to tell my grandmother that, on the contrary, when she went to the hamam she completely disorganized the entire house. Warming to her subject in the face of my grandmother's disbelieving attitude, she said that here she was, starving, with none to prepare a meal for her; her children were hungry too; and because Hacer had already been twice told to throw away all the dolmas and had spent the entire morning cooking, she felt that the rest of the day would go by in similar fashion until we would all die of hunger. This considerably enraged my grandmother, who thought the whole accusation very unjust indeed; then she added chaos to chaos by impetuously ringing for Murat and ordering him to run immediately to the butcher to buy meat, as everyone was hungry. Murat, who was hungry himself, went with great haste lest my grandmother change her mind again. She, with great indignation at being so unjustly accused, went off in a temper to the kitchen to instruct Hacer to leave everything and prepare luncheon because my mother, worn out with all the embroidering she had done that morning, was starving.

She suddenly recollected that henna had to be applied to her hair and called Feride away from the kadin-gobegi, demanding to know why·the henna had not been prepared before this time. Her obstreperousness affected us all, but me in particular, so that I was continually fractious, eventually reducing İnci to weak tears of rage.

"If you go to the hamam," she ground out at me through tightly clenched teeth, "you will come home looking like a lobster. I shall hold your head under the boiling water until you die and pull your nose until it is as long as an elephant's nose!" Sufficiently intimidated, I fled to Hacer, who gave me sugar to eat and sat me on a high chair so that I could watch what she was doing. But the hot smell of food overcame me; and in any case I was far too excited to sit still for very long, so I demanded to be lifted from the high chair and went in search of my grandmother. I discovered her in her bedroom, and as she was in a gracious mood she permitted me to enter just inside the door to watch what Feride was doing. I could not help laughing when I saw her, because she looked so funny. She was sitting in a straight-backed chair in front of a long mirror; Feride, beside her, was placing layer after layer of clean white paper over the revolting brown mess of henna that covered her hair. A silver cup with the remains of the brown mess adhering to its sides stood on a low plaited stool beside them, and next to it was a Moorish table piled with snowy towels and a tray of small gold hairpins.

Because my grandmother had henna on her hair, she was unable to go to the salon or the dining room, so she stayed in her room and ate lokum out of a large dish on her lap and drank rose sherbet. She then languidly refused the tray of luncheon brought to her by İnci, saying she was not hungry and that she needed very little to keep her going. I begged to be allowed to eat the tray of refused food, and permission was indulgently granted; but my mother was furious when she heard of it and sent İnci to fetch me to the dining room. I regretted having to leave the close, scented atmosphere of my grandmother's room and bit İnci's finger on the way downstairs in revenge.

After luncheon was over, Feride reprepared all the bathrobes and lingerie İnci had so carefully packed during the morning. Feride put little bags of lavender between each fold, annoyed because İnci had forgotten to do this. The smell of lavender always lingered in our house, for all the drawers and cupboards were full of the herb, which was tied into little muslin bags and placed between the linen.'

Every year the wild, gaunt-looking gypsies used to gather it in the hills and then come down to the city to sell laden baskets full of its sweet perfume. Lavender grew in a corner of the garden too, but we always bought from the gypsies. I remember a merry-eyed gypsy girl who used to come to the house when I was small. She would stand in the street singing her lavender song and then she would be brought into the house by Feride, who would bargain astutely for the lavender. Hacer would make Turkish coffee for her to drink, and I would steal into the kitchen to look at the dark, alien face of the gypsy girl as she sat on the table and swung her long, bare legs. Sometimes my grandmother would order Hacer to give the gypsy a good meal; afterward she would be called to the salon to read the future for my mother and grandmother, who both had a childlike belief in such things. She would be given a cushion and would sit on this, just inside the door, afraid to advance too far into the elegant room, careful not to put her bare, dirt-grimed feet on the carpets. Having read the amazing things revealed in her shining crystal ball and thoroughly fevered my imagination, she would take out a handful of dried broad beans from a bag attached to the wide belt she wore, extricate a handkerchief, remarkable for its cleanliness, and some blue glass beads, and commence the fortunetelling all over again. When this was finished, my grandmother would toss her a gold coin which she would catch dexterously. I remember that she had long slim fingers, the filbert-shaped nails always tinted with henna, and a brown little face with a wide mouth that always seemed to be laughing. She wore strange, exotic garments of every hue, and her shining black hair had twisted through it many brightly colored glass beads. She would tell us about her life in the tents and of her husband, who made baskets to sell to the peasants or sometimes to the owners of rich houses in

İstanbul. Oddly alluring, she gave one the impression that she was as sharp as a monkey, and I used to imagine a fine, swashbuckling husband for her, with swarthy face and gleaming white teeth and gold earrings dangling, flashing in the sun as he moved his leonine head. He would be a tall, muscular man, with a magnetism to match the strange charm there was about her. I was very disappointed one day when he accompanied her to our house, hoping to sell one of his baskets to my grandmother for Murat's use. He was small and thin and ugly in a frightening way, with a pock-marked face and a cruel mouth and eyes that looked as if they were perpetually narrowed by avarice. He exuded danger and dark deeds on a windy night, and I was very much afraid of him. He was jealous of the gypsy girl who was his wife, and I noticed that she was very subdued in his presence, the laughter dimmed in her eyes. He was very free with Feride, who became taut and haughty and almost incredibly like my grandmother in a rage. He slapped Hacer's rolling backsides several times, roaring with laughter each time she protested. I fled from the kitchen to the salon, my eyes for some reason or other blinded with tears. I felt a helpless, childish rage against him and his coarseness, and pity for the poor, merry gypsy girl he had married.

I did not know that life and people are seldom what one expects them to be.

When my father arrived home that evening, hampers of food, which had been parceled by Feride, were stacked in the hall, and the packages containing the clean linen and various other sundries stood beside them. My father commenced to laugh when he saw them, remarking to my mother that all the world knew when my grandmother was going to take a bath.

She came down the stairs as he was saying this, her hands blazing with jewels and a large, brightly colored silk scarf tied over her head. She looked extremely odd with her small, slender body and swollen head. The drying henna and the innumerable towels still covered it, but she had made a concession to polite society by winding her gay scarf over them all so that she could eat in the dining room with the rest of the family. "I am going to the hamam tomorrow," she said, and my father, with a very grave face and making a gesture in the direction of the parcels, said that this was not difficult to understand. He frowned, however, when he heard that I was going, saying that I was too big for this sort of thing now. My grandmother very soon overrode his objections and with a pretty little display of femininity promised that this would be the last time she would take me.

When my father finally gave in to her cajolery, I was so excited I could scarcely eat a thing, for the thought of his almost certain refusal had been gnawing at me all day.

Murat arrived at the front gates with the polished phaeton and the restive, impatient cream-colored horses, their harnesses jingling musically each time they tossed their beautiful heads. Feride handed to Murat the things needed for our day and then importantly returned to the house to escort my grandmother, who was perfectly capable of conducting herself, into the carriage. I walked behind them feeling rather grand, and Murat looked reproving when he saw me, making the expected remark that I was too big to be taken with the women. Secure in parental permission, however, I ignored him and took a tight, defiant hold of my grandmother's hand. When we arrived at the hamam, the attendants came out to meet us, bowing very deeply to my grandmother but looking a little startled and uncertain when they caught sight of me beside her. They did not make any remark, however, but led the way to the disrobing room that had been prepared for us.

I had difficulty in keeping up with my grandmother's quick, disdainful steps but nevertheless refused to let go of her hand. We passed through a vast marble hall with divans grouped against the walls and little frosted glass doors that opened off to the private rooms. There were many women lying about on the divans, and in the center of the hall was a pool and a fountain, the waters making a cool, tinkling sound as they rose and splashed into the stone basin.

Many bottles of *gazoz*, a type of soda water, stood cooling in the pool, for this was a communal room and it was here that all the women would eat and gossip when they had completed their washing. We passed through without looking to right or to left; in fact, I kept my eyes firmly on the ground as I had been warned to do. Feride had taken hold of my arm and, stealing a glance at her, I noticed the disdain on her black, finely featured face, the nostrils lifted as though there were a bad smell beneath them. Up a flight of stairs we went and were shown to a small room where we started to undress ourselves. I was the first ready, and then Feride went to assist my grandmother. An attendant hovered outside the door, waiting for orders; when we were ready, Feride called to her and handed her our soaps, eau de Cologne, and the large silver cup that was used for rinsing our bodies.

We wore *takunyas* on our feet, a sort of wooden sabot. Mine were painted gold, I remember, with richly colored red roses outlined on the fronts, and my grandmother wore black ones with jewel-studded heels. We made a terrible noise with them on the bare stone floor. She looked very elegant in her rose-colored bathrobe, her hair caught back from her ears and temples with little gold-topped combs. Feride managed to convey all the dignity of the East in a plain, severe white robe wrapped closely about her lean figure. Solemnly we left the disrobing room and followed the attendant to the room where we would wash ourselves and later eat all the food we had brought with us.

Again we had to pass through the communal room where some of the women were still washing themselves, while others lay about on the divans. There was great noise in this place, and the women shouted across each other's heads, their high-pitched voices carrying the scandal and the bits of gossip they had all retained until this meeting in the room of the hamam—for nowhere else would gossip be so spicy in the relating.

As graciousness and sociability were the keynotes of my grandmother's mood on hamam days, she naturally halted our little procession while she inquired after the healths of the women, who, a little overcome by this magnificent condescension, were practically reduced to silence.

My grandmother looked at the naked young girls with the critical eye of a connoisseur; now and then, when a figure displeased her, she would clap her hands together in a very expressive gesture denoting disapproval, saying that so and so was too thin altogether, that her backside rattled, and that she would never be able to find a husband until her figure improved. "Give her plenty of *baklava*," she advised the mother, and everybody would feel embarrassment for the blushing girl and the affronted mother, but my grandmother was always unaware that she embarrassed anybody.

Next she singled out a ripe young beauty for approval and patted the plump thighs appreciatively. This drew the attention of all the mothers of sons, whereupon my grandmother stated, with great simplicity, that if *she* had a marriageable son, this was the very girl she would select for him.

The small girls eyed her with dislike, but as she did not notice this it did not matter. She only had eyes for the budding, well made young maidens who were thirteen years old or thereabouts, and she would tell some delighted mother at great length that she would certainly be well advised to marry such a daughter as soon as possible to the strongest young man that could be found.

"He will know how to delight her," she would boom loudly, "but make sure he is as strong as a lion; otherwise, with those fine legs of hers, she will kill him."

This caused a great silence until the women suddenly caught sight of me lurking in the background and gasped with horror that a young man of the advanced age of five years had been brought among them, a witness to their nakedness.

They curled into the most unnatural positions, trying to cover their bodies and sniggering into their protective arms rude remarks about my male organs. My grandmother frowned at this levity, however. She might be outspoken herself regarding other people's property, but none might dare to make a remark about hers.

Sociability temporarily suspended, she drew herself up haughtily and made a sign to the patiently waiting attendant that she was ready.

Our little procession moved on again, the clattering of our takunyas effectively drowning the remarks that were being made about me, and about my grandmother, too, for that matter. Before we reached the room where we were to wash, we had to cross a narrow channel where the dirty water was running to the drains. We could not cross this, however, until we had all solemnly spit three times into the dirty water and said "Destur bismillah" to appease the evil spirits that always lurk in dirty places. In old Turkey one had to be very civil to the evil spirits. If one did not say "Destur bismillah," meaning "Go away in the name of God," the evil spirits of the drains might very likely feel insulted by the lack of respect shown toward them and give one a push in the back guaranteed to land one face downward in the channel of dirty water; they might even cause one side of one's body to become temporarily afflicted with paralysis. Therefore we never took any chances with them. We were always most respectful. Having on this occasion discharged our obligations, we were able freely to cross the dirty water and proceed without any further hindrance to the washing room.

This room was very large, but because it was for private use there was only one *kurna*, or large water basin, in it, instead of the twenty or so in the communal washroom. In one side of the marbled wall was a niche where Feride immediately placed our baskets of food. The attendant put the soap, the towels, and the eau de Cologne on another shelf and left us, and Feride promptly pulled a curtain, made of rough toweling, into position over the arched doorway so that none might catch sight of us at our ablutions. She then proceeded to wash the kurna and the walls and the floor with soap that had been brought with us for that purpose. While she labored, my grandmother exhorted her to wash everything three times, otherwise it could not be said to be washed at all; and if every place was not perfectly clean, evil spirits would cling to the dirt and perhaps do us some injury while we were washing. I sat on the cleaned part of the floor, apprehensive lest Feride fail to wash everything thoroughly, and visualised grinning, destructive demons lurking invisibly in the air, waiting to pounce on me when I disrobed.

Perspiring freely by the time she had finished, Feride placed more towels about the floor for us to sit on and then lay down herself and blew soap bubbles to amuse me and make me forget all about the evil spirits. Washing was the worst part of the visit to the hamam; for Feride, like İnci, had no mercy on me and lathered me from head to foot three times, making sure I could not escape from her by holding me securely between her strong legs. She put on a sort of loofah glove on her right hand and scrubbed and kneaded my body with it until great ugly lengths of black dirt were brought to the nearly bleeding surface and released. Despite my fierce cries she never relaxed; and just when I thought the worst was over, she repeatedly filled the silver cup with what seemed to me practically boiling water and threw it over my head and body until I finally emerged, smarting and tingling all over and looking like a lobster.

While my grandmother was being subjected to similar treatment, with the wily Feride all the time admiring the delicate, unlined texture of the creamy skin, I was forced to lie down to rest, bored by this part of the day and longing for the excitement of the food to be given me. Food always had twice its appeal if offered in the hamam. I did manage once, however, to slip out of the room unnoticed and wander into the communal room, without my bathrobe, thinking to refresh myself with the sound of the cool fountain that played there.

The women watched me with a sort of hostile interest, sharply calling the younger children to their sides, and I stood alone in the middle of the large room, awkward and shy, yet reluctant to return to the steam and overpowering boredom of the private room. A fat Armenian woman called me over to her and offered me an apple, but I had been taught never to accept anything from anyone outside my family, so I could only thank her and decline the offer, though my stomach turned over with longing to bite at the cool red apple in her hand.

She coaxed me to her side and put a fat, kindly arm about me, whereupon a young woman called impudently: "Madame! It would have been better to have brought your husband here. Why, he's not as big as my little finger, and I doubt if he would be of much use to you."

The other women laughed coarsely at this, and the fat Armenian woman grew red with anger and annoyance.

"It would be better not to let the grandmother hear you talking like that about him," she said, and many more remarks were passed about me. Some of the women stopped eating to see if there was going to be a fight between the fat Armenian and the young Turkish woman. I escaped and ran back to the private room, to the more kindly influence of my grandmother and Feride, and even my posterior seemed to be blushing with the dreadful sense of embarrassment that I felt.

When I got back, my grandmother was resting and Feride was in the act of setting out plates of food on a white tablecloth that was spread over a section of the floor. We all sat cross-legged in our bathrobes and ate with great appetite the *lahana dolmasi* (stuffed cabbages) which the despised Hacer had somehow managed to cook to perfection after all. We ate *köftes*, a savory meat rissole; *börek*, a pastry stuffed with white cheese, eggs, and parsley; *tursu*, a salad consisting of pickled vegetables, mostly cabbages, green peppers, and fat golden cucumbers.

An attendant brought us iced gazoz to drink, and then we ate Feride's specialty, kadin-gobegi, and afterward were so overcome with sleepiness that my grandmother became quite querulous with my slowness in finishing. She brusquely ordered Feride to clear away the dirty remains of our feast and said that she wished to sleep. I curled myself up in a ball beside her, belching unashamedly to show my appreciation of all the good food I had eaten, and then I went to sleep too.

When I awoke, the day at the hamam was almost over.

My grandmother was in the act of bathing herself for the last time, and Feride, noticing my awakening, promptly seized the opportunity to wash me again. Renewed by her sleep, she put as much energy into washing as though the dirt of centuries lay over me.

The day was dying. Crockery, dirty linen, and the silver washing cup were packed away by Feride. The empty eau de Cologne bottle lay forlornly in the center of the floor: it would not be wanted again.

My grandmother put on her rose-colored bathrobe, helped me into mine, and we went down the long echoing corridor to the room where we had left our clothes in the morning, a lifetime ago it seemed now.

I averted my eyes as we passed the groups of remaining women. Many of them who were there in the morning had already gone home, but those who still remained called out respectfully to my grandmother, wishing her good health and continued prosperity, but she was in no mood for trivialities. She ignored them all. The time for sociability was over for another week.

```
   *        *
        *
   *        *
<><><><><><><>

   3

<><><><><><><>

   *        *        A Purely Masculine Subject
        *

   *        *

        *                T
   *        *            HE LONG HOT SUMMER SPED BY AND MY
grandfather's death was eclipsed for me by the autumnal approach
of my sixth birthday and—*circumcision!*
```

Circumcision was only a word to me, but as time went on it
became the most exciting word in the world. It cropped up frequently in my parents' conversations. My father would start the ball
rolling by perhaps remarking that Ali, the son of the local school-
master, had been circumcised a few days ago and that the whole
neighborhood was still talking of his bravery. This was the signal
for my grandmother to look disbelieving, furiously clack her knit-
ting needles, and remark disparagingly, "What! That unhealthy-
looking child! Impossible for him to show any bravery; it isn't in his
blood!" And she would go off at a tangent into some long story
about his father and his grandfather and their lack of bravery until
I would begin to wriggle impatiently and she would check herself
and end triumphantly, "Wait until they all see *my* grandson."

And because she meant me, a hot thrill of pride would surge
through my veins.

My mother would contribute in her cool voice: "You are quite
right, of course. My son will be as brave as a lion, and we shall all
be proud of him."

Nobody ever explained what this terrible ordeal was that lay before me and required the courage of a lion, and I was too timid to ask, though I was becoming more and more curious about it. One day I asked İnci to explain, but she only laughed and told me to wait and see. So then I flew to Hacer for advice, and she popped freshly made baklava into my mouth and grinned coarsely. She made a gesture somewhere in the lower regions of my anatomy, but I did not understand and probably looked very puzzled, for she sobered her grinning and told me to run away and not to be bothering my head with such things. My mother was little more explicit but at least she tried to form some sort of picture in my mind. She told me that all little Moslem boys had circumcision and that it would be the start of my "manhood" and that lovely new clothes were to be prepared for me, for the act of circumcising was a great ceremony in Turkey. I thought about her words but, without knowing it, she had given me a new problem to wrestle with in my already overflowing mind. What had she meant by the word "manhood"? Had it anything to do with my father, whom I had heard referred to as a "man"? It was all very odd to a small boy's mind, but the conversations had the desired effect of making me impatient and eager to experience circumcision.

Every evening I used to climb on my father's knee and ask when it would happen. He would pretend to look very grave and would ask my mother if I had been a good boy that day. The answer was always Yes. Indeed, since the idea of circumcision had taken hold of me, I had walked in saintliness. So then my father would promise to arrange everything before my birthday, and I would swell with pride and the days could not pass quickly enough. It became my custom to wait each evening at the side of the house for my father to return from his business. When I saw him turning the corner, I would run to open the gate for him and examine his bulging pockets, usually filled with toys or sweets for Mehmet and me. One evening he was carrying a large cardboard box under his arm; when I demanded to know what was inside it, he told me it was my circumcision robe. I was almost delirious with excitement and begged to be allowed to carry it into the house. In the hall we met my mother and I pointed out the box to her, almost bursting with pride with the thought of what it contained. She restrained my high enthusiasm and I rushed off to find Mehmet and İnci to tell them the news. Mehmet was now two, and he commenced to cry because the robe was for me and not for him. He wanted a new dress too, he wailed. İnci popped sweets into his mouth, telling him to stop crying, that he was lucky not to be having circumcision, since it would hurt him. It was the first time anyone had mentioned anything about hurt, and I felt the first chill of apprehension. I remember that İnci stared at me with round, appalled eyes because she had told me something she had obviously been warned to keep to herself. I rushed from the playroom, down the stairs and into the salon, in my panic forgetting to knock at the door and wait for permission to enter. As I burst in, my father looked at me in astonishment.

"What is the meaning of this?" he demanded sternly. And I burst out passionately:

"Baba! İnci says it will hurt me. Will it?"

My father looked swiftly at my mother, then back to me and replied:

"Nothing will hurt you. It's all very simple and quick, and now let us look at your robe and see if you like it."

The subject was dismissed, but I noticed that my mother gathered up her sewing and quickly left the room. I knew she was going in search of İnci, and I had a moment's swift regret for what she was about to say to her.

However, my father's words had partially reassured me, so it was with a light heart that I went out to the hall table, where lay the precious package, and brought it back to the salon. My mother returned in time to open it for us, and I stole a glance at her face. She looked very composed, but there was a slight tinge of color in her cheeks.

The robe was the most beautiful thing I had ever seen. Blue it was, thick blue silk that slid against the face, embroidered lavishly with threads of gold and silver and rose. There was a blue cap in the same material, a sort of fez, and written across the front, in letters of brightest gold, was the word *Maşallah*.

I was so overcome with emotion that I could not speak, and my grandmother imperiously called for Feride and Hacer and İnci to come and see the pretty thing. Amid their exclamations and cries of delight I strutted proudly as a peacock and was only shaken once, when I saw Mehmet put out a small, tentative hand to take the hat. Fortunately, İnci coaxed him away from the shining wonder, and my heart began to function again.

After this I became consumed with impatience. I wanted a definite day to hold in my mind, and my shadowy fears began to grow bolder, threatening to swamp my mind. İnci had told Mehmet it would hurt. My father had assured me it would not. I trusted my father implicitly but I trusted İnci too. I could not remember a time in my life when I had not seen her black laughing face bent over me. She was as much a part of life and existence as were my fingers and toes. I commenced to have frightening dreams, but there was no one to whom I could run for consolation. Oh, the dim, incomprehensible fears of childhood and the total inability to share or lessen those fears!

At times I would run to my mother, putting my head in her lap and bursting into floods of tears. She would take me on her knee and I would smell the comforting, familiar smell of her eau de Cologne as I nestled against her shoulder. She would ask me to tell her what was the matter, but shame and pride forbade me discussing such a purely masculine thing as circumcision with her. But one day, unexpectedly, fear and doubt became things of the past —things to be looked back on with amusement and a certain lingering shame.

That morning dawned differently from the others. In the first place my father did not go to his office, and all the house was caught up in the bustle of extra cleaning. Poor Hacer was almost beside herself in the kitchen, with my mother and grandmother constantly going to inspect what she was doing. Feride was ordered to finish her work upstairs quickly in order that she might assist the near-hysterical Hacer. İnci was taken from Mehmet and me and we were left in the garden with my father, who would have been almost certainly better in his office, since the uproarious house was no place for him. In the middle of the afternoon I was whisked off to be bathed, an unheard-of thing, since my normal bath time came prior to going to bed. While İnci was drying me, she told me that I was going to be circumcised. Just then my mother arrived, in a flutter, with a bottle of her own especial cologne and practically drenched me in its sickly, overpowering smell, damping and flattening down my curls with it and rubbing it across my body. İnci screwed up her little button of a nose and said I smelled like a woman, then quickly stuck her tongue between her teeth to make me laugh. When they finally let go of me, having powdered and perfumed me to their hearts' content, the blue robe was lifted from its box and lowered over my head. The cap was placed over my flattened hair at a becoming angle, for İnci had a great sense as to how a fellow should wear his headgear. I could hardly stand still with excitement and was several times sharply reprimanded by my mother, who was trying to pull white socks over my dancing feet and fasten intricate silk slippers. Yet even though I was excited, my stomach was playing funny tricks; and when Feride appeared with a little tray of fruit and milk, it revolted in no uncertain fashion. However, I was forced to swallow some milk, even though it tasted like poison, and then I was taken down to my father. He held me at arms' length and laughed at my timorous face. Hacer and Feride came to inspect, and Mehmet, clinging fiercely to İnci's red skirts, suddenly burst into loud howls—whether of envy or horror I shall never know. He had to be hurriedly taken away, for my grandmother's frown of displeasure threatened to make him worse. The salon was full of people. Feride helped my mother dispense liqueurs and bonbons, and there was a great deal of noise and laughter, with everyone drinking my health and crying "Maşallah." It had been arranged that circumcision should take place in the house of our neighbor, who was a colonel in the Ottoman Army, for his son and half a dozen other children were also to be circumcised. Presently the front doorbell trilled and the colonel was brought into the salon, very erect and military-looking. The mere sight of him and what he represented was enough to completely unnerve me. He chucked me under the chin and boomed in a terrible voice, "Well, we're all ready for you."

I felt like a lamb being led to the slaughterhouse. My stomach turned over and did a somersault without any help from me at all. It felt as if it were pouring away. My mother came over to me and put her arm about my shoulders. After the colonel had tossed off his liqueur in one gulp, having waved Feride and her bonbons indignantly away, he joined my father. Presently they came and took my hand, and we went out with the cheers of the guests echoing after us. My mother stayed behind, for it is not the custom in Turkey for the women to be present at a circumcision. For fear my silk slippers should become soiled, my father carried me across the little side path that divided our house from the colonel's. The front of the house was crowded with children, and one or two of the bolder ones had even entered the garden to get a better view of the circumcision robes. I refused to look at them and buried my face in my father's shoulder. The interior of the colonel's house was decorated with flowers and silver streamers. There was the same bustle here as there had been in our house; and as I was carried through the long hall, I caught glimpses of the native servants entering and leaving the salon with trays of drinks. I was taken to a small room that had been especially set side for the use of the children. There were six or seven other boys there, all a little older than I and similarly robed. They talked animatedly, showing no sign of the burning fear that was now rapidly devouring me. They greeted me in a grown-up fashion and I envied their composure. My father and the colonel left us, going to pay their respects to the adult guests. When we were alone, the other boys, the oldest of whom was eight, strutted proudly about the room, talking in a very off-hand way and wondering which of us would be the first to go to the doctor.

Then a clown appeared, dancing in and out between tables and chairs and playing a flute. Presently a second one came to join him. This one juggled deftly with oranges; and they both looked so funny, with their exaggerated eyebrows, their white faces and red noses, that soon we were all laughing merrily and even I was beginning to forget my cowardice. An orchestra could be heard tuning up in the salon, and then a woman's voice broke out in a little plaintive melody that reminded me of Hacer. Suddenly I commenced to laugh louder than any, and the clowns were delighted and redoubled their efforts to amuse us. But they did not know that I was laughing because I had had a vision of fat Hacer's leaping, merry breasts. More and more clowns appeared, and we eagerly crowded round them. They played gay little airs on their flutes and we children jigged lightheartedly about the room. The oldest of us, the son of the imam, was very fat and pasty-faced and wore huge, disfiguring spectacles. Suddenly one of the others snatched a clown's hat and put it on his head. He looked so solemn and funny, with his eyes blinking owlishly behind the thick lenses of his glasses, that we roared with spiteful laughter. He looked immeasurably silly as he just stood there, quite still, while we shouted with laughter until the tears poured down our aching cheeks.

The colonel appeared in the doorway and commanded us to go upstairs. Clowns, laughter, excitement, were all forgotten, and even the orchestra no longer played from the salon. We all held our breaths and looked a little fearfully around us. My father came over and took my hand, and we followed the others up the stairs. How slowly I took each stair! And how each one passed seemed to seal my doom inevitably!

The fat boy was just in front of us with the imam, his father, who was saying:

"Now there is nothing to be afraid of. You are the oldest boy here; therefore you must be the bravest and set an example to all the others."

But the poor fat boy only trembled violently and looked slack with fear. The room we entered was at the far end of a long corridor, a large room that overlooked the gardens. I remember that I looked out of one of the windows, across to our garden, and I saw İnci and Mehmet playing together on a rug which had been put out for them. I wanted to run to them, but there was no escape. My father's hand held mine reassuringly. He had seen my involuntary glance through the window, and I think he wanted me to know that he understood.

In the room were eight beds, arranged dormitory-wise, four down each side. Each bed was covered with fresh linen, lace-edged pillows, and a blue-silk coverlet. In the center of the room was a large table loaded with sweetmeats and fruit and glasses for drinks. All the clowns had followed us and were dancing and tumbling all over the floor, playing their flutes, juggling with oranges, and throwing their absurd, tall hats into the air. My father showed me my bed, for I was to sleep in this house for a day or two. It was under a window, and I felt momentarily happier, for, from here, I could watch the garden and see İnci and Mehmet at their play. The doctor came in.

Instinctively I glanced away from him and over to the fat boy. His cheeks were wobbling with terror and his knees trembling so violently beneath the long robe that I wondered how they ever supported him at all. His fear communicated itself to me. I wanted to run, to shout, to call for my mother, to feel the comfort of İnci's arms about me. I looked at my father and felt my lower lip begin to quiver uncontrollably. He stooped over me, and still I have the memory of his face, that kind gentle face, that lonely, shut-away face I loved so dearly. He was willing me to be brave, and his fingers closed tightly over my icy hand.

"It's all right," he comforted me softly, so that the others should not hear. "Just be brave for one little minute more and then it will be all over."

The doctor looked at all of us standing so docilely with our fathers and commenced to shout with laughter.

"What!" he said happily. "Eight children in one room and not a sound to be heard!"

He looked at me.

"You are the youngest," he said, "so you shall come first."

He took my hand and peered into my face.

"I don't really believe you are afraid," he said gently. "There is no need to be afraid, you know! I never hurt good boys, and your father tells me you are a *very* good boy indeed. Come!" he insisted to my stubborn, disbelieving face, "you will see. I shall not hurt you."

He took my arm and led me to an adjoining room, a small room that was bare enough to strike fresh terror into an already terrified heart.

The colonel stood me on a table that had been specially placed in the center of the room. I faced the window, the colonel on one side of me and my father on the other. The doctor busied himself with a black bag and boiling water; after a minute that seemed a year, he approached the table.

"Now just be a good child and stand still," he commanded, but it was unnecesary for him to waste his breath, for I could not have moved if I had tried. My legs were rooted immovably to the table and my body was icy cold. I turned my head away as I caught sight of a little shining instrument, and the doctor said heartily: "Come, Hüsnü bey! Let us see what sort of a man your son is."

My father lifted my robe, baring my legs and the lower part of my body.

"Open your legs," commanded the doctor, his voice no longer sugared but the voice of a man intent upon performing some duty. "Wider!" he roared.

I tremblingly obeyed. I remember that the colonel held my ankles from behind me while my father pinioned my arms tightly. The doctor came nearer. I closed my eyes and was ready to die. There was a slight stinging feeling and suddenly it was all over.

I had been circumcised and my fears had been groundless. Nevertheless, I screamed lustily. Screaming was such an exquisite relief to my overwrought nerves that I continued long after the need for it was over.

The colonel carried me back to the large room, meeting the second victim in the doorway. I was put into bed, and clowns played their music and turned somersaults for my benefit and I felt proud and important.

I had intended to eat many sweets, but Nature had her way with me and very soon I slept.

When I awoke, the circumcision was over for everyone, and the music of the orchestra came faintly and sweetly from the salon. The clowns had all gone. It was night and the stars looked very near and brilliant in a cloudless sky. Laughter and music and the chink of glasses came stealing up from downstairs, and all the other boys slept. I was drowsy and contented and I turned on my side and went to sleep again.

The next morning I awoke to sunlight and peals of laughter. The foot of my bed was heaped with presents, and I sat up quickly and commenced to undo them. The terrors of the previous day had vanished, and everyone boasted of his remarkable bravery—all, that is, except the fat boy. And he turned out to have a sense of humor, for he told us that when the doctor came over to him he had neighed like a horse. In the midst of our laughter a colored servant came in with a tray of breakfasts. There was the customary white cheese, grapes, boiled eggs, bread and butter, wild-cherry and rose jams, and tea served in small glasses with slices of lemon.

The servant mocked our inability to get up and walk, remarking on our appetites, which, she said, were surprising, since yesterday we had rejected every offer of food and she had thought perhaps we were delicate children. All this was said with a twinkle in her eye to abash us for the cowards we had been less than twenty-four hours before. After breakfast our mothers visited us, promising that upon the following day we would be taken to our homes. I asked my mother why she had not been to see me the previous evening, and she replied that she had but as I had been asleep she had not wanted to awaken me. She said she was proud of me because some-one had told her I had been a brave boy. I blushed with shame, trying to explain that I had not been brave at all, but she laid her cool fingers over my mouth and would not let me finish.

"Sometimes the weakest of us are the bravest," she said. Mehmet had sent me lokum to eat and had cried for me during his breakfast. I was so touched by this that I resolved never again to be impatient with him when he could not follow a game.

I kept that resolve for quite three days.

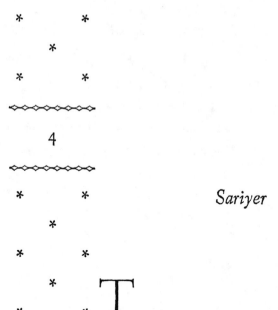

4

Sariyer

THE MOST BEAUTIFUL PRESENT I HAD RE-
ceived for my circumcision was a big rocking horse, brought me by
my Uncle Ahmet.

. Uncle Ahmet was my father's brother. He was big and jolly and
very good-looking. In his younger days he had been the despair of
my grandfather's life but after his marriage to a young and wealthy
girl he had apparently settled down. I loved him and his wife, too,
for they had no children and used to spoil me atrociously.

The day after I arrived home from the colonel's house, Uncle
Ahmet and Aunt Ayşe arrived in a horse-drawn cab, laden with
presents. They had come unexpectedly but there was a great joy
in welcoming them, with us children making most of the noise and
refusing to be hushed. My uncle brought many stuffed animal toys
for Mehmet and butter and cheese and eggs from his farm for my
mother.

Aunt Ayşe was a lovely shy person, most surprisingly blond,
with large dark eyes. I think she was a little frightened of my
grandmother, for she hardly ever opened her mouth in her presence
or expressed an opinion. I discovered later in life that she need not
have been afraid, for my grandmother had a great liking for her
and her money. Her greatest respect in life was money. The day

they arrived, the house was soon filled with noise. Our squeals of delight, coupled with the loud, hearty laughter of my uncle, and the orders screamed by my grandmother to the servants, the chattering voices of my mother and my aunt, all served to give a stimulus, a sort of artificial gayety to the drowsy old house. My rocking horse was borne off to the playroom by my uncle, I following slowly and painfully, for I was still unable to walk properly. Mehmet was lifted, chortling with joy, on the lovely horse, and I was bitterly jealous because I could not yet do the same. My uncle played with us for a long time and promised me that he would ask my father's permission to take me back with him to Sariyer, which was the name of the place where he lived. I loved to stay at Sariyer, for it was much bigger than our house and had vast gardens and an orchard and many greenhouses. Also, there was a gardener there who, contrary to all accepted ideas, loved little boys. It was the custom for my family to spend three months of every year at Sariyer. Usually we went there during May, when the heat of İstanbul began to become unbearable, but this year my grandfather's death and my approaching circumcision had kept us in the city all through the interminable dust and heat and flies of summer. We had suffocated beneath mosquito nets and insufficient fresh air, for the windows had been fitted with fine netting in an effort to keep the insects away, and the shutters were tightly barred at night. Still the mosquitoes found entry, filling the dark nights with their whining music. So it was the middle of that fateful August of 1914 that eventually brought my parents to Sariyer. Permission was readily given for me to return, on the following day, with my uncle and aunt; the remainder of the family were to leave İstanbul as soon as my father's business activities permitted. I was very excited to be traveling without the restrictive eye of İnci or my grandmother. I helped İnci to pack clothes for me and lovingly stroked my rocking horse, for this was to come with me. Mehmet's lamentations of grief I ignored and could not be persuaded to leave the horse for my father to transport, being convinced that if it were left after me Mehmet would pull off all its lovely mane and no doubt do other irreparable damage.

Murat drove us to Galata Bridge, where we were to board the boat that would take us down the Bosporus to Sariyer.

Murat was a grumpy, miserable old man who immediately made difficulties over my rocking horse. My uncle, however, eventually managed to persuade him that there was plenty of room for it in the phaeton. Murat, in darkest retaliation, prophesied that it would get damaged on the boat. Unlike my uncle's gardener, he had no love for small boys and thought it beneath his dignity to drive us to Galata Bridge, where, he said, all the riffraff of İstanbul gathered. He liked best to be seen driving my mother and grandmother, both heavily veiled, around the quiet green squares of Bayazit, to one of the big houses to pay a brief morning call.

Driving across the Galata Bridge behind the high-stepping horses was an adventure in itself. In those days there was even less traffic control in İstanbul than there is today—and God knows there is little enough today. That morning, horse-drawn cabs, carts, porters carrying beds or other furniture on their shoulders, gypsies stepping out into the road beneath the very feet of the flying horses, peasants riding their mules—all were in danger of being knocked down or overturned, for Murat, with a fine disregard of human life, drove like the wind and was more autocratic than any sultan.

Boarding the boat was fraught with difficulties, for I lost sight of my horse and in the resulting confusion wailed long and loudly and would not be pacified, despite my aunt's repeated assurances that she had distinctly seen Murat give the horse to my uncle. In the end, however, the horse was discovered to be safe and sound, importantly seated all by itself and looking over the rail of the boat with glassy eyes. Uncle Ahmet bought *simit*, a sort of crescent-shaped bread studded with pistachio, and we fed the crying sea gulls that followed us.

The journey took two hours and I was beginning to be bored with inactivity when the boat station of Sariyer came in view.

It was good to be on land again, to catch a glimpse of my uncle's greenhouses through the trees that enclosed the gardens from the curious eyes of the boats. Servants met us, taking our meager baggage, and I swung happily along the dusty road, clinging to my uncle's strong hand and keeping a half-fearful lookout for snakes, for which Sariyer was notorious.

That night I slept in a cool little room overlooking the house garden, a wilderness of tangled briars and tobacco plants with their hot, hurtful scent, and roses which were not considered good enough for the famous rose garden. Jessamine trailed through the windows and the night was very quiet. I missed the sound of the sea, for the Bosporus was on the other side of the house and could not be heard from my room. I also missed İnci's clever fingers to undo my buttons. My aunt had sent an old servant to look after me, and she fumbled over my clothes and over my bathing. As a crowning insult, she omitted my evening glass of milk and closed the door after her when she had put me in bed. İnci had always left my door ajar, so that I could go to sleep to the sound of my parents' voices from downstairs and to the comforting clatter old Hacer made when she washed the dishes after the evening meal. I lay in my little bed, listening to all the unfamiliar sounds that assail one away from home. Furniture seemed to creak extra loudly and shift itself, and the shadows in the corners were alive with fearsome things.

Fidèle and Joly, the house dogs, padded restlessly up and down the path under my window, sometimes brushing through the shrubs, sometimes stopping to bark ferociously—at some unaccustomed noise perhaps, or merely because they were bored. When they barked, Hasan the gardener or Thérèse the Greek cook would hush them to cease their noise. Once a big black cat climbed on the branches of a tree opposite my window, and my heart leaped in terror, for it seemed so large there, so still and evil in the dusky light. Yet for all my little fears I slept soundly, awaking next morning to the friendly voice of my aunt bidding me get up.

We had breakfast in the garden, my uncle fresh from a dip in the Bosporus. Afterward I played with my aunt and the dogs, big, lovable Dalmatians, who gamboled on the smooth lawns, chased the innumerable kitchen cats, and licked most of the gleaming paint off my horse.

When I had been there a few days, my uncle announced one

morning that he was going to his farm in the hills and proposed
to take me with him. My aunt was asked to prepare snacks for the
journey, for the farm was two and a half hours' drive from Sariyer.
The phaeton was brought round and in we climbed, settling ourselves with much laughter amid the cushions. My aunt's face
was covered with a thick motoring veil—a veil that fluttered in the
breeze and sometimes tickled my nose. When we arrived at the farm,
dogs leaped out to greet my uncle hysterically. They seemed very
big and fierce to me, and I clung tightly to Uncle Ahmet's coattails.
The dogs wore great iron collars around their necks; and because
wolves always first attack an animal by the throat, these collars were
heavily spiked for protection.

We lunched in the farmhouse, in a low dining room with an
uneven stone floor and a big open fireplace large enough to roast
an ox. The furniture was primitive and hand-made, but the meal
that was served to us was delicious. There were roast fowls piled
on a mountain of pilau—rice cooked in butter and chicken water;
swordfish straight from the sea and served with parsley, slices of
lemon, and various kinds of salad. There were dishes of grapes,
watermelon, and some kind of heavy sweet made of shredded
wheat, butter, syrup, and chopped nuts. Wine was served in
carafes, and my uncle, answering the appeal in my eyes, poured
a little into my glass. After the meal Turkish coffee was served
under the lime trees, and my elders seemed drowsy, lying back on
their chaise longues, their eyes half-shut against the glare of the
sun on the grass.

I wandered away to explore. I went into the empty stables that
smelled of horses and leather and I discovered seven or eight puppies playing in the straw. They were so soft and fluffy that I could
not resist taking one of them into my arms to pet. The rest played
about my feet, trying to climb up my legs. Suddenly two large
dogs sprang in and I dropped the puppy to run, but the dogs were
on me in a thrice and I thought they intended to eat me. I commenced to scream. A farm laborer came running and I heard my
uncle's voice in the distance. My legs threatened to collapse and,

ignominiously, I wet my trousers! The farm laborer told me, in his difficult peasant Turkish, not to be afraid. The dogs were the father and mother of the puppies and only wanted to play with me. I mistrusted, however, their idea of play. The peasant tried to press bread into my trembling fingers with which to feed the dogs. But before I could take it, the dogs voraciously snatched it from him. The puppies, scenting sport to be had, got joyously under my feet and succeeded in knocking me down into the straw. So there I lay struggling, with dogs and puppies crawling over me and I screaming like one possessed. I was eventually sorted out of the doggy mess by my uncle's capable hands and taken, in floods of tears, to be changed and washed. My aunt and uncle were roaring with laughter, and the louder they laughed, the louder I bawled, feeling their amusement to be adding insult to injury.

After that disgraceful episode, I took care ever afterward to avoid the stables, and I was glad when we returned to Sariyer.

My uncle used to bathe every morning before breakfast, and I used to watch him from the dining-room windows, running down the garden to meet him when he was returning to the house. Some mornings I was taken with him, and he taught me how to swim. We had fun splashing about in the chilly water and came to breakfast with great appetites. Now my uncle was very fond of grapes; he could eat with ease two or three kilos each morning. Because of this, my aunt was miserly about cutting from the house vine, which spread out over the terrace like a canopy. She treasured those grapes and would tie each cluster in little muslin bags to prevent birds or bees from blemishing the fruit. And she never gave my uncle enough of them—at least in his estimation. Instead, dishes of market grapes were set on the table, which would cause heated words between them, he saying that one of the few pleasures of his day was to reach up to his own vine and cut as much as he wanted. He would come on to the terrace each morning, eyeing with disgust the market grapes arranged so temptingly but so futilely for him.

"H'm!" he would remark disparagingly, ringing a little silver handbell for the parlormaid, who would timorously emerge from the house knowing full well what was to come. "What are these grapes doing here?" he would demand, to which she would reply sadly, "Bey effendi, it was not possible to get any from the vine this morning. . . ." and stand there before him, looking down at her feet, her face and neck slowly reddening. Before my uncle could any further embarrass her limited intelligence, my aunt would appear to ask what was the matter.

"The grapes, hanim effendi—" the parlormaid would begin.

"These grapes, Ayşe," my uncle would interrupt, waving to the parlormaid to go away. "Why cannot we have our own grapes instead of these half-dead-looking specimens?" Then he would stick out his lower lip, looking charmingly at my aunt, and maybe she would sigh and proffer the grape scissors without another word.

Having got his own way, my uncle would be instantly repentant, contenting himself with one outsize bunch and one meager one, calling upon my aunt to witness his amazing economy. But victory was not always so easy. The results largely depended upon my aunt's mood, and she could very easily turn her face to all cajolery. So my uncle formed a plan. I was shamelessly instructed to pamper and pet my aunt, and when her mood was judged to have been softened sufficiently, to look appealingly to the house vine and beg for some of its grapes. This I did, and my aunt responded in the way my uncle had prophesied, but I sometimes wonder how much she guessed of his villainy. For he would come to the table buoyantly, his face wreathed in smiles at the sight of his favorite grapes; but my aunt would now and then look thoughtfully at him, then turn toward me as if wondering how far she was being made a fool of between us.

I used to spend most of my days in the gardens, my aunt sitting sewing under a magnolia tree and keeping an alert eye on my activities. I loved the magnolia trees with their shining green leaves, the thick, creamy texture of their flowers, and sometimes I would pluck one, giving it to my aunt, who would place it behind one ear, suddenly looking exotic and strange. There was a pool in the middle of the grounds, and I would peer into it for hours, watching the lazy goldfish with Fidèle and Joly panting beside me. They had adopted me as their own property, following me everywhere and howling dismally if I left them to look for Hasan. They were forbidden the rose garden and the kitchen garden but lived in the hope that one day an unsuspecting person would leave one of the wall doors open for them to slip through. Hasan would let me pick up the overripe apples that had fallen to the ground and on rare occasions he would give me peaches to eat, warm from the day-long sun on the southern walls. Once I let the dogs come with me, and it was the only time I saw Hasan really angry, as opposed to his not infrequent grumblings. He fussily hunted the two dogs off the carrots and onions, beat them from the raspberry canes, and swore luridly when they trampled his strawberry beds. I took to my heels and ran, Fidèle and Joly, having had enough of sport, flying after me, and Hasan's curses filling the air with vengeance.

My uncle had a rowboat, and in the cool of the evenings he used to take me fishing. I used to look down into the Bosporus, into the clear blue waters, and watch for fish, my uncle amused by my exclamations of delight. He used the line and we sometimes hooked mackerel or small tunny, and great would be my excitement to see them flapping and gasping on the floor of the boat. Once I saw a school of dolphins and watched breathlessly as they leaped through the air. Then we rowed home in the twilight, with stars beginning to prick the green evening sky, with mackerel or tunny at our feet and my uncle telling stories. Riding the Bosporus effortlessly, hearing and yet not hearing the voices of the shore people and the sirens from the big boats. They were good times for an almost six-year-old to remember, times that have lived on in the memory long after the pleasure has died.

One afternoon, during siesta time, which was taken in long cushioned chairs on the veranda, I awoke to laughter and heard

my aunt saying, "You must be tired, traveling in this heat," and the
voice of my mother replying that it had been quite cool in the
boat and that she was not tired. I jumped up and ran into the hall
and there stood my smiling family, in various attitudes of arrival.
I was so happy that I could not speak for a moment or two but
just stood there fingering the soft stuff of my mother's dress, going
redder and redder with suppressed emotion. My mother unwound
her veil and stooped over me.

"How brown you are!" she exclaimed, kissing me, and suddenly
my feelings were loosed and I started to chatter. I flung myself
on İnci and Mehmet, only realizing at that moment how much
I had missed them. Immediately the comedienne İnci started to
roll her eyes at me, and I roared with laughter, turning somersaults to show my appreciation. My father restrained my high spirits
and put his hand on my head. He seemed quiet, unlike himself,
and I was too young to know or understand that Germany and
England were at war, too young to know the difference that these
far-off countries would make to Turkey and my own life.

We sat on the veranda, where the vine sheltered us from the
afternoon heat of the sun. Extra cushions were arranged, a maid
brought glasses of iced water and Turkish coffee, and I climbed
on my father's knee. He was absent-minded and did not take any
notice of me, intent upon discussing with my uncle the kind of
school I should be sent to. My uncle was opposing the whole idea,
saying I was still too young to be sent to school in these troubled
times; and here a secret look passed between them that puzzled
but meant nothing to me. The subject was dropped and they commenced to talk of other things. I was too young to follow their
meaning but, in after years, my mother pieced most of it together
for me.

That night, lying in bed in a bigger room which also held
Mehmet, I could hear the voices of the grownups as they talked
together on the veranda. There seemed to be a difference in their
voices, an argumentative note not usually discernible. There was
less laughter, more urgency—and that was odd when the ladies

were present. I crept from my bed and leaned out through the open window. I looked down on the thick mat of the vine leaves, which looked pale green in places where the light of the lamp shone through. It was very still and I could hear every word of the conversation. My father appeared to be attempting to persuade my grandmother to sell our house! He said there was war in Europe and that none knew the day our country would be in it too. He said that anything might happen and that, in view of the poor way of his business lately, we ought to cut down on expenses.

"Nonsense," came my grandmother's voice crisply. "Why should a war in Europe make any difference in our lives? All my children were born in that house, Hüsnü, and two of yours. I came to it when I was only thirteen, and I would rather die than leave it now."

Here my uncle interposed.

"Hüsnü is right. The house is too big for you now. It has been too big for years, but when our father was alive it was not our business to interfere."

"I should hope not indeed," said my grandmother, but her voice did not sound so harsh: perhaps this was an old argument.

"We have enough money," she went on. "And Hüsnü has your father's business—"

"I have told you I am selling it," came my father's voice, sharp with finality.

There was a silence and I shivered in my thin nightshirt, although the night was warm. I felt the tension in the air. I could not have explained my feeling or defined it in any way, but it is a fact that I was aware of a strangeness, an alien influence hanging over my family. Years later, when I began to record family events in diary form, my mother most faithfully reconstructed that night at Sariyer—the night when a small, inquisitive boy first felt the cold breath of insecurity.

My mother broke the little silence.

"Selling the business?" she said, bewilderment in her voice, as though powerless to understand what strange force was driving my father.

"It is necessary to sell it if we are to survive at all. When my father died, I had hopes of reviving the business on a large scale, but, as you all know very well, events were against me. Oh, it is impossible to explain all these things to you and make you understand. There are so many difficulties: labor, export, bad representation abroad; and now the war in Europe writes finis to all my hopes of markets there. If Turkey comes in—and in my opinion she will— I shall have to go. Ahmet will go. And who will look after things here? It is better to get rid of it now, and if one day I come back— well, with our name it is easy to build the business again."

Again there was that frightening silence, a grim, uneasy sort of silence that paralyzed me. These conversations were the first hint of the changes that were to come. I was tearful standing there, insecure, and wishing passionately for life to stay as it was now— no, not as it was now, but as it had been yesterday when I had gone fishing with my uncle, helping pull in the mackerel, and we had rowed home singing, under an evening sky.

This time it was my grandmother who broke the silence, obstinate, wayward, still indomitable.

"Because you may be called to the war, Hüsnü," she said—"and I must say the possibility seems remote to me, although no doubt you think me a stupid old woman—it still seems drastic to sell your business. Your father and your grandfather built that business, and surely this war which you talk about cannot interfere with the selling of our carpets to Persia and Europe. There must still be people left in the world who appreciate beauty."

She was answered by a shout of laughter from my father, strange laughter that sent little shivers down the spine.

He said: "Mother, I kiss your hand and have a great respect for you, and I know you will forgive me if I say you are talking nonsense. When Turkey is in this war, nobody will care about our carpets or the business my grandfather built so diligently."

"Very well then, Hüsnü," declared my grandmother, unexpectedly capitulating; "I do not understand why this war can make so much difference, but you are a man and know these things better than I, so sell your business if you wish, but leave me my home if you please."

My father sighed heavily, the sound ghostly and distinct through the vine. Perhaps his eyes appealed to my uncle, for presently I heard the deep voice of Uncle Ahmet saying:

"Hüsnü is right, Mother. You must let him sell that barn of a house and find a smaller one, and you must get in supplies of food. Prices are rising; the peasants are commencing to hoard their wheat. It is better to provide now against the day when the shops may be empty and you and my sister Şevkiye have to look after yourselves."

"I wish I knew why we are all so gloomy," said my grandmother, "and why we have to look after ourselves. Where will Hüsnü be?"

"God knows," said my uncle feelingly.

"Even if he goes," continued my grandmother, determined to be fractious, "he will be an officer and will be able to send us many things. He will surely not see his family hungry."

My father said quietly: "The Ottoman Army has too many well trained officers already. They will not want more officers; they will want good material to feed the guns."

I did not know what he meant, but apparently my mother understood, for she made a little moaning sound of protest, and my grandmother was silent for once.

I could hear my mother softly crying, and my heart began to pound and my skin to prickle uncomfortably. What had happened to my mother and my jolly father? What was all this queer new talk of war and what was "war"? I was wide-awake and suddenly sleepless. I would have liked to have called down to the little group sitting so still under the protective old vine that listened to their tragic secrets. I did not know why I was afraid, but I was old enough to realize that I had eavesdropped on a conversation not meant for my ears.

The next morning, after İnci had dressed me, I ran impatiently downstairs, anxious to know what change there would be in my parents. They seemed perfectly normal. My mother was as calm as ever and my father smiling-eyed. I felt a great relief. Perhaps the night and the darkness had played tricks with my imagination and I had never heard their conversation at all.

My uncle greeted us merrily and cut great clusters of grapes from the precious vine, with a fine disregard for economy. All that day I seem to remember that my father sat idly in the gardens, sometimes throwing sticks for the dogs, or playing with us children. He asked me if I would like to go to school, and when I enthusiastically replied in the affirmative, he said he would make arrangements when we returned to İstanbul. I timidly asked him if we were going to leave our house. He looked startled for a moment, and I thought he would ask me where I had learned this, but he did not, only sighing a little and saying that perhaps we would have to leave.

Before going to bed that evening, I sat playing alone on a corner of the veranda. My father and my uncle sat sipping wine and quietly talking together. I listened idly to what they were saying and heard the strange, new word "war" repeated over and over again. The word appeared to dominate all thought lately and cropped up with unfailing regularity whenever the men were alone together.

My father was saying:

"The German officers are not training the Turkish Army for the sake of their black eyes."

My uncle was inclined to disagree. "But if we go into this new war, we are finished as a nation. Already we have lost our empire and have just come out of the Balkan War, defeated and belittled. Surely Enver's conceit is not so great that he will see his country in ruins?"

"When a man is trying to create history about his name, there is little he will not do; and Reşat is powerless, which is perhaps just as well, since there is little to choose between the two of them."

"What treasonable talk is this?" inquired my grandmother's voice sternly, and I looked up at her, as much surprised by her silent approach as the two men.

"Treason is a word that has very little meaning these days," replied my father, and his eyes caught mine, for I was watching him intently.

"Where is İnci?" he demanded. "Why is this child sitting here with us at this time of the night?" and he violently rang the hand-bell.

After that I heard no more disturbing talk of "war" or of anything else, for my parents were most careful to see that I was fully occupied, or safely in bed and asleep before they commenced their unsettling conversations. Those days at Sariyer passed swiftly, and we children grew brown beneath the sun. My father began to fish with my uncle during the eventide and sit idly during the day in the gardens. The ladies would go for short drives, pay calls on the one or two big houses in the district, and sip Turkish coffee in the cool of the afternoon, under the spreading branches of the magnolia trees.

They looked so gay and elegant there, seated on their chaise longues, chattering like magpies, the sun washing their vivid silk dresses to shades of pastel. Sometimes I used to stand at a little distance from them, watching them embroidering or lifting the coffee cup to their lips with white languid fingers that flashed fire as the sun's rays caught the gleam of their rings. Perhaps the parlormaid would come across the lawn to them, her apron dazzlingly white against the somber darkness of her dress, and I would feel nostalgia clutching at my heart for I knew not what. Vague fears would commence to tremble formlessly in the mind, and I would want to catch and hold that brilliant, vivid scene for ever. But at last the day came for us to leave Sariyer; and returning home to İstanbul and Feride and Hacer was filled with its own excitement.

My aunt wrapped parcels of food for us, and Hasan presented my mother with a bouquet of roses.

As the boat passed the bottom of the garden, we waved gaily to my uncle and aunt and all the servants who had gathered there with them, and none of us knew that we were saying goodbye to a life that had gone from the world for ever.

My aunt waved her scrap of pink handkerchief, and I did not know that in after years, whenever I saw just such a pink wisp of cambric, it was to bring that day before my eyes again. I did not know of the long years of poverty ahead or that one day this I, this happy boy, would eat the grass because he was hungry.

None of us knew—how could we?—that our casual goodbye was indeed goodbye.

Unthinking, unconscious of our destiny, uncaring, we sailed into the morning sea, turning our backs on Sariyer and the good life that was over.

5

The New House and Other Things

URAT, WITH THE PHAETON, MET US AT
Galata Bridge, less bad-tempered this time about my rocking horse,
and traveling at a sedate pace because my grandmother was with
us. On this occasion incautious pedestrians were quite safe from
the hoofs of the horses, but I was bored, longing for speed.

Once home, life very quickly resumed its normal tempo again,
our holiday a thing of the past and already beginning to lose its
bright shape in the memory. No more talk of "war" threatened to
disturb our peace of mind. It was arranged that I should start at the
local school, and several days were taken up with the preparation of
new clothes, and a smart leather satchel was purchased. Hacer made
tray after tray of *lokma*, a heavy, syrupy sweet, for it was the custom, thirty-five years ago, for newcomers at school to provide sweets
for the other pupils. I was taken to school by my father, full of
importance and pride. We were met at the entrance by the *hoca*,
a teacher who looked very fierce—or, at least, seemed so to me.
However, he patted my head kindly enough, and my first impres-
sions were somewhat allayed. He wore a large black beard, a black
robe to match, and a white *sarik* bound about his head. We followed him into the school, which consisted of one classroom. There
were no desks, no chairs, no books, indeed, no evidence to connect

it with any scholastic activities. Twenty or thirty children were seated cross-legged on cushions on the floor. The hoca sat on the floor also, but on a bigger cushion and away from the children. The trays of lokma were brought in by Murat, who gave a sour look at the hoca. The latter peered into the trays, took a few lokma between his fingers, and popped them into his mouth. He chewed ecstatically, his eyes raised to heaven, then bade Murat place the trays on the floor, while he himself arranged the children around each tray. I was told to say goodbye to my father and kiss his hand, which I did, feeling vaguely uneasy, for I did not like the hoca and did not think he was liable to improve upon closer acquaintance. I was given a place on the floor with the others and listened disconsolately to my father and Murat driving away. I was soon called to attention, however, by a smart rap on the head from the hoca's large stick. It was about ten feet long, which enabled him to chastise any child without moving from his cushion. I cannot remember any lessons from that day and am inclined to think that there were none, save occasional readings from the Koran. I best remember my horrible fascination as the stick of the hoca descended on some luckless pupil's head. It descended on mine too, frequently, and no matter how hard I tried to dodge it, the hoca was always quicker than I. Other refractory children were put in the various corners of the room and made to stand on one leg, with their hands in the air. They looked extremely funny, but I was afraid to give way to my mirth for fear the hoca should stand me there in similar position. He used to preface all his remarks with "Padişahim çok yaşa" (Long live my sultan), and we had to chant it after him.

That evening my father closely questioned me about the school, appearing to have been suffering from the most terrible misgivings all day. I described it to him and noticed the glance he exchanged with my mother. My grandmother was highly indignant that an ignorant hoca should dare to beat her grandson.

"Ahmet was right," declared my father firmly. "He must be sent to the French school at Gedik Paşa."

So ended my first and last day at the district school, İnci lamenting the trays of lokma, which she evidently considered far too good to have been eaten by the hoca and his pupils. Arrangements were made with the principal of the French school; a smart gray uniform was ordered for me, and primers and notebooks were put into the leather satchel. In September of 1914, one month before my sixth birthday, I started school again.

The French school was entirely different from the district school. In the first place there seemed to be an abundance of teachers and many classrooms. I learned to say *"Bon jour, m'sieu,"* or *"Bon jour, mam'selle,"* as the case might be, and to count to ten in French. I made many new friends at the school. The majority of the pupils were Turkish, from families in the same social strata as my own, but quite a few were French or Armenian. I soon learned to go to school by myself and would meet my friends on the way. We would bow to each other and affectedly say, *"Bon jour, mon ami. Comment allez-vous?"* for it was the fashion to ape our elders and to speak French in public, a rather grand and adult thing to do.

Sometimes my new friends would visit me at home, and I began to grow away from Mehmet and İnci. I would refuse to play babyish games with Mehmet; and when he used to stagger into a room where my friends and I were gathered, I would peremptorily ring for İnci and tell her to take him out of the way.

One evening, after I had returned from school and was sitting in the salon telling my mother about my day, my father arrived home with a porter from the market place who was carrying several large tins. They were given to Hacer, and my father afterward explained that these tins must be filled with storable foodstuffs.

"The situation is serious," he explained to my grandmother's wooden face. "I shall go myself to the market tomorrow. Palace gossip suggests that our country will go to war. Enver and Talat Paşa are strongly pro-German; and if I have to go away, I want to feel that everything possible has been done for your comfort."

My mother's face grew serious, and I knew that a discussion was imminent. I half expected to be sent away, but my father said I might stay, adding:

"When I am gone, you will be the only man in the house; therefore you must know how to guard your womenfolk, eh?" And he playfully pulled my ear.

He stood leaning against a console table, and for the first time I felt him to be old. I did not know he was only twenty-six; perhaps if I had, I should still have considered him old, for twenty-six is an enormous age to a child. That evening he looked white and tired. Had my father been born in this age, in another country, he would not have fought in any war. He was essentially a man of peace, a good Moslem who feared his God with an awful fear and believed in an afterlife; a man who was appalled by the poverty of his people and who, in his own small way, attempted to alleviate it. The carnage and brutality and utter senselessness of war tore his heart for the ordinary man who was caught up in the military machine. I have no picture of him, and his face refuses to emerge clearly from the mists of time, but my mother represented him as a thinker, a bit of a dreamer if you will, a man more fitted for the leisured life than the life he was afterward to know. He had sure knowledge of Turkey's muddled politics, the schemings of the peacock Enver, the treacherousness and greed of his subordinates, the weakness of the sultan, and the lack of organization and unpreparedness of Turkey for a new war.

That evening, I remember, he told my grandmother that he had received an offer for our house, too good, he estimated, to refuse. She looked thoughtful and said:

"I do not know how we shall manage in a smaller house; and there are the servants to be considered too."

"Hacer must go," declared my father—and one wonders how it must have hurt him to talk like this to his womenfolk, he who only wanted to heap fine gifts on them. "Feride," he continued, "must take over the kitchen. You must arrange these domestic problems yourself, but Hacer is to go."

"Oh, dear," said my mother, "is it really necessary for Hacer to go?"

"Yes," said my father. "One day gold will buy nothing for you.

Whatever amount of stocks we get in now will only last a certain time, so the less mouths there are to feed, the better. Today the colonel told me that the Army is buying so fast that the shops are emptying. Murat and the horses must go too: there will be no place in a new house for a phaeton."

"No!" said my grandmother violently, standing up so quickly that she knocked over a bowl of roses that stood on a little bureau. "I refuse to part with Murat."

Fascinated, I watched the water from the overturned bowl spreading darkly on the carpet.

"This is no time to think of grandeur," said my father. "You have not seen the poverty outside your house or the bewilderment on the faces of the soldiers, with their patched uniforms and their worn-out boots. You cannot be expected to understand politics or know that our country is under the heel of the Germans. We're riddled with German influence and capital, even though we may appear to be only sitting on the fence."

"I don't understand a thing you say," grumbled my grandmother. "And if you only want Hacer to go because of the food she eats . . ."

But though she paused, nobody enlightened her. My father had done with explanation.

After that, quantities of food would arrive at the house for storing, and the kitchen became alive with the sickly smell of jam making and Hacer was told she would have to go. My mother moved through this activity serenely and calmly, never, to my remembrance, betraying her feelings. But my grandmother remained stubborn and intractable, spending most of her days paying calls, as though suddenly making up for a lifetime of neglected duties.

She would sit proudly and coldly in the phaeton, ablaze with jewels and hauteur. She would have to give in to my father, but she intended to go down fighting.

A new house was found and bought, at a higher price than had been anticipated. The price of everything had risen, and many of the shops remained closed for long periods each day. More and more men were taken to be soldiers, and presently one saw mainly women in the streets. Servants and mistresses and prostitutes, they all had to eat and would spend their days tramping the streets in search of an open shop. Bewilderment and resignation were to be seen in all their faces but no resentment. That came later.

The new house seemed very small after the large, rambling old konak where I was born. No longer had I a room to myself but shared one with Mehmet. There was no playroom, and we children had to use the dining room if our parents required the salon to themselves.

The garden was large and had many fruit trees and a pocket-handkerchief lawn, with a lime tree standing in the middle of it. When my grandmother first saw it, she snorted with disgust—if one may use such an inelegant term in connection with my grand-mother. She demanded how she could be expected to live in a house that size and wanted to know where all her furniture would go. She made it quite clear that she had no intention of selling any of it.

When I first saw the house, my father said to me: "I hope I shall see you here as a grown man, my son, and myself as an old man. But if anything happens to me, then you will have to take my place. Perhaps many times it will be difficult for you, but it will be your duty to look after your mother and your grandmother."

I could not bear to hear my kindly father talk like this and I threw myself on him, weeping as if my heart would break.

The house stood on a hill, and from the upper windows we could see the Marmara, but faintly from this distance, and more gray than blue. A laundry had been built on the side of the house by a previous owner as a haphazard afterthought, and a fig tree grew in the middle of it. There was no proper roof on the laundry, only a sort of terrace built of wood, with a hole left for the fig tree to emerge triumphantly, so that in summer it could spread its glory outside the bedroom windows. In winter, rain must have often come through, but because it was only a laundry, no one seemed to care. Only in İstanbul could such a lovely, enchanting thing be found. Later on, after we moved there, İnci would spread a carpet across the terrace; and my mother would lie there with us on cushions, watching the sun through the leaves of the fig tree, now and again stretching upward to pull the ripe, purple figs with a stick that had been specially made for that purpose.

But before we moved in, men erected chicken coops at the end of the garden and furniture was arranged, but to the satisfaction of none, for the smaller, darker rooms looked unbearably over-crowded with my grandmother's unwieldy furniture. She never liked that house and seemed a different person for the short while she lived there. The day before we moved in, my father bought a ram, for this is a tradition still observed in Turkey today. Its horns were painted gold, its woolly coat red and gold, and a large red ribbon was tied about its neck, the bow sitting coquettishly under one ear. That night I could not sleep, for I was excited and at the same time sad for the poor beautiful ram that would be killed on the morrow. Next morning a butcher was called. With my father reading extracts from the Koran, the ram's throat was slit; and as the blood poured down into the street, a great shout went up from the watching crowd. "Hayirli olsun!" they cried, meaning, "Let this house be lucky for you!"

My father turned to us and said, "Bismillahir rahmaner rahim," which can be very roughly translated as, "I go into this house in the name of God."

Then the little ceremony was over and the ram was taken away to be cut up for distribution among the poor people. The same evening, after sundown, my father went to the mosque to give thanks for the new house.

So into the new house we went, and strange indeed it was that first evening. There was the garden to be explored and the joy of discovering ripe pears and quinces on the little trees. It was ex-citing to open the garden gate that led to a path to our neighbor's home and to a big field that was just waste ground, dotted here and there with a few stunted fig trees. Strange it was, too, to see Feride in the kitchen, to know that never again would one hear Hacer's laughter or see her fat buttocks straining under her skirts. Strange to play in the dining room for the last half-hour of the day before bed, although we discovered that a satisfactory "house" could be made beneath the table. And then to go into the salon, with its tall narrow windows fronting the hilly street, to see my mother and grandmother there, thoughtfully looking round them at the clumsy, heavy furniture made for a roomier house. And strangest of all it was to go up the stairs and see Mehmet's little bed alongside mine— strange, but comforting nevertheless—and to hear İnci's breathing all through the night, knowing she was there within call, in the little scrap of room that opened off ours and was barely wide enough to hold her bed or the cupboard for her clothes.

The newness wore off and we became accustomed to the sight of Feride in the kitchen, and I still continued at school. One evening when I returned from school, I saw that my mother had guests. I flung my satchel on the hall table, washed my hands, and went into the salon, which my greater years or the slight relaxation of discipline now gave me the right to enter freely.

A very elegant-looking lady was seated on the sofa drinking Turkish coffee; two children, about my own age, sat demurely with her. My lighthearted entrance was somewhat checked by their presence, for I had not realized that children would be there. My mother, however, introduced me before I could turn tail and run to find İnci.

"This is our neighbor, Madame Müjgan," she said, and I had to step forward and kiss her hand.

"This," continued my mother, bringing forward the girl, "is Yasemin and her brother Nuri."

I bowed to them both, then retired a little shyly; but my mother rang for İnci, and we were told to go into the garden and play together.

Once out of the presence of our elders, our shyness melted and we talked to each other freely. Nuri, I discovered, was two years older than I and Yasemin one year younger. From then on we frequently played with each other, our friendship being smiled upon by our elders. Nuri was very jealous of his sister and seemed to resent the quick friendship that sprang up between her and me. He would suddenly leave us in the middle of a game and go stalking off by himself to sulk. He was a heavy, handsome boy, unable to bear the sight of his sister hero-worshiping somebody else. One day he and I had a fight and arrived at our homes with blood-stained noses and a couple of ripe, black eyes. Our outraged parents forced us to apologize but, although we were civil enough before them, we continued the feud in private for many weeks.

One other day stands out in memory. Yasemin and I were playing alone together in our dining room. We were playing the age-old game of "husbands and wives," and I was proudly returning from my "work," greeting her with a passionate kiss, when a sharp slap on the backside put *paid* to that. İnci had discovered us and went to inform my mother, who apparently blushed deeply, locked me in my room, and escorted a tearful Yasemin to her own home. It appears that the two ladies talked long and earnestly, later informing their husbands of this dark deed. The upshot was that Yasemin and I were separated and forbidden to play with each other again. So Nuri got his sister back again. I would see them playing in their garden together, and if Yasemin were to catch sight of me, she would give a little precocious, flirting tilt to her head, ignoring my placatory smiles. Life was full of resentments for me just then. I was very hurt and puzzled by my parents' attitude toward the kissing of Yasemin and angry that nobody would give any reasonable explanation as to *why* I should not kiss her. I became suddenly troublesome at home and at school, being surly with my teachers, who promptly reported this behavior to my father. One other night I refused to eat my dinner, demanding that İnci should serve me with the sweet course first. When she refused, I bit her hand and, knowing that trouble would arise from this behavior, added insult to injury and pinched her hard. She howled with pain and rushed to tell my mother. My father was very angry. He beat me with a stick, then sent me to my room without anything to eat. In my room I angrily kicked all the furniture, thereby hoping to damage it. I tentatively used some of the swear words I had picked up from the other boys at school, half expecting that the house would fall on me with the wrath of God. When nothing happened, I used the words more freely, shouting them aloud to the empty room. To make matters worse, I could see Yasemin and Nuri playing in their garden, uncaring of my misery.

I was so hungry I wanted to cry. After Mehmet and İnci slept, I debated with myself whether I dare go downstairs and raid the larder. Before I could summon enough courage, however, my grandmother crept stealthily into my room with a slice of bread and white cheese and a glass of milk. I ate ravenously, and she whispered that she had been unable to bear the thought of my hunger but that I was not to tell my mother that she had given me anything. I promised fervently and soon went to sleep.

I had been at the French school a little over two months, when one morning, upon arrival, all the pupils were told to go into the music room instead of their classrooms.

We were very curious, especially as all the teachers were also gathered there, and we wondered if we had done something awful. Presently the director of the school arrived, going to the dais and looking sternly down at us. At least we thought he looked stern.

We said, *"Bon jour, Monsieur le Directeur,"* and he replied in kind.

Then he spoke in Turkish, which was very unusual, but he wanted to make sure we all understood him. He said:

"My children, this country is at war. This is a French school, and my country and your country are now enemies. This school will be closed indefinitely. You may all go home now, and God bless you."

His voice cracked and his little goatee quivered mournfully. And that day, too, my father told my mother that a pact had been signed between Turkey and Germany, and that our country was now in the war.

Thus ended an era for us, quietly and soberly, and with no indication that these times would never come back again.

About this time, I became acquainted with Bekci Baba. There is still a Bekci Baba in Turkey, but the "Baba" has been dropped and his duties are less onerous than they were in the old days.

Every Bekci Baba is attached to a police station, and thirty-five years ago many and varied were his tasks. During the day he would bring vats of drinking water to the houses, and during the night he became our guardian and our watchman.

He used to carry a large thick stick, the bottom of which was bound with an iron rim. This was very useful when he wanted to beat a miscreant, or knock him unconscious until the police arrived. It was also Bekci Baba's duty to beat the drums during Ramazan, or any other religious Bayram. He had to announce important tidings or give warning if there was a fire in any part of İstanbul. This latter warning was the signal for all the young men in the district to leap from their beds, hastily collect the one and only pump allotted to each street, and rush madly and with wild cheers to the scene of the fire.

I had never seen Bekci Baba, for during the day, when he called with the water, I was never allowed into the kitchen; and at night, when he turned watchman, I was generally in bed and asleep.

But one night I was lucky, for I was lying in my little bed, wide-awake, looking out at the evening sky. The pale light from the street gas lamp shone faintly into the room, and there was a great stillness everywhere. Not a soul seemed to stir in the streets, and only now and then could be heard the faint, far barking of a dog. Suddenly a noise came out of the quietness, a heavy *tak-tak-tak*. The sound grew nearer and I heard a voice crying something, but it was too far away for me to distinguish what it said.

My father came out into the hall. He was calling back to my mother and grandmother in the salon.

"Bekci Baba is coming. He's shouting something but I don't know what he's saying. There must be a fire somewhere."

I began to feel excited up there in my little lamp-lit room, and I sat up in bed to listen. The noise of Bekci Baba's stick was nearer now. It went *tak-tak-tak* on the cobblestones, and the old man shouted: "Fire! Fire! There is a fire in Beyoğlu," spacing his words out carefully and clearly, so that none should misunderstand.

I jumped out of bed and ran to the window.

Bekci Baba was coming up the road, a fearsome-looking figure with his dark cloak flapping out behind him and his stick thumping the ringing stones. He stood for a moment under the gas lamp in front of our house and, to my heated imagination, his face looked ghastly.

The poor wavering light from the lamp leaped and flickered over his face, now lighting, now shading the prominent cheekbones and the cadaverous eye sockets.

My father called out to him, "Where is the fire, Bekci Baba?"

"Beyoğlu!" the old man rasped, and was off again on his way, his cloak still flying out behind him and his stick going *tak-tak-tak*, far into the distance.

For a long time after I ceased to hear his voice, I heard the echo of his stick coming back to me, ever fainter. Probably Bekci Baba was still shouting of the fire in Beyoğlu.

6

The Changing Scene

I

IT WAS THE END OF 1914 AND TURKEY WAS at war. How little that meant to me then or to my family, save perhaps my father, who had the gift of vision and foresaw things more clearly.

Just at first there was no change in my home. It is true that I no longer went to school, but the events of the house continued without change.

One evening our neighbors were to dine, and, war or no war, food must still be served, wine decanted. My grandmother took an active interest in this little quiet dinner party. She felt she could not trust Feride to do everything properly and lamented the loss of Hacer.

One of the dinner dishes she particularly wanted prepared was the lahana dolmasi, of which she was very fond, and she spent the entire morning complaining to my mother that Feride would ruin them. Eventually she marched into the kitchen herself, tied a large apron over her black-satin dress, deposited her many rings in a safe place, and started to prepare the lahana dolmasi herself. She explained to Feride that although she had never *actually* cooked them, she nevertheless knew perfectly well how to do it.

Apparently Feride watched her noisy preparations with a great deal of misgiving and found difficulty in getting on with any other work, since my grandmother continually got in her way.

I was allowed into the kitchen to watch. I was directed to do this, that, and the other—all the dirtiest jobs, incidentally.

She called Feride to her side and gave a demonstration of how onions should be chopped, looked up directions in an old cookery book, then disagreed with them. She chopped onions with great gusto, calling upon my mother and İnci to witness her handiwork. While my grandmother busily explained to us how capable she was, Feride was frantically trying to interrupt, to tell her the cabbage leaves were boiling over and what should she do with them? My grandmother disregarded her. My mother said thoughtfully that it did seem to her that rather a lot of rice was being prepared, surely too much for a quiet dinner party of a few people? My grandmother airily disregarded her too and proceeded to wash and drain the rice. She then began to mix her finely chopped onions with it, and poor Feride, unable to stand the strain any longer, burst into tears. My grandmother paused in the mixing, looking with astonishment at the violently weeping Feride, and asked what was wrong. Between the paroxysms that shook her, poor Feride gasped that the onions first had to be cooked with şam fistigi (nuts), in olive oil *before* being mixed with the rice. My grandmother paused uncertainly, then demanded from my mother what the cookery book said. The cookery book, unfortunately, said the same as Feride.

My grandmother looked down at her messy fingers and the piles of wasted rice mixed with the wasted onions, then rinsed her hands under the tap, declaring she was finished with cooking. Amid a great silence she untied her apron, put all her rings back on her fingers again, and told Feride that she could make the dolmasi herself—the way the cookery book advocated. She declared she would never set foot in the kitchen again, having expected a little gratitude from Feride, not tears. She then went haughtily out to sprinkle eau de Cologne on her hands. Afterward she complained of the smell from the cabbage leaves and was all for having them thrown down the drain and vine leaves substituted. My mother restrained her and led her to the salon, still grumbling. She then commenced a long tirade, pointing out the shortcomings of Feride and the merits of the absent Hacer.

That evening, despite my grandmother's poor opinion of Feride, a dish of beautiful lahana dolmasi appeared on the table, and my grandmother told everyone she had made them herself. When she caught my astonished eye, she stared so haughtily at me that it was I who was forced to blush and look away first. Indeed, she half convinced me that she was right.

Our guests arrived early and were taken to the salon, where a bright fire crackled merrily in the white china stove. There İnci served little dishes of lokum.

Yasemin and Nuri, very demure, were on their most polite behavior. In the dining room they sat with Mehmet and me at a smaller table in a corner, while our parents ate at the big walnut table in the center.

During dinner my grandmother talked vivaciously, even being prevailed upon to sip a little raki, which brought the color to her cheeks.

Just as dessert was being served—slices of yellow watermelon in a silver dish surrounded with ice—there came a strange noise that sounded like drums. Everyone at the big table was suddenly stilled. I, noticing the silence, looked at them and saw the color ebb from my grandmother's face and my mother's hand unsteadily reach out for a fruit knife.

My father said: "They are playing the drums tonight: that must mean an announcement of some sort. Let us hope it is good."

Our neighbor, Orhan Bey, replied: "They play the drums during Bayram or Ramazan, but tonight is neither. What can it be?"

"They play the drums for war also," said my mother faintly, and we all looked at her, surprised that she should interfere in a masculine conversation.

"Şevkiye hanim, I hope you are wrong. I sincerely hope you are wrong."

Orhan Bey spoke jerkily, fussily, unable entirely to hide his own fear.

The faint drums beat on and we finished our dessert almost in silence. The grownups toyed with the melon, and my grandmother peeled a tangerine, cutting firmly with her knife into the bright skin, making it stand out around the fruit like a flower. She quartered it with deft fingers, then put it on her plate and sat looking at it with far-away eyes, as though wondering how it got there. The drums came nearer, and I started to tremble; the fear of my elders once again communicated itself to me.

They left the table, the ladies huddling by the window and my father and Orhan Bey going into the hall and opening the front door. I crept out after my father and stood beside him in the darkness. The drums were nearer now. They sounded their doom, their terrible message; and even to this day I cannot bear the sound of drums. We could hear Bekci Baba calling something, but he was too far away for us to distinguish what it was he said. My father put his arms around my shoulders and I pressed against him, feeling intolerably cold and miserable. Then the figure of Bekci Baba turned the corner of our street, a man beside him beating mournfully on the big drum. They came nearer, the drum beating ceaselessly. *Dan-dan-da-da-dan-dan* cried the drum, and Bekci Baba came under the lamp before our door to shout his shattering news.

"Men born between 1880 and 1885 must report to the recruiting center within the next forty-eight hours. Who fails to do so will be prosecuted."

And *dan-dan-da-da-dan-dan* went the drum, and my heart echoed its melancholy.

Orhan Bey shouted, "What does it mean, Bekci Baba?"

And the reply was: "War! War! Don't you know your country is at war?"

Bekci Baba moved off, and the old, old man with the drum followed him, to spread their news further.

We went in to the ladies. There they stood by the window, like three flowers blown in out of the black night, their silk dresses spreading about them and their faces pale to the lips.

Madame Müjgan started to speak, then swayed uncertainly and fainted in my mother's arms. Yasemin and Nuri ran to her, shouting *"Anne! Anne!"* And İnci was dispatched for eau de Cologne with which to massage the wrists and forehead of Madame Müjgan. While my mother was busy with her, Orhan Bey put his arms about his two children and said, "I was born in 1885—" and broke off, too full of tears to say any more. He pressed his children closer to him, so close that Yasemin cried out that he was hurting her, and then he released them, looking at them for a moment or two with the eyes of a sleepwalker: the eyes of a man who no longer saw two frightened children before him but the long dark nights in the stinking trenches, the gun flashes now and then lightening the sky, and finally the long dark night of death.

Presently his wife recovered. He took her on his arm and with great dignity thanked my mother for her evening and for what she had tried to do for his wife. He bade us good night. My father went with them across the garden, the two children tightly clutching his hands. Mehmet was taken away to be washed, and I stayed in the salon with my mother and my grandmother. ·

"Ahmet was born in 1885," said my grandmother.

She repeated it softly, over and over again, like a litany.

The next day my father left home early, for he was going to Sariyer to see Uncle Ahmet.

All that long day the house was a dead house. I tried to play in the garden with Mehmet, but I was bored and uneasy, sensing accurately my elders' alarm. There was no sign of the children from next door, and the first hint of there being anything out of the ordinary about the day came with the arrival of the cook of Madame Müjgan. I was on the back porch at that time and heard her asking Feride if the *bakkal* (grocer) had arrived with the bread. Feride replied that she too was waiting for him, since she had no fresh bread for luncheon. They talked for a few more minutes in whispers; and although there seemed to be a great sense of urgency about their talk, I could not distinguish anything. I was left with the queer, empty feeling of there being something

wrong, but I could not put a name to what it was. The morning
wore away. İnci set the table for luncheon, but still no bread appeared. Feride eventually told my mother, who treated the matter
lightly, saying that no doubt the bakkal had forgotten us this day,
and she gave permission for Feride to go out to buy bread. We
waited over an hour for her to come back, my mother growing more
and more impatient; but when she did come wearily back, she had
no bread.

"What is wrong?" asked my mother, very surprised.

"There is no bread anywhere, hanim effendi," replied Feride.
"Since I left here, I have been standing in a queue, with the people
killing each other and breaking each other's heads to get near the
baker's door. Some of them were buying twenty loaves at a time.
Every family in the district is there, with all their children and
their servants and all of them trying to get a loaf each. The baker
had sold out before it was my turn." So we sat down to our meal,
grumbling that we had to eat the previous day's bread. We did not
know that one day we might be glad to eat bread a week old.

During the afternoon, Feride again went to hunt bread but again
returned with empty hands. This time she reported that the shop
was shut and that, although the queues were greater than ever,
nobody knew when the shop would open. Nerves were uneasy that
day and tempers snapped easily. My grandmother, her face pale,
sat reading the Koran, decorous and pious-looking in her black
dress. My mother, her hands strangely empty, sat for most of the
day in front of one of the windows, watching for my father's return. What a difference there was already in them! Looking at my
grandmother reading the Koran so soberly, it was difficult to find
in her the amusing old lady who had only yesterday made us all
laugh at her culinary efforts. My mother was very white, her pale
face emphasized by the dark stuff of her dress; and her hands were
busily twining and untwining all the time in her empty lap. Once
she asked İnci to fetch her a glass of wine; the request was so unusual that, momentarily, İnci forgot all her good training to stare
at her in wide-eyed surprise.

My father returned in the middle of the afternoon, having been

unsuccessful in finding my uncle. My aunt had told him he had
left that morning, early, for the recruiting center and that she did
not know where he now was. She was, my father observed, very
distressed.

He had called at the Sariyer recruiting center on his way back
to the boat station, but all had been confusion and uproar there.
Harassed officials roared instructions, and civilians were herded
like cattle, hungry, hopeless, and apathetic. No one had been able
to give news of my uncle. In fact no one, it appeared, had had time
to listen to my father's questions, and at one time he had been in
danger of being herded with the other conscripts. My mother mentioned the incident of the bread and he laughed tiredly. The
streets, he said, were full of panic-stricken people, all looking for
something to buy and store. News of Turkey's entry into the war
had swept fear into İstanbul, and rioting was taking place in some
quarters.

He went out himself to seek bread and returned after many
hours with one small hot loaf in his hand. He looked ineffably
weary and dispirited, and there was a long scratch down one side
of his face, inflicted by a panic-maddened woman who had tried
to snatch his bread.

Dinner was a sober affair, with us children being urged to hurry
and our elders silently making a pretense of eating. Gone were the
leisurely, laughter-filled nights of good eating and good conversation, with my grandmother tossing off sparkling, malicious epi-
grams and my silent, shy mother offering only her grace and beauty
as a contribution to the dinner table.

The next morning Uncle Ahmet came to say goodbye to us.
Mehmet and I greeted him quietly; there was no noise, no fuss this
time, for our parents' faces set the pattern for our behavior. He
had brought boxes of bonbons for us, and we were sent into the
dining room while they discussed the serious business of war in the
salon.

Some things in life stand out sharply in the memory, making a
picture so vivid, so clear-cut, that the mind's eye retains them

indelibly for ever. Such a precise memory I have of the November day that my uncle visited us for the last time. Sharp and cold was the morning, with sunlight playing behind the scurrying clouds. The house was peaceful and still, as if great things were not happening all around it. The odd-job man was sweeping the terrace of the last fallen leaves. Feride was creating a good appetizing smell from the kitchen and İnci was pegging out the washing in the little side yard. The washerwoman sang lustily in the laundry, uncaring of the drafts that swooped moaningly from all about her. What cared she for war? And what cared Feride or the young İnci for war? Everyone that morning had something to do. I stood with my nose pressed against the windowpane and looked out upon the windy rustling garden that held its own wild winter beauty; Mehmet played busily on the floor. My father came into the room to decant some wine and, perhaps because I looked dejected, or perhaps because İnci was not there to guard us, he told Mehmet and me to go to the salon and play there.

In the salon my uncle was drinking Turkish coffee, looking unhappy. Nobody took any notice of us, so I sat down in one of the chairs. My mother looked at me, perhaps wondering why I was there. My uncle was talking about my aunt, saying that her health seemed to be getting worse. There was a peevish, worried note in his voice. Then he mentioned the farm, saying that most of the men had registered with him and who would look after things in future, he did not know.

My grandmother sat very silent, looking at Uncle Ahmet as if her eyes could never see enough of him, her eldest-born. She was an unemotional woman, but that day the tears were seldom far from her, only her fierce high pride beating them back. I suppose she was realizing for the first time in her life what war might do to families. For the first time, I think, she saw herself as a defenseless, ignorant woman who knew nothing of events outside her own small world, the world which held only sociability, women's gossip, and formality. And the last two men of her family were going from her. I am quite sure she did not pause to consider my mother's or my aunt's feelings. Naturally cold and a bit of a despot, she saw things only in relation to herself. She was losing her sons, might lose them for ever, but my mother and my aunt were only losing their husbands.

And although my grandmother had a high opinion of husbands, she had a higher opinion of sons. It is trite to say that little escapes the eye of a child, but nevertheless it is a fact; and I knew my grandmother better then, if more inchoately, than she would ever know herself. She had no time for self-analysis, and Freudian theories had not yet burst over İstanbul. My mother, too, I knew, and the latent streak of hardness there was in her, so that in after years, when hardness had become her chief characteristic, I was not taken by surprise, having all along recognized its deep-down existence. I could not write a true picture of them today were I not looking back with the eyes of a child to pictures I had thought dead; but just as these pictures today bring back so vividly places, scenes, and conversations that are gone, so too do they recall in part the *sensations* I felt as a child. That November day, for instance, I *knew*, as if she were screaming her thoughts aloud, what was going through my grandmother's head.

When she asked my uncle to stay for luncheon, I knew she was prolonging the fatal moment of goodbye; and when he refused, she seemed to shrink into herself, looking small and lonely in her tall chair. He said he had many things to attend to in Sariyer and was anxious about my aunt, and all the time he carefully avoided her eyes, perhaps feeling that if he looked at her too closely he too would break down.

Presently he stood up to go, and I can still see his tall figure dark against the windows.

"I shall be leaving tomorrow," he said. When my grandmother inquired for where, he shrugged his massive shoulders and replied that he did not know.

He leaned over his mother, kissing her hands, and she murmured a prayer over his bent dark head. One hand escaped from his kiss to stroke his cheek tenderly.

Uncle Ahmet swung Mehmet on his shoulders, took my hand

in his, and went out to the hall. My father said he would accompany him to Galata Bridge, and Ahmet beat his foot impatiently while İnci helped my father into his overcoat. Then they were ready and we were kissed. My uncle put his hand over my hair; then I saw his mouth suddenly quiver, and my inadequate heart longed to comfort him. Down the short path they went to the street, and at the corner they turned to wave to us; then they were hidden from our view, and we went back into the house again, Mehmet and I—two small boys who knew of no way to relieve the partings.

That evening Orhan Bey came to bid us farewell. He too was off the next morning to a place he did not know. We drank his health and wished him well, Mehmet and I holding our glasses high with the others. And down the street the drums beat for someone else. For in those days going away to the war, any war, was a brave and noble thing to do; and as the young men left a district, the band would play outside each of their houses, the Turkish flag being handed to the newest recruit. And all the youths with their wild, wild hearts leaped and danced and shouted, the better to drown the noise of the women's weeping. When they were leaving their homes, the band played a song of unbelievable sadness, and everyone commenced to sing:

> "Ey gaziler yol göründü
> Yine garib serime
> Daglar, taşlar dayanamaz
> Benim ahu zarima. . . ."

(O wounded ones, I am coming to take your place and my heart is crying because I am leaving my beloved ones. The mountains and the stones cry with me. . . .)

Orhan Bey bade us farewell and left for his own home; in the street the band still played.

The next day my father again hunted for bread and once again tried to see my uncle. He came home very late, and my grandmother immediately asked if he had seen him.

"Yes," replied my father, "I caught a glimpse of him as they marched him away."

"And did he look well in his uniform?" demanded my grandmother eagerly.

My father said gently: "He had no uniform. All the men wore their own clothes and carried bags on their shoulders. They had no marching boots, and armed soldiers kept between them and the crowd. And all their wives and mothers and sweethearts were there. I followed with the crowd, and they were put in a building in Sirkeci. We all waited, hoping for a sight of them, but nothing happened; and in the end the soldiers guarding the building sent us away."

My father ceased talking and his eyes looked bitter. He had seen Uncle Ahmet ordered and pushed and prodded by the butts of the guns of the peasant soldiers; he had seen a soldier kick one of the men; but he did not tell these things before my grandmother.

The next day my mother prepared a bag for my father, made like the bags the other men had been carrying across their unaccustomed shoulders. Nobody mentioned anything about his going, but we all knew the day would come. So my mother sewed a bag for him, working the coarse white linen bag with exquisite stitchery. And I think she sewed her heart into that bag, too, for, after my father had gone, we who were left saw nothing of her heart.

My father's business had been sold, and now he spent the days at home, awaiting his turn, impatient at the delay. It seemed as if the Government would never call him; and now that he knew he would have to go, he wanted to be away, to be done with the waiting that tore the heart and whitened the cheeks.

But the day came at last. The same drum beat out its poignant message, the same Bekci Baba stood under the same lamp and delivered his ultimatum:

"Men born between 1886 and 1892 must report to the recruiting center during the next forty-eight hours. Who fails to do so will be prosecuted."

And *dan-dan-da-da-dan-dan* mocked the drum.

My father had been called at last, and we thought that nothing worse than this could ever happen to us.

He went the next day to the recruiting center, and all the remaining young men of the district seemed to go with him. When he returned I was in bed, but I was not sleeping, even though I could not hear what they talked about.

It was a gray day when he left us, a gray cold day in early December; and because so many others were leaving with him, the band was going to play them all out together, from the lives they had always known to the bleakness of the battlefield. Feride packed the coarse linen bag with cakes and pies and other delicacies she had prepared for him. My father stood in the middle of the salon, already gone from us in spirit, looking about him for the last time. His face was secretive and closed, an alien soldier's face that had no right in this elegant, smiling room. My mother stood close beside him, and she too had that alien, shut-away look. But my poor huddled grandmother, who could not go to where these two had gone, sat in the windows and listened for the drums that would take away her youngest son. İnci brought in Turkish coffee, Feride following with the packed linen bag, and Mehmet ran to pull at her skirts, not understanding what all this fuss was about or that his father was going away. I went to my father and put my arms around him, and he lifted me up in his arms.

"You will be father from now on," he said, and I pressed my head against his face and felt a tear drop on my cheek. Whose tear was it, mine or his? Perhaps it fell from both of us, for tears tormented both of us. Feride and İnci burst into loud wailing, their soft hearts inexpressibly touched, but my mother stared dry-eyed. She had, I think, shed all the tears she would ever shed in some more private place than this. And now her frozen heart was able to look on this farewell scene almost with tranquillity. My grandmother prayed without stopping and then she began to mutter: "My eldest son and my youngest son. My eldest son and my youngest son. They have taken you both."

The distant drums began and my father put me down, drinking his coffee quickly.

He said, "Şevkiye! Don't look like that! Smile for me. I shall come back again—"

My mother's frozen face relaxed to give him her old, dazzling smile, and my father said to her, "You would make a better soldier than I."

They stood there facing each other, smiling their brilliant smiles, not touching each other yet insolubly merged into each other. The band came nearer, and now we clearly heard the drums and the *zurna*, a primitive clarinet, and the shouting of the following children.

My mother's eyes flew away from my father's, and the lovely miracle was broken. She picked up his heavy bag and handed it to him and they kissed like strangers, those two who had no need of kissing. My grandmother held out her hand for his gesture, and Feride and İnci then came forward to pay their tribute to him. They were crying bitterly, and he patted their heads, as if they were children again, like Mehmet and me. He swung his bag over his shoulder and went to the front door and the crowd that waited outside. The band played softly and mournfully, and my father kissed us children, then said his goodbye with lips that were wooden and stiff.

An old man came forward and handed him the Turkish flag, and the people all shouted "Padişahim çok yaşa," and my father stepped into his place among the other recruits. The waving and the cheering went wildly on, but there was no need to drown the weeping from our house, for the women did not weep. They stood there gently smiling, and the band played for my father:

"Ey gaziler yol göründü
Yine garib serime
Daglar, taşlar dayanamaz
Benim ahu zarima. . . ."

Then they turned the corner, out of our sight, with only the sound of the cheering and the singing voices and the noise of the band coming ever fainter back to us.

We went into the empty house.

7

Week-end Leave
and the New Bride

WE DID NOT KNOW WHERE THEY WERE taking my father; and although we asked Bekci Baba he could only say that the recruiting center might have some information.

The next day Feride was sent to inquire and came back to tell us that my father's age-group was at the Hasan Paşa Mosque, waiting to be sent away. My mother was excited and bade my grandmother get ready to accompany us to the mosque, as perhaps we would be able to catch a glimpse of my father before he left. We made our way through the crowded streets, my mother and my grandmother heavily veiled, the latter volubly protesting at having to walk and lamenting loudly for the vanished Murat and the phaeton.

Hasan Paşa Mosque was built in a garden, high above the street. When we got there, there were many other women and children, also come to try to see their menfolk before they left İstanbul. Crowded in the garden were the soldiers, looking down at us and searching for their loved ones. One of the soldiers shouted down to us, calling my grandmother by name and telling us that my father was somewhere in the garden. We looked at the soldier wonderingly, for who was this rough-looking person who dared to call my grandmother by her name? Suddenly my mother recognized him, telling us that it was the man who lived opposite us. I could hardly believe her. That soldier in his drab gray uniform, with his hair cut close against his head, could surely not be the elegant gentleman from across the way who had so proudly carried his wife on his arm each evening when taking her for a stroll. It was impossible: Where was the similarity between this soldier and the frock-coated, fezzed man from across the street?

My curiosity ebbed as I saw my father walking to the edge of the garden. There was quite fifteen feet between us, and the garden stood so high from the ground that it was not possible for each to see the other clearly.

My grandmother called to him, asking if there was anything he wanted, but he shook his head and said sternly, "Take the children home and do not come here any more." So we waved our handkerchiefs to him and left. There was nothing else to do. We could not wait there all night, and we could not bring my father home again. A few days after this, we learned that he had been moved to Selimiye, on the Anatolian side, for training; and one day my mother took me there with her, hoping to see my father. But it was impossible and we returned wearily home.

When we arrived home, we found that Madame Müjgan and her children were with my grandmother. My mother begged them to stay for dinner, for I think she felt their presence would help us forget our father's absence.

It seemed odd to have guests without my father being there, and to see my mother sitting in his place, at the head of the table. The talk was naturally about the war and their absent menfolk, with my grandmother still inclined to grumble over changed conditions. She was horrified by the war lust manifest in the bloodthirsty youth of the district, the only youth she ever saw, and those only from her window, for she could not be persuaded to go out on foot. And she was piously indignant that the sultan and his Government should be so inconsiderate as to leave all the women without their men to protect them.

But we others were growing accustomed to the idea of war, and even to the absence of my father. My mother seemed a different person without him, more competent now that she had not his shoulder to lean on, more decisive and less inclined to sit doing pretty, useless embroidery. She made an effort to instill some scholarship into me, since there was no school to which I could be sent, but it was not a success. She had not the teacher's patience, and I, no inclination to learn from her. She was very affectionate with us but curiously detached, and it was not possible for a child to want to run to her, or sob against her shoulder his small fears. We children appeared to be the merest incidents in her life and my father a sort of god.

One day, Aunt Ayşe came to visit us, bringing a tall gaunt maid with her as chaperone. She looked very thin and was distressed by having to travel without my uncle, saying that the noise and confusion in the streets frightened her. She asked for news of my father, and my mother told her where he was. My aunt replied that Uncle Ahmet was outside Turkey altogether, then sat twisting her hands as though that knowledge were a fearful knowledge to hold and to be outside his country, the most terrible thing that could happen to Uncle Ahmet. During dinner that night she ate little, although Feride had been at pains to prepare all her favorite dishes. She sipped a little red wine and coughed continuously, apologizing blushingly, saying that she had had this cough for many months now and that it would not go or respond to the various herbal treatments her cook had recommended.

During dinner, Feride appeared with a letter for my mother. It had been brought by the batman of a certain captain whom we knew very well. He said that my father was well but unable to write, for he was undergoing a very rigorous officers' training which for some reason or another made it impossible for him to communicate with my mother himself. The captain went on to say that at the end of the initial training period, probably by the coming week end, my father would be given a few days' leave.

Feride stood by while my mother read this out to us, and she was as excited as the rest of us and there and then began to plan what my father would be given to eat. My aunt smiled wistfully. But my grandmother triumphantly held out her glass for more wine and said: "You see! They will make him an officer. Did I not tell you that always?"

Then we all drank my father's health and felt proud and happy. İnci was dispatched to tell Madame Müjgan of the good news and to request that she should come and drink coffee with us. Mehmet and I were taken to bed, but the women sat long in the salon, their happy voices floating up the stairs and my mother's laughter now and then ringing out purely, just as in the days when my father had always been with us.

Aunt Ayşe left for Sariyer, and we had two more days to prepare for my father's arrival. In those days the Moslem week end was Thursday and Friday, and no cleaning could be done during that time. Thursday morning dawned clear and cold, and İnci had no time to waste with Mehmet and me. Once we were dressed, we were severely cautioned not to get ourselves dirtied, but a twinkle lurked behind the severe voice, for today was a happy day, not to be spoiled by tears. That day the house was enchanted. Clean curtains were hung in the main rooms, a great orgy of polishing went on, and silk cloths and lace cloths were placed everywhere, just as at Bayram. But this was better than Bayram, for our father was coming home.

Many neighbors called, and my mother drank endless cups of Turkish coffee with them. My grandmother held a sort of court among them, all five fingers of one hand decorated with exquisite rings and jewels blazing about her neck. She was her old arrogant, despotic self again and commanded royally.

Feride and İnci worked like slaves. Flowers were found and arranged; glasses were polished until they shone with a thousand eyes; and silver made a note of glory against the mellow walnut of the great buffet. Morning slipped by into afternoon and still my father did not come. Mehmet and I waited for hours in front of the door, until finally the raw air drove us shivering indoors. Everywhere in the house was a sense of expectancy. The hall was all

a-glitter with the sheen from the freshly polished floor and with
the reflection of the giant silver trays in the patina of the table, an
English table my great-grandfather had once brought back from
his travels. A copper mangal, a sort of brazier, gave off heat to thaw
a cold and weary voyager, and the chrysanthemums from Sariyer
glowed brightly in a corner. The house waited for its master and
nothing more remained to be done. But still the afternoon passed
until it was evening and time for İnci to light the six tall lamps in
the salon and the smaller ones in the hall.

Mehmet and I were disconsolate. Would our father not come
after all? We opened the front door for a last peep into the evening
gloom, letting in such a gust of cold air that İnci sharply ordered
us to close the door immediately. But I had seen a soldier turning
the corner, and I thought it was the captain's batman come with
another message; I shouted to my mother to come. The soldier
called to me, and then I knew it was not the captain's batman after
all, but my father. I ran to him, throwing myself with violence
into his outstretched arms, and Mehmet came flying after me.

We went into the house together, and there was my mother in
the hall, all a-tremble with happiness and flushed rosy-red, wearing
a wine-velvet dress and rubies to glorify her neck.

Such laughter and tears there were suddenly, such excited ques-
tion-and-answer, for the master of the house was home again, and
the old house creaked in its joints and was content to shelter such
radiance.

My father looked drab in his uniform and said he only longed
for a bath and a change of linen, for the coarse Army underlinen
chafed his skin.

He was gay and talkative, glad to be home again, hiding his
unhappiness at being in the Army. He said he would be training for
several more months, adding that that was all to the good, since it
meant he would remain at Selimiye and might occasionally be permitted to come home. He mentioned the commanding officer, a man
who had been a great friend of my grandfather's; but he only touched
lightly on him, saying that one could not expect favors in the Army.

German officers were attached to the unit—Prussian upstarts he called them, adding that there was no love lost between the Turkish officers and the strutting Germans. My mother shone quietly for the two days he was at home, but on the last evening I wandered into the salon on a conversation that was to puzzle me for a long time.

"Anything may happen," my father was saying earnestly, adding, "but if I am not here at that time, I would like the baby to be called Muazzez—or Arif, if it is another boy."

Here I saw the ever alert İnci look across to them—she was pouring coffee at a side table—and I was intensely curious, wondering what baby they were talking about.

I had not the courage to ask questions and, in any case, the subject was abruptly dropped, since my father noticed the proximity of İnci and my own staring face.

When my father left to go back to his unit, everyone was cheerful, for this time we knew that he was only going as far as Selimiye and might soon be back with us.

"Au revoir," my mother called gaily to his handwave, and Mehmet and I remained to watch him out of sight.

Then we went back to İnci and daily routine, and we none of us knew that this was the real goodbye.

Some weeks later a letter was brought from my father. My mother kept that letter all through her life, and it is in my possession today, almost the only souvenir left from those times:

. . . so you see we shall be leaving Selimiye almost immediately. Our training is not finished, and what they intend doing with us nobody knows, so for the time being we march with the rest. We shall leave by train, so come to the railway track tomorrow morning. I cannot give you a time but I would like one more glimpse of you before I go. Let the children come too. There is nothing more that can be said here, but I pray God all goes well with you. I leave you and my unborn child in the hands of God and kiss from your eyes. . .

My mother cried over this letter; but my grandmother was offended because my father had not mentioned her, and she sulked a little for the ingratitude of all sons when they take a wife. Mehmet and I were excited to be going to the railway tracks. They ran across the bottom of the big waste field behind our house, and although they could not be seen from the house, very often one heard the rumble of the infrequent trains. It seemed very romantic to us that our father should travel in such a fearsome monster as a train, and we greatly envied him.

İnci said to me that day: "Perhaps soon you will have a baby brother or sister. Would you like that?"

"No!" I replied, appalled by the thought of a new baby in the house, for perhaps some subconscious memory lingered from Mehmet's babyhood, when I had been continually hushed into silence.

"But perhaps it will be a lovely baby sister," persisted İnci, until she finally aroused my curiosity.

"Who will bring it?" I wanted to know.

"One of the pigeons in the garden, one of *your* pigeons, will bring it from your father."

"This morning?" I asked. "Or tomorrow when we go to the tracks to see my father?"

"No, silly!" said İnci.

I immediately lost interest in the arrival of such a remote baby.

"Did my pigeons tell you?" I asked finally, not quite able entirely to dismiss the subject. When İnci replied that they had, I sat and thought about her words, then dragged Mehmet off to the garden to look for the knowledgeable pigeons. They strutted at the bottom of the garden and seemed to think we had brought bread for them, but to all my questions they only answered "Coo-coo," in their soft, throaty voices. Mehmet maddened me by rushing at them, his arms flapping, and they took fright and circled irritatingly above my head.

"Tell me!" I shouted at them, and they replied, "Coo-coo," "coo-coo," curving and diving and circling until I sadly decided that İnci must have some very special knowledge of pigeon language.

Next morning we were wrapped in heavy overcoats and scarves and taken with my mother and my grandmother to the bottom of the waste field, where we could see all the passing trains. It was bitterly cold and many trains passed that day, all of them overflowing with soldiers who shouted and sang and waved to us, but my father was not among them. Trainload after trainload passed, and still he did not come; after two hours we children were almost crying with the cold, stamping our feet in an effort to keep warm.

"Perhaps he has already gone," said my mother, her voice despairing. "Perhaps he passed this way when we were still sleeping."

On came the thundering trains, bound for Edirne and God knew what hell afterward. On the other line we saw a Red Crescent train come in, and I felt my mother shiver beside me as she said to my grandmother:

"An ambulance train, Mother! I wonder if they are sick or wounded soldiers?"

And my grandmother replied, "Stop tormenting yourself like this."

The Red Crescent train slipped past with its weary travelers, and then another train, coming in the opposite direction, caught our senses. With such suddenness that we were almost startled, we saw my father's face at a window and his white handkerchief waving to attract our wavering attention.

"Look!" Mehmet shouted. "It's Baba!"

My mother waved to him and threw reckless, last-minute kisses, half laughing, half crying in her excitement.

As the train roared past, my father leaned far out of the window and shouted: "Goodbye! God bless all of you!"

And my mother cried back to him, "Not goodbye, Hüsnü!"

But the train had passed on, so perhaps he never heard what it was she said to him, those last poignant words which she did not know were to be her last spoken words to him.

One little moment more we saw his outstretched hand and the waving, waving handkerchief, then that too was gone and he was gone and the cold morning seemed suddenly colder. We returned home to a warm fire, but the chill that was in our blood took a long, long time to thaw.

But life still had to march on, and the slow, agonizing days of waiting for news had to be lived through. Then other problems began to present themselves, creeping insidiously into the normal pattern of life and disrupting it. First arose the problem of food. For weeks past, Feride had been using our reserve stocks, and my mother became alarmed by the rapidity with which they were depleted. Six of us to be fed several times in a day made great inroads on flour and sugar and rice.

Feride spent more time hunting open shops than she did in the kitchen. Our bread consumption was cut to the minimum. Sweets with luncheon became things to be remembered, and fresh milk was scarce and costly. When it could be bought, it had to be boiled for several minutes before it was safe to drink, and it was almost half water. The odd-job man was dismissed, since formerly he had always had all his meals in the house. The washerwoman was for the moment retained, since she only came once a week and was deemed a necessity.

My grandmother professed to take no interest in these domestic problems, but many times I heard her grumbling voice declaring that in her time six servants had been necessary to run her house and that now my mother expected to get the same results with two and a washerwoman. My mother ignored her. She had ceased to be a lady of leisure and was frequently to be found in the kitchen these days, during Feride's shopping expeditions. Prices had suddenly become fantastic; and when food could be bought, treble its normal price was asked. But our trouble was not then one of money. When my father sold his business, he brought all the money home to us, in notes and in gold, and it was decided to keep this large amount in the house, since banking systems were deemed to be too intricate for my mother to understand. So the undefended money lay in the house, many thousands of lire dangerously reposing in a flat wooden box in my mother's bedroom. And none realized the danger of that arrangement.

My grandmother had no money of her own. My grandfather,

according to old Turkish custom, left everything with my father, merely stipulating that my grandmother should be cared for all her life. Since this was the usual manner of leaving possessions or property, my grandmother felt no resentment. She had many fine pieces of jewelry, and the lack of ready money was no drawback to her. She had never been allowed to handle money in her life, rarely went out anywhere, and had no knowledge of the value of anything. She got impatient if my mother complained of the dearness of things and could not be made to understand why sweets were no longer served with luncheon. She had a great appetite for the heavy, syrupy Turkish sweets, made with butter and eggs, and accused my mother of trying to starve her now that there were no menfolk in the house to defend her. She would imperiously demand fruits or bonbons and sulk when she was told she could not have them. She complained that her Turkish coffee was not sweet enough and took to secreting little packets of sugar about her person, tipping a little surreptitiously into her cup when my mother was not looking. As the winter grew more severe, she became more and more cantankerous and would sit huddled over the fire in the salon, wrapped in numerous shawls. Morose and irritable, she found fault with everything, and her appetite was insatiable. One morning she threw us all into a flurry by announcing over breakfast that she was going to Sariyer, where she insisted she would get more to eat than she was getting with us. She demanded that Feride should accompany her, remaining with her during her stay with Aunt Ayşe. My mother indignantly opposed the idea, asking what she was expected to do without her treasured Feride. My grandmother grunted, implying tacitly that she neither knew nor cared. She wanted Feride and that was all there was to it. However, in the end it was all arranged to everyone's satisfaction. Feride would accompany my grandmother but would return to us that same evening. We bolted our meager breakfast, and Feride tore herself in little pieces trying to do too many things at once. But at last we got them off, my grandmother having her last little grumble because she had to travel to Galata Bridge in a hired cab.

Mehmet and I followed my mother into the kitchen, where she

was going to take Feride's place for the day. She wore an apron over her pretty dress, and we were set to work to help her. I was put to peeling potatoes, a job I loathed only a little less than I loathed the taste of potatoes. Mehmet was given the easiest things to do and staggered happily about, taking the dried cutlery into the chest in the dining room, hanging cups and managing to break a few.

"Times are changing," said my mother to me, conversationally, briskly shaking out the freshly washed kitchen cloths. "Perhaps there will be many things you will both have to learn to do until this war is over. When your father comes back again, everything will be all right, but until that time we must all learn to look after ourselves. Your grandmother is old and she does not understand things, therefore we must have patience with her."

She sounded hard and a bit impatient, and I wondered why she spoke of my grandmother like this. She felt me watching her and said:

"She is a very good woman but she will not accept the fact that there are many things we cannot get nowadays. All those little luxuries your grandfather used to bring her—" And she broke off, pondering on the changed conditions. Her hands looked red and ugly, and I was horrified to see that they looked like Feride's or İnci's. All their smooth, cool whiteness seemed to have disappeared. She caught my look and smiled at me, then glanced back to her rough hands and seemed proud of them. I thought she was very brave. She was only twenty-two at that time, well born and accustomed to the sheltered life that only the well born women of old Turkey really knew. Yet she had taken on her shoulders the responsibility of us children and my grandmother and was so sensitive to the welfare of her servants that she shared their work willingly. She could not sit idle while two servants did the work of four; and, despite the fact that she was a shocking cook in those days, she was always ready to help in the kitchen, humbly learning from the experienced Feride.

During my grandmother's sojourn at Sariyer, we received a

letter from my father. He was somewhere near Edirne; he was well but worried because no letters were being received from us or from Uncle Ahmet, to whom he had written repeatedly. He wrote of his longing to be with us and of the appalling misery of the Turkish soldier. It was the first news we had had for many weeks, and it was like a tonic for my mother: we heard her lilting, singing voice again about the house.

My grandmother brought back news that Uncle Ahmet was at Şam, in Syria, and that my aunt was more ill than we had suspected. Sariyer, she said, was in a shocking condition, with all the young men having gone to the war and only the old ones left to look after the estate, with no supervision to guide them. She brought back eggs and chickens and fresh butter, eagerly saying that Feride could now make for us some nice, heavy, sticky sweets. My mother was going to veto indignantly any such idea, but perhaps the old lady looked pathetic, for she suddenly relented and let my grandmother have her way. The visit to Sariyer had done a lot of good for my grandmother. I think the state of things there had depressed her unutterably, for now she began doing small things about the house and stopped complaining, appearing genuinely glad to be back in the sane, healthy atmosphere of our house.

One day the wife of the local imam paid us a surprise visit. She was a vast caricature of a woman, with treble chins and a bosom that shot straight out like a board. She sat very upright in the salon, obviously not desiring the presence of Mehmet and me. My mother apologized for us, explaining that İnci had so much else to do that she could not be expected to look after us exclusively. The imam's wife nodded gravely and said she quite understood, but her hard eyes raked us with positive dislike, and I felt quite sure she did not understand at all. She settled herself comfortably near my grandmother, beginning to talk in a penetrating, sibilant whisper. She related that a certain well known gentleman of our slight acquaintance, a rich, eccentric old gentleman, was looking for a wife! She put a world of meaning into that one word.

"Why?" demanded my grandmother blankly, and with such astonishment in her voice that the imam's wife huffily sniffed that she did not know but that it was no unusual thing for a gentleman to want a wife. Energetically my grandmother replied that it was highly unusual for the gentleman in particular. The imam's wife made no comment, and then my mother came in with coffee and for a while the subject was not discussed. But as though drawn by a magnet, the visitor could not keep away from the matter for long. This time she came straight to the point and propounded the amazing suggestion that my grandmother should marry him herself. We were all astounded. Taking our astonished silence for approval, she continued by saying that the old man had himself expressed a great preference for my grandmother. He only waited for her to give her decision before formally declaring his intentions, when, we gathered, he would eagerly leap like a young man into the arena and carry her off for himself. There was an astounded, disbelieving silence when the imam's wife had finished speaking. I sat on the floor gaping foolishly until my mother, with an exasperated, angry note in her voice, told me to go out of the room immediately and to take Mehmet with me. I rushed in search of İnci to tell her what I had overheard. Her reaction disappointed me, for she sagely nodded her crinkly head and said that she knew all about it. I refused to believe her; but she assured me that every servant in the neighborhood knew, for they had been informed many weeks ago by the old man's cook—who was too astute to let much pass her ear.

I could not imagine anyone wanting to marry my grandmother, for she seemed incredibly, unromantically old to me, though İnci pointed out that she was still several years short of fifty and a recognized hostess in the district. What this had to do with her marriageable qualities I did not know, but İnci assured me they were both very important. I heard no more about the matter for several days, for my mother would not discuss anything of such a delicate nature before us. Neighbors took to more frequent visiting, to my usually hospitable mother's annoyance, for she had to provide coffee for them, and sugar was short. Madame Müjgan breathlessly arrived to give her advice. She pointed out what an excellent match this would be, since the old man was fabulously wealthy, owning many coal depots and wharves and heaven knew what else. And—best of all in their opinion—he had no tiresome relatives to interfere, except a nephew who could be trusted to behave. My grandmother noticeably weakened, and my mother grew more and more tight-lipped, seeing the whole situation as a farce.

"Have you lost your senses?" she demanded one day in exasperation. "What do you suppose Ahmet and Hüsnü will say to such a marriage?"

My grandmother replied that Ahmet and Hüsnü had their families around them, that she had nobody to care about her, and that she did not wish to grow old and lonely and a burden to all about her in this house. My mother turned her face from such reasoning, and a coldness blew between the two of them. Mehmet and I were insatiably curious for knowledge, anxious to know the outcome of such an odd, unorthodox courtship, but little enlightenment came our way. Then one day my grandmother defiantly announced that her mind was made up and that she was going to marry her rich old man. Mehmet and I wriggled with excitement; but my mother received the news coldly, merely saying that she would immediately set about listing my grandmother's furniture and belongings, as she supposed she would be taking them to her new home. Never was a marriage arranged with such lack of warmth, such formality. New clothes were prepared for everyone, and Feride drew again on our precious food stocks, for a reception was to be held in our house.

On the marriage morning Madame Müjgan, the imam who was going to perform the ceremony, and his capacious wife and several neighbors gathered in the salon to await the arrival of the bridegroom.

My grandmother looked pale and composed and utterly magnificent in gray watered silk, a material all the rage at that time in İstanbul. The old man arrived in his carriage, his nephew assisting him into the house, for he was very gouty. The imam read from the

Koran, and after a few minutes my grandmother became a bride again for the second time in her life. Congratulations, false and unreal as a winter's sun, broke out, and liqueurs and bonbons were distributed before the more serious eating really began. My mother drank to the couple's health but looked forbidding and was nothing more than politely formal to my grandmother.

Later in the day the bridal pair were handed into their elegant carriage, and my grandmother, looking suddenly lonely, was driven to her new home.

In the evening three porters from the old man's house called for my grandmother's furniture. For the next hour or so they were busy removing it, and things kept shifting in the salon and in the dining room until I had the fearful thought that nothing would be left for us.

Last of all they stripped my grandmother's room; that, for me, really was the end of her, for when the room was empty, I peeped inside and saw that nothing of her was left there. The patterned curtains swung in the little breeze I made with the open door, and so little impression had my grandmother ever made on this house, that it seemed to me as if she had never lived here at all. The empty room echoed gently when I said "Grandmother," and I shivered and ran to find İnci, who was always at hand when a small boy needed comfort.

8

Muazzez Makes Her Debut

AFTER MY GRANDMOTHER'S MARRIAGE, the house seemed larger and, it must be admitted, more peaceful. The remaining furniture was rearranged and I moved into her empty bedroom.

Occasionally during the afternoons my grandmother would visit us, for she still lived quite near Bayazit, but she never mentioned her husband and my mother never inquired after him. By tacit agreement his name was taboo. Later on in the year, in the fine spring weather, Mehmet and I were given permission to visit her. But this we did not like doing, preferring to see her in our own house, for her husband had no affection for small boys; in particular, he disliked Mehmet and me. At another time my mother paid an afternoon call with us, but the old man stayed in his own little sitting room the whole time we were there and made it so abundantly clear that we were unwelcome that my mother decided never to set foot in his house again. We were also forbidden to visit there, but nevertheless, when the days were fine and we were supposed to be playing safely in the garden, we did sometimes manage to escape. My grandmother's new home was very beautiful, with exquisite old tapestries and Chinese vases which we were told were very valuable. He was a bit of a connoisseur in his way and loved beauty. The gardens were expansive and well kept, but my grand-mother had a temporary look in that house, as though she had rested there but for a moment. The servants were all old retainers who had been there for years and knew their job so well that she had no conceivable right to interfere with them. This restraint, this lack of freedom in her kitchen, made her feel lonely for Feride and İnci and the other servants she had trained from childhood. As I have remarked before, the old man did not like Mehmet or me. He was very jealous if my grandmother gave up any time to us, resenting us in some queer, illogical way, and telling her over and over again that she must give up her visits to our house. He said our family was dead for her, that she had married him and that he required some attention from her. All of this I learned many years later, but when I was a child I saw him only as a cantankerous, horrid old man who was completely unlike my own beloved grand-father. One other thing I learned later in life. He had expected from his marriage that she should share his bed with him: upon her adamant, astonished refusal, he informed her that he could, if he wished, insist on this right. She, apparently, sharply and coldly reminded him that as he was well over eighty years old, he should be contemplating his death and not setting himself up as an *amoureux*. This plain speaking had considerably affronted him, and huffily he had warned her that if she were to continue in this atti-tude, she need not expect any benefits from him. Since my grand-mother *was* hoping for benefits from him, she thought it better thereafter to hold her peace, though still continuing in her firm refusal to become part of his bed. Later, a bitter quarrel took place between them, and he refused her permission to visit us. And a hus-band's will in those days was not to be lightly disregarded. My mother did not know of this quarrel, and Mehmet and I were sent to find out what was wrong. We met the old man in the street, almost at his own door, so to speak.

He was carrying a large stick and asked me where I was going. Tremblingly I replied that I was going to see my grandmother, and he lifted his heavy stick to bring it down on our shoulders. I quickly dodged out of his way, dragging a surprised Mehmet after me, and the stick dropped shatteringly to the ground from his fingers. Nimbly I picked it up and ran away with it in the direction of our own home to pour out the story to my mother breathlessly. She grew white as she listened and banished the offensive stick to the kitchen. Later on, a servant of the old man called for it, bringing with him an insulting message that we were to be kept out of his master's way. Never have I seen my mother in such a passion. She put on her veil, asked Feride to accompany her, and, leaving us in İnci's care, went off to my grandmother's house.

When she told me the story in after years—with much laughter for things so far behind her—she said that she had marched boldly to the old man's room, ignoring alike the alarmed faces of my grandmother and the servants. She had thrust open the door of his private sitting room, leaving the terrified Feride outside to wait for her, and told him what she thought of him—and a good deal else besides, I gathered. He had been as astonished as the rest of his flurried household and had listened, unwillingly, to most of what she had to say before sufficiently reviving to ask her to leave his home.

Naturally this dispute did not make relations any less strained between the two families—if anything it widened the breach. Once my grandmother secretly managed to visit us, but she was in such fear of being discovered that my mother asked her not to come again.

I thought she was hard with her, not listening to her complaints, not giving a word of comfort; and I felt near to tears as I saw my grandmother hurrying furtively away from our house: she seemed to be a little lonely old woman without a word of comfort in the world.

In Turkey in the old days there used to be a month called Aşure Ayi.

Aşure is a sweet cooked with wheat, sultanas, figs, dates, dried beans, what you will, the whole being boiled for several hours until the result looks a little like aspic jelly. The legend of aşure is that when Noah in the Ark found himself running short of supplies, he ordered all the remaining foods to be cooked together for one last gigantic meal. This was aşure—or so we were told.

During the Ottoman Empire, days a month used to be set aside each year for the making of aşure in all the houses of the rich, who afterward distributed it to the poor. When my grandfather was alive, it used to be made in our house, fat Hacer being an adept at it; but latterly my mother had discontinued the habit, for Feride was uncertain of the recipe and my mother too cautious nowadays to waste any precious food. But it was made in my grandmother's new home, and a huge silver pot of it sent to us. Feride was immediately ordered to give it to the poor, and my mother sent a message to my grandmother not to send anything more to us. If my mother had anything to do with it, the breach between them would never heal.

After that I remember Ramazan. None of us kept the fast, although in my grandfather's day Ramazan was the signal for the entire household to fast and pray the prescribed five times in a day. With the closing of Ramazan comes the Şeker Bayrami, when all manner of sweets are distributed, especially to the children. This particular Bayram was unbearably sad for us, and perhaps that is why I remember it so well. My father was no longer with us, my grandmother had remarried, and my mother was, although I did not know it, pregnant with her third child. And she was alone in this great empty house with two small children and her faithful Feride and İnci. That Bayram morning İnci dressed us in new clothing—for new clothing is as necessary to a Bayram as are the sweets and the celebration. We were taken sedately downstairs to the salon, where my mother sat alone, in a pretty silk dress and with all her rings sparkling on her reddened fingers. A few neighbors called to congratulate the Bayram, then went away again, and I saw my mother quietly crying to herself.

What an emotional, unhappy Bayram to remember when only happiness should have been present.

Later that same week we were taken to Madame Müjgan's house to stay for a few days, for we were told that our mother was not well. We were inclined to be tearful, but I remember that İnci whispered that perhaps when we came home again the new baby would have arrived. So that made us feel better, and we proudly boasted of this to Yasemin and Nuri, who were bitterly jealous that they had no new baby to boast about.

The last evening we spent in the house of our neighbor, Mehmet was inclined to be fretful, calling for İnci; but he was eventually persuaded to sleep by Madame Müjgan's upstairs maid.

I lay there in my little narrow bed, listening to the street sounds drifting in through the window. Somewhere I could hear Bekci Baba crying his news of a fire, and sleepily I remembered the night I had seen him for the first time. Then I remembered the shivering, mournful beat of the drums the day they came to take my father away, and I felt suddenly lonely, lying there in an unfamiliar room. I wondered if the pigeons had brought the new baby yet and finally drifted into sleep to the sound of Bekci Baba's voice. He still cried of a fire that raged somewhere in the city; but a fire was not exciting to me, for I had never seen one and I did not know that the wooden houses and konaks of İstanbul were a heaven-sent opportunity for enemy spies. I did not know that one day I should see my beloved İstanbul burning, burning to the empty skies.

The next day İnci arrived to take us back home. On the way across the gardens she said to me:

"Your pigeons have brought a lovely baby sister for you. Aren't you pleased?"

I was uncertain until I had seen the wonderful baby, so I reserved my judgment, and İnci thought I was sulking and laughed at me.

Upstairs in my mother's room, all was arrayed as if for a wedding. Lace pillows supported my mother's dark head and a satin quilt dropped almost to the carpet. Mehmet and I stood awkwardly in the doorway, uncertain whether to advance into such grandeur or not, but my mother smiled and called us over to her. Excitedly we ran for her kiss, my grandmother fussily warning us not to jump on the bed.

"Where's the baby?" we wanted to know and my mother pulled back a lacy sheet and we looked down at a little dark head and a red crumpled rose-leaf of face.

Mehmet said, "Why doesn't she open her eyes?"

And my mother laughed and replied that she was sleeping. She put her hand against the baby's dress and drew out a long white box.

"See what she has brought for you from your father," she said, and we took the box in delight, discovering chocolate bonbons inside, a rare luxury nowadays. We were happy that the baby had not come empty-handed and disposed to regard her more kindly.

The days passed by, those sunny May days of 1915, and one day my mother was downstairs with us again and we became accustomed to seeing the baby sleeping in her white cradle on the terrace. Mehmet and I would peep at her curiously, anxious for her to open her eyes and smile at us. She was so quiet, lying there, such a remarkably docile baby, that we quite grew to love her, for no matter how much noise we made, she still slept on. We were never hushed for her sake, and I think our love for Muazzez dates from that time.

About this time too, my grandmother started to disobey her husband and visit us whenever she pleased. One day she helped my mother compose a letter to my father, telling him of the birth of his daughter, but we never knew whether he received the letter or not. Neighbors began to alarm my mother, hinting that his long silence might mean that he was dead, and advised her to go to the War Office for information. But this she would not do, perhaps fearing to hear what they would say.

Aunt Ayşe paid us a visit from Sariyer, eager to see Muazzez. She looked so different that I could scarcely recognize her, she was so gaunt and white and her cheeks so sunken. She started to cry when she saw Muazzez, and I remember that I fascinatedly watched her. The tears poured down her face, and Mehmet plucked uncertainly at her sleeve, distressed to see such sorrow, his small brown face looking unhappily at Aunt Ayşe. When her tears ceased, she commenced to cough in a sickening sort of way, and my grandmother, who sat out on the terrace with us, looked impatient and tapped her foot, as if she abhorred such a display of emotionalism.

I stood there pondering about crying. Everyone seemed to cry nowadays and for no reason at all, in so far as I could see. Rebelliously, I wished my father back with us again. I had not thought about him for weeks, perhaps for months; yet suddenly there he was before my eyes, and my heart ached with longing to see him come striding onto the terrace, to hear him call out to us in the old way. And I felt a great lump rise in my throat and I did not know that crying was infectious. Afterward I heard my aunt say that Uncle Ahmet had been blinded somewhere in the desert and that she could not understand why the authorities did not send him home to her. Her unhappiness nagged at the heart, even phlegmatic Mehmet noticing it and trying to climb across her knee to console her. My mother told her we would all come to Sariyer later in the summer, when Muazzez was a little older and in a better condition to travel. And my aunt sighed and asked if we remembered last year there.

I listened to her soft voice rising and falling, but in my eyes was a picture of Sariyer. I saw the old house set among the trees and heard again my uncle's merry laughter. I went fishing with him on the Bosporus and slept again in the little rose-scented room above the tangled old garden. I heard the ships' sirens as they passed in the night—and yet I never left the terrace. But the memories were so clear and insistent in my mind that for a split second in time I was back again in Sariyer.

When my aunt left us to return home, I felt sorry that she had to go. She looked so little and lonely that I yearned to protect her from the world she found so hard now that my uncle was not beside her.

She did not kiss us, I remember, but stood fondling our heads, reluctant to leave yet anxious to return to Sariyer, where news from Uncle Ahmet perhaps awaited her.

"We shall come in June," said my mother confidently, as if nothing might happen to disturb that promise. Aunt Ayşe left, and I never saw her again in my life. I never saw Sariyer either, for many years afterward, when I visited it, nothing remained but a tumble-down house and a garden choked with weeds. The Sariyer I knew and loved was no more, vanished like its long-dead owners. Yet that Sariyer still shines clearly for me today, just as Aunt Ayşe's face emerges out of the mists of time and shines too. There are some things in the heart that do not die, and the loves of early childhood are the strongest loves of all.

*   *

*

*   *

<><><><><>

9

<><><><><>

*   *   *A Long Farewell*

*

*   *

*

*   * M̲UAZZEZ MUST HAVE CONTINUED TO BE
a quiet baby, for I remember next to nothing about her from those
days. Looking back, I find it is easier to remember all the strange,
unquiet things that happened. I suppose all memories only need a
little shaking-up to restore again places and things and people.
Certainly I have had little difficulty in delving back to the past.
Letters and photographs and later-day conversations have brought
all these long-dead days before the mind's eye again, in some cases
with startling clarity. For instance, I still recall the day my grandmother came to take Feride away from us.

It was high summer, and we played in the garden under the eye
of my mother. She was sewing clothes for Muazzez, who kicked
on a rug, İnci being inside in the house working. Feride's singing
voice drifted out from the kitchen, and a great peace lay about us.
It was a cloudless, blue, shining day, and I had a surge of happiness for no reason at all. Never had my home looked prettier, standing there squatly and compactly in its green lawn, the flower beds
a blaze of color, the house blindingly white where the sun's long
fingers touched it, blotched with gray, lacy patterns where the
leaves of the vine and the fig tree sheltered it. Recalling that scene
now, did an uneasy peace linger in the sky above it, I wonder,

*   101   *

making the tranquillity stand out all the more sharply by contrast because of the things to come? That morning remains etched on the mind, one of a series of pictures that will never die while I live.

My grandmother called toward noon, coming across the grass to us, severe in her high-necked gown.

İnci followed her almost immediately with a tray of iced sherbets, cooling, effervescent drinks that tasted of roses.

My grandmother sat down in the chaise-longue my mother pushed forward for her, unveiled her hot face, and held her hand to us children to be kissed. She was disposed to be gracious, praised the looks of the baby, gave my mother some entirely unwarranted advice regarding her embroidery, and was altogether so charming that I felt she must want something. For my grandmother was never known to waste her charm on us.

She lay back in her chair, talking animatedly and fanning herself with a little ivory fan which she carried everywhere with her. My mother sewed tranquilly, replying to the other's rapid questions in her light, low voice that seemed to blend so well with the dreaming mood that was upon the house that magic day. My grandmother finished her sherbet, then came to the main point of her visit. Her husband, she said, was giving a very big dinner party that night to some business acquaintances and she was distracted to know how she would manage, since her cook was in bed sick and the other servants did not know how to cook any of the elaborate dishes she wished to give the guests. Here, she paused, eyeing my mother uneasily, but the latter never betrayed by as much as a flicker of the eyelids what it was she was thinking. She sewed peacefully on, and Mehmet, thoroughly bored by this woman's talk, commenced to pull grasses from which to suck the sap. I hovered uncertainly behind my sister's rug, and my grandmother began to display the faintest trace of irritability.

"Well, Şevkiye!" she demanded in her old bullying voice, all the sweetness gone. "Did you hear what I was saying, or have you been dreaming all this time?"

"Of course I heard," returned my mother, looking at her steadily, "but I cannot suggest anything. Perhaps your cook will be well enough to get up and prepare everything and then go back to bed again."

"Don't be silly!" said my grandmother waspishly, the control beginning to go out of her face. "Well, I suppose I shall have to manage something. You could not spare Feride, could you?"

"No," said my mother very gently, and I marveled at such control and discipline. My grandmother's mouth folded obstinately.

"But only for the one night," she begged. "I shall send her back tomorrow morning."

My mother did not reply, and my grandmother talked on and on, putting forward all sorts of reasons why she should have Feride with her.

In the end, worn out by such volubility, such unceasing persistence, my mother gave in, but on the condition that Feride be returned to our house that same evening.

Sulkily my grandmother agreed to this; however, she could not afford to be too sulky, since my mother was quite capable of changing her mind. But I think my grandmother had hoped to retain Feride until her own cook was well again. It mattered nothing to her that İnci and my mother would have to do all the work of the house between them—although if you were to ask my grandmother to do anything, she would be highly indignant and explain to you that she was not a servant.

Once she had gained her own way, she hurried off, refusing to stay for luncheon but stopping on the way to tell Feride what had been arranged for the afternoon.

My mother sighed after her but made no comment to us.

After she herself had gone to the house, Mehmet and I continued to play listlessly, for the sun was very hot. The grass was burning to my hand, the pigeons cooed sleepily, and the whole romantic little scene was so peaceful that it might have been something in a dream.

I think, too, that the mood for dreaming was heavy upon me that day, or was I only weighty with prophecy? It is a fact, though, that I remarked to Mehmet—or so my mother in after years assured me—that it would be a pity if all this peaceful life were to be swept away. Mehmet, it is to be assumed, would have only looked at me drowsily, his black eyes uncomprehending; perhaps it is also to be assumed that he would have asked me what I meant. And if he had I could not have explained. There were no words yet in my vocabulary to express my only half-formed, inarticulate thoughts. The white house, the green lawn, the brilliant flowers: all seemed threatened with annihilation, but where were the words to tell this picture? The dark flash that had for a moment lit my imagination would have been dismissed as a silly, childish fabrication. With Mehmet's drugged eyes holding mine, I might have forgotten the threat that had hung in the bright air, the dark hand that had hovered over me.

Little things stand out from that day, all of them unimportant then but having their own sad value in after years. Luncheon was hurried, with Feride anxious to get away; and İnci was sent to look for bread, for she had a way of insinuating her lithe body between the crowds in a manner the more solid Feride could never emulate. Madame Müjgan came across from her garden in the middle of the afternoon, Yasemin and Nuri trailing hotly after her. My mother and she sat idly talking until evening crept into the brilliant sky, and Madame Müjgan was begged to stay to dinner. My mother was loathe to eat alone these days and welcomed the little diversion her neighbor made.

Madame Müjgan talked of the war and her husband, but my mother, I thought, seemed anxious to discourage this trend in the conversation. She rarely mentioned my father; and even to Mehmet and me she spoke of him so seldom that after a while his face would rise before us like the face of a stranger, or the face of someone well loved a long time ago, now only vaguely seen or recognized.

For long periods at a time we forgot him altogether and could not imagine him ever again in the house. The squat white house he had bought for his family now seemed a woman's house, and it needed an older imagination than mine to give it back my father's lounging figure or my uncle's laughter. My grandfather had receded far into the distance. He held no place in this house; he had never known of its existence. Their male figures were dimmer now, and every day they dimmed a little more, waving their ghostly hands in farewell.

The day would no doubt come when they would be back with us again—as İnci not infrequently reminded us when we were disobedient—but in the meantime they had lost their authority with us.

The sun dropped lower down the sky, and the faintest breeze blew through the long grass. The ladies drew little cashmere shawls about their shoulders, and İnci came to take Muazzez to bed. Mehmet and I gathered our playthings and then took our guests, Yasemin and Nuri, to wash before dinner. Yasemin splashed cold water across her face and her reflection glimmered palely in this place of uncertain light. She said, catching sight of herself, "How odd I look!" and there was a doubtful note in her muted voice, as if not recognizing herself.

The dining room was filled with a lucent, tender green light, and all the windows stood open to the empty garden. The snowy table set with damask and glass and silver, with plates of cold food, looked cool and remote, a dish of black and white grapes making a somber mark in the center, like a bruise on a white face—like Yasemin's face so lately seen in the mirror, her eyes like bruises in the pallid ivory of cheek and nose and forehead. Wine chilled in a cooler, and we children were allowed for this once to sit at the big table.

İnci appeared from upstairs, her day with Muazzez finished, and my mother told her not to bother about waiting at table but to eat her dinner quickly, then go to collect Feride. She was so anxious to have the absent Feride back in the house again that she told İnci the table could be cleared the following morning. Never had I known such a thing permitted before, Mother being most punctilious in having the house in order before she retired for the night. After İnci had gone, we few were alone in the house, and a great, waiting silence seemed to descend upon us, even though wine flowed in the glasses and the ladies' laughter tinkled.

Dinner over, we left for the salon, leaving the debris of the table, which looked a little vulgar now, as tables always do after a meal has been eaten. My mother made coffee on her little silver spirit lamp, and we sat there in the lengthening dusk that shadowed the salon, a little tired now that the day was over. Presently we would go yawning to bed, and the square white house that held us would creak and grumble and mutter before settling into sleep under a summer sky. Yasemin and Nuri were petulant with tiredness, and Mehmet nodded by himself in a big chair. It was nine o'clock and long past bedtime. Madame Müjgan gathered her children and we roused ourselves to walk with them across the garden to the little gate between the houses. We bade them good night and came back again along the white path glimmering in the dusk; a little bit of a moon was rising in the clear sky. My mother waited for us in the French windows of the dining room. She looked unreal and ghostly standing there, like a figure in a play, so pale she was in her pale clothes. The house by night looked withdrawn and secret, a little frightening in its tall shroud of trees. We went in to my mother, who tightly shuttered the windows, the dirty, littered table looking like a table in a dead house. I helped to fasten doors and windows and then we went up to bed together, a tall golden candle lighting our way. The house seemed incredibly quiet without İnci and Feride.

"How will they get in?" I asked.

"Who?" asked my mother, puzzled.

"İnci and Feride," I replied, and she laughed at my anxious face, telling me that they had the front-door key. Suddenly Mehmet said that he wanted İnci, and commenced to cry. My mother put her arm around him, and he sobbed that he was frightened.

"But there is nothing to be afraid of," said my mother amusedly. The image of Mehmet's fear had imprinted itself on the dark air, and I began to feel vaguely uneasy too. When my mother kissed us good night, I begged her to leave her door open as well as ours.

She seemed so reluctant to give in to our fear that Mehmet commenced to weep again, and her own face began to reflect his terror. I do not know why we were so unaccountably afraid that night. Perhaps a little bit of the future impinged on the consciousness. Or perhaps—but I do not know. I only know that having slept contentedly in the dark for years, that night both Mehmet and I were unwilling to see the candle taken out of our room and across the landing to my mother's.

Before she left us she stood a few moments at the window, and the *tak-tak* of Bekci Baba's stick could be heard coming nearer to us. My mother sighed imperceptibly.

"Bekci Baba is a great comfort," she said, adding, "I wish he could stay outside this house all night."

Then she recollected herself, closed the window a little, and went across to her own room, where Muazzez slept peacefully. I lay sleepless for a long time after she had gone. Street noises drifted in; two cats were fighting in the gutter, hissing and spitting at each other with cold, rapacious felinity. The house was very still, the bedroom door a dark cavern; and as the street noises gradually died, I had an odd sense of waiting. I waited and the house waited and the empty staring sky waited, but I do not know for what it was we waited.

But I grew tired first and slept, and wild dreams threshed to and fro in my brain. How long I slept I do not know, but I remember waking to a terrible crying from my mother. Or was the crying only part of my dreams? Someone was shaking my shoulder, telling me to get up quickly and run—*run.*

My tortured mind could only absorb the one word "run," so still enmeshed in violent dreaming was my mind. Mehmet whimpered like a little animal, and I caught his hand as he ran blindly past me, swinging myself from the bed, bemused, bewildered, wondering if this horror were still part of a nightmare. My mother was screaming; there was no control left in her voice; but what it was she said I shall never know—only guess at, perhaps—and the unendurable nightmare persisted. In the dark doorway clouds of thick, acrid, eye-smarting vapor caused me to choke; but my mother, with Muazzez wailing in her arms, inexorably pushed Mehmet and me before her down the dark stairs, with the hot, thick vapor burning our throats. Blindly we stumbled, terror-stricken and half-stupid with sleep. A great dark red lick of flame belched upward to meet us.

"No! No!" screamed Mehmet, hesitating and dragging on my hand to impede progress.

"Fire!" I shouted, suddenly wide-awake and comprehending, but my mother pushed me on and I dragged Mehmet after me, his feet slithering reluctantly on the stairs.

"Run!" commanded my mother in an awful voice, a voice to freeze the blood in the marrow; and she forcibly impelled me onward, with such force, indeed, that Mehmet fell on one knee, letting go of my hand. She swooped down on him, frantically tearing him by the shoulder, shouted to me to hold her skirts, and ran like the wind through the narrow pathway through the flames. For a moment that seemed an eternity, she wrenched at the overheated front door, swinging it open for us to fall into the daylight of the street. Oh, to remember that night when the enemy spies set fire to the wooden houses of İstanbul, when they burned like matchwood under a summer sky! The street was daylight, for all the houses on both sides were a lurid, blazing mass.

"The garden door!" my mother was saying piteously, but we had not been able to get to the garden door, for the flames in our house had been worse in the back. Did we stand foolishly in the flaming street for one petrified moment? Who knows? Memory has shut down on that, for I can only coherently remember running along the street, clutching my mother tightly while she sought a way to turn off, to reach the waste field that lay at the back of our house, at the bottom of the garden. The street was full of humanity gone momentarily mad: maidservants, old men in their nightshirts, screaming, petrified children. Great fiery rafters from the derelict, deserted houses came tumbling down. One fell in my mother's path, and I heard her give a sort of gasp of horror, a moaning,

inhuman gasp. Our bare running feet pattered on the hard cobblestones, and our breath emerged harshly from our chests, while all
the time the fires crackled merrily. We went down a dark street
this time, with no falling rafters to block our path. Frantic men
and women were at their doors, wondering if the fires would spread
to threaten them too.

"God save us! What a terrible night!" said their grotesque faces,
but we panted on to reach the open fields. The waste field at last,
soft grass under our bleeding feet, and mass hysteria to greet us
under the fig trees.

Mehmet and I fell on the ground, sore and bleeding, our hearts
thumping to the bursting point, our thin nightshirts bound with
perspiration to our shivering bodies. My mother laid Muazzez
across my lap and leaned against a stunted little tree in a posture
unendurably touching and desolate.

"My money!" she said over and over again, "and all my jewelry."

And suddenly, like a mad thing—and indeed I believe the dark,
feathery wing of madness touched her brow eternally that night—
she darted away from us on her weary, bleeding feet.

"*An-ne! An-ne!*" I shouted in a fresh paroxysm of terror. "Don't
leave us; oh, don't leave us!"

And then I started to cry in a weak sort of way, for I had no
energy left to put into crying.

But my mother ran unheeding of my crying voice, stumbling
a little, falling over, picking herself up to forge ahead again.
Muazzez lay on my knee, wrapped in a little lacy woollen shawl,
and I bent over her, wearily trying to hush her whimpering.
Mehmet plucked at my sleeve, wanting sympathy too, and I put
an arm about him and drew him against my shoulder. We watched
the fires and our own house burning with the rest, and our brains
were numb, no longer functioning properly. Even fear and tiredness had dropped away to leave us mercifully empty. All about us
children were crying and women were wailing, but these were only
external things, having no power over us. Even the knowledge
that my mother had gone back to that burning house could arouse

no emotion, revive no terror. We just sat there, Mehmet and I, and the fig tree stretched above us, and now and again Muazzez softly whimpered.

Before us lay our garden and farther back was our home, our home that had been our comfort and our childish security. The district *tulumba* (firemen) had arrived and were trying to find water, and their frantic shouts echoed to us across the gardens. We could see them running from place to place, trying in vain to stem the fires. They had only one pump, but at least ten houses were burning; and on the other side of the street, which we could not see from here, as many more burned. So they ran and they shouted, throwing ineffectual buckets of water, and the fires roared triumphantly. I was watching for my mother to come back, but there was no sign of her for a long, long time. Then I saw her running to us down the garden path, for it was as light as day, and I plainly saw her figure in its nightdress and the thin white delicate feet running, running, running. . . .

She came to us and flung herself down, utterly exhausted. Her hair hung wildly about her face and in her mournful eyes was a glare, a brilliance, that knew nothing of sanity. She looked toward our house and I looked too, and the last bit of the roof came down into the greedy inferno that waited for it. Our house, like all the others, had blazed up like matchwood, like a piece of paper, and now only its ghostly shell remained to remind us that once we had been happy there.

Still, thirty-three years afterward, I have only to close my eyes to be back again to that night and see our home burning. It is as clear before me as if it had only happened yesterday.

A woman came with a crying child, laid it on the grass beside us, then ran off again to God knows where. Surely she did not hope to go through that hell to salvage anything? My mother stared before her with dilated eyes, and my heart turned over in fear, so still and pale she looked. She said very loudly, as if to make sure I quite understood:

"Everything is lost. Everything. Do you understand that?"

And she fixed me with that hard, brilliant stare, her nostrils quivering; then suddenly she heeled over in the thick soft grass, oblivious to the sounds about her or her ruined, blackening house.

How long she lay there, how long we children sat there, I do not know. I think perhaps Mehmet cried himself to sleep, and even Muazzez at last gave up her whimpering.

Dawn broke over the desolate scene, the fires died down, and only a pall of thick black smoke lay over the empty shells of the houses. The chill of early morning was in the air. Presently, in all that dead, exhausted place, I discerned my grandmother, with Feride and İnci, coming over the fields, looking to right and to left, as though searching for us.

"Grandmother!" I called, but my voice was no voice at all, only a thread of sound, a croak that could not disturb the silence.

I placed Muazzez carefully on the wet dewy grass and stood up stiffly, walking toward the three who were searching for us. I walked haltingly, for my feet were badly torn and the blood had dried between the toes; the soft, dawn air whipped through my thin nightdress like a gale.

They saw me and ran crying to me and put their kind arms around me, my grandmother wrapping me in her coat. I stood looking at them as if they were strangers; and, in a sense, they were strangers, for they came to me out of another life, a gracious, easy, friendly life that might never come again. I told my grandmother my mother was safe, and my brother and sister, too, then led her across the grass to them.

Feride knelt down beside my mother, taking off her own warm cloak and wrapping it around her tenderly. I saw her force cognac down my mother's throat and heard her cough and choke a little with its burning rawness. Then she opened her eyes and looked at us for a moment uncomprehendingly. She looked at each of us in turn, then picked Muazzez up in her arms.

"If you had not taken Feride," she said to my grandmother, "something would have been left of my home. I could have saved the only money I had, or my jewelry—if you had not taken Feride."

Then her stiff body relaxed and the hardness left her eyes. She looked at me, at Mehmet, and at our poor cut feet and smoke-blackened faces, at our quivering, unsteady mouths, and she put out a hand to draw us to her.

"But I still have my two big men," she said, and we fell on her and shed the tears that had been dammed up inside us for too long. Then my grandmother got busy with hot drinks, which she carried in a sort of flannel bag, and we were taken to her home.

And of all that little group, perhaps it was I alone who said a long farewell to my burned home, which had smiled so brilliantly in the sun only yesterday.

10

Trying to Build Again

WE WENT TO MY GRANDMOTHER'S HOUSE, where we were bathed and fed and put into warm beds, while Feride was sent to buy clothes for us.

My mother became very ill with a fever, the doctor calling many times each day, and we were constantly told to keep quiet. My grandmother's house held an alien quality for us, more than the quality of strangeness.

We used to sit out in the gardens with İnci, feeling unwanted in that childless house, and we rarely saw the old man. As a matter of fact, we were so terrified of him that if we ever saw him coming we used to run like the wind in the opposite direction. Nobody knew how long we were going to remain in this house, my grandmother only saying that when my mother was well again something would be arranged. Mehmet and I felt cut adrift, not being allowed to visit our mother, never seeing Yasemin or Nuri, for they had moved to another part of İstanbul, their house having perished with ours. Changes began to take place. Feride one morning bade us goodbye, for my grandmother had found another situation for her, knowing we could never afford her again. İnci left too, with many tears, for she had never known any other service but in our home. Now that she was being sent as a nursemaid to a strange family, even she would be separated from her mother. Saying goodbye to İnci frightened me, for I did not know what we were going to do without her. It was almost like losing a limb, a part of one's self. One morning we were allowed to visit my mother, who lay in her big bed looking like a doll. Her appearance shocked me. Her dark curls had all been combed flat against the sides of her face; her cheeks were pinched and taut from the fever.

Although she reached her hands to us, there was no welcome in her face and her eyes were expressionless. She looked as if coming back to life were too much of an effort for her and that, given the slightest opportunity, she would slip loose. As I grew older and came to a better understanding of things I realized that my mother was a woman predictable only if things went her way. Poverty she had to face; but many people in the world face poverty, if not with contentment at least with resignation. She was unable to do this, yet she was also unable to escape. The sight of her burning house was a far greater shock than my father going to war: the loss of her possessions was the worse blow. With money she could have built a new life: without it she was unable to accept what other people did for her.

It was not so much pride, although that entered in too. It was more an incapability to deal with life on any other terms than with money behind her. I think she had hoped to die the night of the fire. The thought of having to rear three children, one of them an infant, was almost too much for her simple, inexperienced mind to bear. She was sick of a fever for days and emerged from it quite another person. She had always been quiet, but now her silence was a fearsome thing. She had never been known to lose her temper; now she flared into easy rages that were all the more alarming because of her usual chilling quietness. The shy, beautiful young woman came out of her fever with a different personality.

When she was able to get up, she would sit in the gardens, looking at nothing and seemingly unaware of her surroundings. She never once asked for Feride or İnci and would gaze speculatively at the infant Muazzez, who was being looked after by a wet nurse.

One day my grandmother told her that the old man was willing to give us rooms in one of his many houses. My mother listened to her and agreed to accept the offer, but my grandmother had to urge her almost forcibly before she would give her decision. She had one good diamond ring, which she had been wearing the night of the fire, and she asked the old man to sell it for her. I remember that she held it out to him disdainfully, between her finger and thumb, and the sun touched rays of fire from it. As he took it from her, her eyes flickered uncertainly. When he returned and handed her the money from its sale, she thanked him and said she would be glad to move into the rooms he proposed to give her as soon as possible.

The old man replied, but with courtesy, that nothing would please him better, and his cold eyes raked Mehmet and me with such an expression of active dislike that I was quite breathless with astonishment. This old man had centered all his dislike on us children. He had hoped that his marriage would give him children, sons, to carry on his name and his business. I think my grandmother's refusal to share his bed had damaged some part of his pride to such an extent that he could not bear to look on us, the fruits of her life with my grandfather.

To my grandmother I never saw him anything else but coldly polite. She was an obstinate, self-willed woman with a wounding tongue, and I imagine that his pride suffered badly beneath her hands. Looking back, it amazes me to what extent she overrode him, since he could have, in those days, thrown her penniless from his house by simply saying, "I divorce you," three times in the presence of witnesses. Many a wife thirty years ago was a good wife simply because she lived under the threat of those words. With the Atatürk régime all this was done away with so that nowadays in Turkey the divorce system is so complicated that many couples effect a reconciliation long before the slow-moving, intricate machinery of divorce goes into action.

Servants were sent to the house we were to occupy, or more accurately, the rooms we were to occupy. I was permitted to go with them. The house was behind Bayazit Square, two-storied and so old that one wondered what it was that continued to hold it erect. There was no garden and it fronted the narrow dreary street, all its windows covered with *kafes*, closely latticed harem shutters always used in old Turkey to prevent passing males from catching glimpses of the women who moved within the house.

The upper floor was to be ours. It consisted of three large, very dirty rooms, a big square landing with no light save the grayish haze that filtered through the unclean skylight. All the rooms were dark and airless because of the kafes covering the windows. My mother told one of the servants to tear them off, but he trembled with horror to attempt anything so reactionary without the old man's permission.

My mother knew it was useless to insist. She looked impatient, and the servants commenced to scrub the floors. Taking my hand, she led me back to my grandmother's house. She seemed very determined, and I had difficulty in keeping up with her hurrying figure.

These odd, inexplicable moods of hers tormented my heart and gave me a feeling of insecurity. Too much seemed to be happening at once, and I had mental indigestion trying to keep up with events. Lately I clung to her passionately, watching her face anxiously for signs of storm, learning of the coldness of the world before my time. My mother represented love and stability, and, to be trite, children are conservative.

When we arrived at my grandmother's house, she asked to see the old man; finding that I would not be dissuaded from her side, she impatiently allowed me to enter his room with her. He sat in a big chair in front of the window and looked irritable, for it was a day when his gout was giving him its own particular hell. My mother, with remarkable docility, asked if the kafes might be removed from the windows of our new abode. He sat looking at her for a moment or two, while she stared steadily and coolly at him. Surprisingly, he agreed to her request. He added that he would instruct his men to paint the rooms for her and hoped that she would be comfortable there.

His voice was quiet and formal, yet I think he liked my mother in his own way. He probably felt a certain, understandable pity for her distress, but her relationship to my grandmother alienated her.

My mother was pleased with her victory and hummed a little air, a sure sign that things were going well with her. I was overflowing with thankfulness to have her back with us again, even if it were only for a short time. For, ever since the fire, she had been unapproachable, far away from us; and several times I had caught her remote eyes fixed on Mehmet or myself, as though she asked herself what we had to do with her. I smarted under this unawareness, for she was all that we had left, having lost so much from childhood.

When my mother told my grandmother what she was doing about the kafes, the latter was appalled in much the same way as the servant had been earlier in the day. She told my mother she must not do such a thing, that she would be stoned as a prostitute if she exposed herself in this shameless fashion. My mother laughed at her; and afterward, when we were returning to the house, she disdainfully refused the offer of a maid to accompany her, saying that in her new station in life she could not afford the luxury of a maid.

At the house the scrubbing had been finished, and the clean, naked floors gleamed wetly. A man was busy removing the offending kafes from the windows while another mixed distemper in a bucket. They were very polite to my mother, but it was plain to see that they thought her very odd to want the kafes off the windows to let the daylight into these depressing rooms.

She was very gay all that day. Her gayety transformed her so that one could see she looked twenty-two again, beautiful and high-spirited but husbandless. And the menservants were probably prophesying among themselves her downfall. She was an odd contradiction, one moment spineless and the next bounding with immense vitality.

In one way, her own unobtrusive way, she was the forerunner of Kemal Atatürk, for she emancipated herself years before his time. That the people in her new life would talk about her she did not care.

She had always lived in houses that admitted fresh air and she intended to do the same thing here; if there was no garden to protect her from eager scrutiny, then she would have to get used to the peculiar ways of mankind. But fresh air she intended to have even at the cost of her reputation. So she snapped her fingers at the gossipers, acted the lady in her three mean rooms, and lamented the loss of her diamond ring. Now that she had found a home again, her vitality was boundless; color seemed to return to her cheeks, the flesh to the delicate bones. To Mehmet and me her courage was wonderful, and we still think so today. We cannot help admiring her colossal struggle, her intrepid spirit, and even as children we were aware of this courage. We could forgive the lapses into depression and bad temper, the seeming ruthlessness when she banished her children eventually. Today we know these things in their true perspective and can only see the wit, the bravery, and the gayety that transformed three mean rooms in a mean street into a formidable bulwark against the rest of the world.

My grandmother arranged to let us have the most of her furniture, the cumbersome, handsome walnut furniture she had moved from our house upon her remarriage. From her vast stocks she provided curtains and linens and rugs and tapestries that had once graced our salon in my grandfather's house. The three rooms and the dark square landing took on a joyous air, as if they had been waiting for just such a transformation.

The windows stood wide open to the world, and if the neighbors gasped at such audacity in their midst, my mother, I am sure, was totally unaware of it. Naturally, they knew her story, for gossip has a way of traveling in İstanbul as rapidly as it has in any other part of the world. No doubt the good neighbors thought she had brought these "fast" habits from her former life.

The first evening we were established in the new house, we discovered that, so much else having been thought of, we were without lamps or food. My mother went down the naked stairs to the widow who lived beneath, thinking that perhaps she would oblige. Their conversation must have been pathetic: the grand lady in her fine silk dress and the poor, wretched trollop shunned by the neighbors because of her reputed "goings-on." She must have thought it was the sultan himself, no less, who had descended upon her to request the loan of a lamp! Unfortunately she had no lamp, or if she had was far too flustered to search for it, but she produced a scrap of candle. This my mother triumphantly bore upstairs, placing it in a silver candlestick on the buffet. Much had been lost and was irretrievable, but a silver candlestick was a necessity. Nothing less would have done, not glass or china or just plain, honest tin; nothing but a silver one was good enough, for ladies only used the best. . . . In the candlelight the room hid some of its secrets, and the cracks in the ceiling might have been gold-encrusted ornamentations in that kindly glow—if you had enough imagination, and I had much of it. Well, there we were in our new home, in our new clothes provided by my grandmother—and we ate dry bread and a handful of black olives to still the ache in our stomachs. Then we settled to sleep, far away from the murmur of the sea or the scent of the flowers from an almost forgotten garden; and for me, at least, it was as comfortable as the Dolmabahçe Saray. It probably was too, for the white Saray, which looked like an iced cake, had echoing dungeons and no great reputation for comfort—or so I heard afterward.

And I wonder what my mother thought that night as she lay down in my grandfather's exotic bed—the one where I had once played "lions"—with its legs placed in glass bowls of water to prevent the bedbugs from becoming too adventurous. Did she thank God for safe deliverance into a new home, however mean, or did she pray for guidance for the future?

Perhaps. Perhaps not. She was never a religious person, being too impatient to accept the Moslem teaching of Fatalism, and with a mind so hurrying that God must have just flitted through it with barely a hurried nod in her direction. She had been born in Albania, and her unorthodox views of life and religion were derived perhaps from some far-off Christian ancestor who slept uneasily in her blood.

The next morning the *sütcü* (milkman), awakened us by his violent assertions that his milk was the best in İstanbul. Mehmet and I leaped from our shared bed and rushed to the window to see this remarkable apparition who had dared to disturb our dreams.

Always before the sütcü had decorously called at the back door and in a series of sibilant whispers conducted his business with Hacer or Feride, never dreaming of loudly crying his wares for fear of waking the sleeping occupants of the house. This was a great change. In our new life people set their day in motion with the arrival of the milkman, and the sütcü himself had no false illusions about his value, firmly believing in thoroughly arousing any sleepyheads who still remained in bed.

He saw us hanging out of the window and his jaw dropped in surprise because the kafes were gone. He was long and lean and bronzed and wore patched clothing, but it could not disguise the smooth rippling of the muscles under his shirt. He had a several days' growth of beard, and this fascinated us very much. His voice was the voice of Doom.

"Milk," he barked at us fiercely. "Do you want any milk today?"

"No thank you," we said politely, in chorus, and he grinned sourly and stood back to get a good look at us, the paragons of good behavior.

Just then the widow opened the front door, thrusting forward a saucepan which the sütcü silently filled.

Then I heard my mother's pattering foot taking the stairs, and she also held out a receptacle to be filled. She bought yoghurt for us too, a sort of sour junket that we loved to eat with sugar.

With the coming of the sütcü, the street came to life. Doors opened and saucepans were thrust forth and the sütcü did a roaring trade.

My mother called to us from the landing, which had been made into a kitchen, that it was time for us to get up. We commenced to pull our clothes on, fumbling over buttons and tapes. Mehmet exasperatedly started to cry and said he wanted İnci, and my mother swept impatiently into the room. Suddenly buttons and tapes became docile things under her experienced fingers. She showed us both how our clothes should be put on, how held together—which was the most important so far as we were concerned. She explained that for the time being there was no İnci to help us and that we must learn to do these things for ourselves. She was particularly scathing with me, declaring that a boy almost seven years old should at least be able to pull on his boots, even if he were incapable of lacing them.

I hung my head in shame, for every word she said was painfully true and I simply had not the remotest idea of which boot went on which foot. No doubt we benefited from her instructions, for I certainly never remember another occasion of being helped into our clothes.

Later that day, when I was sitting in the so-called "salon," I saw my grandmother coming up the street. I recognized her by her veil, for all the women in the street wore the çarşaf, a sort of black scarf tightly binding the forehead and hair; another piece of material, a peçe, covered the lower part of their faces. They looked unbearably ugly and drab, and I was thankful that neither my mother nor my grandmother wore such things.

I called to her from my little window, and she waved her hand to me and I rushed down to open the door for her. She instructed me to leave the door open, as two of her porters were to arrive with more furniture for us.

My mother greeted her, then mocked lightly.

"But what is this today? No chaperone?"

And my grandmother self-consciously replied that she saw no reason why a poor old woman like herself—she was about fifty—could not walk the daytime streets unescorted.

My mother's emancipation seemed to be affecting my grandmother too, although of course she would never admit that, holding firmly to the argument that whereas perhaps *she* might be rash enough to venture out alone, by reason of her age, my mother could not do the same thing and for the same reason!

Porters arrived with a sewing machine that had formerly been used by Feride for the household mending. There followed a large console table, a little inlaid Moorish coffee table, a wooden chest containing God knew what, and monstrous armchairs that would crowd everything else out of the salon. My mother's face was a study as she watched all these things hauled up the narrow stairs and heaved pantingly into the rooms. When the porters had departed, she asked my grandmother where she thought everything should be put; my grandmother looked taken aback, for naturally, such a thought had never entered her head. In a sudden burst of generosity she had given this furniture to us, expecting pleasure at our reaction and not pointless questions as to where it should all be put. She looked around her, having to admit that the rooms were already overcrowded, but she told my mother she ought to be grateful for that. She felt affronted and took no pains to conceal it. I think she saw nothing incongruous in this lovely old furniture adorning these poor rooms, or the silky Sparta and Persian rugs strewn across the broken and uneven floorboards. She had wanted to install her daughter-in-law and her grandchildren in a fine home and hey presto! had she not done so? Why, then, was the daughter-in-law looking round her so doubtfully, as though ungrateful for all these lovely things? She must have given up struggling with the idea, for she abruptly dismissed the subject of the offending furniture and proceeded to unpack the wooden chest, feeling certain that these treasures would be appreciated. She brought forth curtains, stipulating that they were to be hung immediately. Table and bed linen was dragged out to trail on the floor; heavy silver cutlery, to be used presumably for our dry bread and our black olives; hammered brass lamps that would require a gallon of oil a day to keep them going; a silk-embroidered bed set which, she proudly informed Mehmet and me, had been given to her when she was a young girl for her wedding to my grandfather.

My mother looked at all these old treasures and her eyes filled with tears. They reminded her too vividly of my grandfather and my father and the houses where she had been happy, and I felt she did not want them here, in this house that held no memories. She said nothing, although the tears commenced to drop on to her cheeks. Then she recovered herself and bade me blow the mangal so that coffee could be brewed. I went out to the landing, where lurked the mangal, a table, crockery for everyday use, and several buckets of water. There was no water in the house, although fresh drinking water was supplied each week by Bekci Baba. All other water had to be fetched from the local pump, the meeting place for all the ladies of the district; and only that morning I had staggered back and forth twenty times or more, filling small tin cans. I could not bear to see my mother do such menial work as this. The darkness hid what was on the landing, but the unlovely smell of cooking filled the house perpetually. Cooking facilities were primitive. Charcoal was burned in the big copper brazier, an iron tripod was placed over it, and the pan containing whatever had to be cooked stood on it. After several slow hours a meal was either cooked to perfection or ruined beyond redemption, depending on the sort of cook you were. In those first days with this cooking arrangement, much of our food was uneatable, for my mother was *not* a good cook. She liked good food but had no patience and could not be bothered to do everything the cookery book prescribed. Many years later she became quite an expert, but only when she had already ruined our appetites.

That morning she made coffee for my grandmother, handing it to her on a worn thin silver tray; and if one turned one's back to the window—ignoring the view—one would have thought that İnci had just left the room and that we were back again in the house that had been burned. So firmly was ritual in her blood, that my mother—she who had nothing left in the world, who was poorer by far than the widow who lived under us—saw nothing odd in the fact that she should continue to serve coffee on a silver tray that would have graced a collector's possessions. We saw no incongruity in my mother's gesture either, but remembering that moment so long ago can bring a smile to me today. There they sat, those two elegant ladies, in a slum room and sipped coffee from a silver tray. The old order was established once more, and presently my grand-mother would forget herself and look for the bell to ring for İnci to clear away. . . .

That day, before she left, she pressed gold money into my mother's hand, the latter protesting that she was not in need of it since she still had the money from the sale of her ring. My mother had very little knowledge of the value of money and absolutely no true knowl-edge of food prices. If she wanted something, she had to have it; and if it seemed to cost many gold coins—well, unfortunately that was life and we were in the middle of a war. Consequently, traders robbed her, demanding exorbitant prices for their wares.

She was always too shy to argue with them, feeling it beneath her dignity, but I had begun to notice that the other women in the market place paid much less for their foodstuffs than she did. If I remonstrated with her, she would hush me impatiently, but there came a time when she began seriously to worry about her money. It was inconceivable that my grandmother could continue to sup-port us. We had already heard that her husband had been almost insane with fury when he discovered that she had moved all her furniture without consulting him. Still, food continued to be our biggest problem; and one gold coin seemed to have very little pur-chasing power—especially if one patronised the Bourse noir, which my mother did.

At about this time in my life, I became initiated into the purely feminine mystery of acting as nursemaid. My mother had formed the habit of shopping alone, usually after the morning's meal was over. She would leave Mehmet and Muazzez in my charge, to my disgust, for I hated to be held responsible for everything they did. My duties mostly consisted of saying "Don't," but occasionally I would give Mehmet an exasperated slap, which would make him roar so loudly that once the widow rushed up to see what was wrong and afterward complained about me to my mother. When my mother remonstrated, I was resentful, blind and deaf to every-thing save my intense dislike of looking after the younger ones.

One day my mother found more difficulty than usual in getting bread for us. Latterly, our whole world revolved on the one word "bread." She had spent most of the morning at the baker's, returning weary and empty-handed. She went out again in the afternoon, with the same result. Toward evening she set off again, telling Mehmet and me not to make too much noise, since Muazzez was sleeping. For a while we played quietly, then Mehmet became tired and fretful, and we gathered our toys together, putting them into a cupboard on the landing and returning to our favorite corner seat to watch for our mother's return. It was getting dusky and my mother seemed to be away for an unusually long time. The street was deserted, and presently we heard the widow go out, closing the front door conspiratorially after her. We watched her black dumpy figure disappear down the street and we became uneasy, knowing there was now nobody in the house save ourselves. Perhaps some memory of the darkness that had preceded the night of the fire came up to catch us by the throat, causing us to talk in whispers and now and then look furtively over our shoulders into the darkening room. Mehmet was sleepy and begged to be allowed to go to bed, but I was loath to part with his company. I longed for my mother's return. I wished the lamps were lit but dared not touch them, on my mother's orders. We continued to sit there, but still she did not come; the room grew darker and the street was silent as the grave. There was a little mosque near the house, and from our corner window we could see it quite plainly, its one slender minaret piercing the gloom. More clearly to be seen, and within one of its windows, was the tomb of a holy man, with a candle—lit by some pious aspirant—burning steadily in a glass holder. The muezzin had mounted the lonely minaret and was calling the people to prayer, but we could not see whether anyone was entering the mosque or not, for the entrance faced in the opposite direction to us. The muezzin's voice was mournful and mysterious, the liquid Arabic notes rippling from his tongue like strange music. When he had finished reading Ezzin and had left the minaret, the night seemed stiller and blacker than ever. Only the candle still winked brightly on the holy man's grave. Suddenly I began to be afraid. Fear and hunger and tiredness combined loosened my tongue.

"Dead man is coming! Dead man is coming!"

Mehmet looked at me in the semidarkness and his lip started to quiver. He looked in the direction of the candle and began to howl with fear too. We rushed from the window and over to the sofa, which was draped with an old Persian prayer mat, and this we pulled over our heads, whispering in terror. We whipped up our fear to a greater frenzy, telling each other that the holy man had got out of his grave because he was cold and lonely there and was coming to take us back to his grave so that we could keep him warm. We shivered and our teeth chattered, and scattered remnants of İnci's ghostly lore kept coming back to keep our terror at fever pitch. We lay clasping each other in desperation, muttering that the holy man must be very near to us now. We pushed each other in our extreme agitation, pulling the too small prayer mat first over his head, then over mine. In the midst of all this, I heard footsteps, slow, furtive footsteps.

"Here he comes!" I yelled, panic-stricken in earnest this time.

The footsteps drew nearer and nearer, entered our front door, and mounted the stairs slowly, wearily, heavily, just as I supposed a long-dead holy man would walk. My heart was ready to stop for ever as I lay under the prayer mat, with Mehmet screaming his lungs out, until a stern hand pulled the mat away from our faces.

"What is this?" inquired my mother's voice.

I was so relieved to see her that I was totally unable to reply, but Mehmet managed to stutter "D-Dead man!" and then went off into a fresh paroxysm of wailing. My mother strove to make him cease, sorting him out from where he had wriggled beneath me and trying to wrest the corner of the prayer mat, which he clutched tightly, from his fingers.

When she had finally extricated him, it was discovered that he had wet his pants a couple of times over, and looked as if the slightest cross word from my mother would cause him to do the same again.

11

The End of Sariyer

LIFE WAS BY NO MEANS DULL IN OUR STREET. From the arrival of the first early-morning sütcü to the departure of the last evening *yogurtcu*, there was noise and bustle and arguing and laughter. I used to sit in my corner window, a pile of cushions placed on my chair so that I could see the better, and watch the street vendors leading their lazy-looking mules up and down, up and down, crying their wares and shouting insults at each other. There were the eggplant sellers, the tomato sellers, and traders with great, glowing heaps of lemons, and, in their seasons, the watermelon sellers and grape sellers. They would lead their mules drowsily, enormous baskets strapped on either side of the beast to display the eggplant and the tomatoes and the tender young French beans. They would cry hoarsely to the listening houses that no finer vegetables than theirs were to be found in any part of the world. A shrill housewife would demand the price and, upon hearing the reply, would commence to abuse the seller. Perhaps even a battle would ensue, the trader and the housewife each vying with the other for the honors of the slanging match. Sometimes other housewives would join in, defending their representative. A few of the other traders would listen skeptically; and after a while the battle of words would reach such a pitch that the combatants had to search deeply into the opponent's antecedents in order that fresh fuel might be added to the fire. There was never any danger of either side running out of words, even if it meant reiterating the same ones over and over again. It was nothing to hear one of them informing the other that he was a son of a donkey or that he was the husband of a prostitute, or the father of innumerable illegitimate children. These were mild epithets against the stronger ones that could be used if the housewife really got into her stride. She usually bested the trader, for she almost always had grown sons, ready to defend her honor should he reply to her in like manner. And, of course, there were always the other housewives, who would think nothing of setting upon the poor unfortunate seller, beating him with whatever came to their hands, while their children would rifle the laden baskets that lay across the back of the phlegmatic mule.

There were a great many children in the street, dirty-nosed, underfed children who were tougher at seven or eight than many a man is at forty. Mangy cur dogs explored the dustbins, which were left outside the houses, for we were no respecters of authority in our street. Thousands of cats, in all stages of growth and development, ranged the rubble heaps and chased the rats from the sewers, and were even capable of eating each other when their hunger became maddening. Through all this wretchedness and dirt and poverty my mother walked with her proud firm step, and the other women eyed her suspiciously and murmured against her because she thought so little of their censure that she had torn the kafes from her windows and walked among them as shamelessly as a prostitute. The small boys threw stones after her, and the men leered into her veiled face as she passed through their malevolent ranks like a queen. She would not allow us to play in the street, for, despite her destitution, she retained her snobbishness. Our daily exercise depended on the amount of time she had left over from her shopping expeditions. She rarely bought from the street sellers, having no bargaining capacity and being shy before the cold, appraising scrutiny of the other women, who automatically crowded their doors to see what she bought and how much she was foolish enough to pay for it.

She bought in the local market place, hiring a street urchin—always to be found in the markets—to carry her wares in a basket slung over his thin shoulders. She would walk home before him, direct him upstairs to the smelly landing, tip him, and send him away. Mehmet and I were always given the job of sorting the vegetables into their respective places, for in those days she soiled her hands as little as possible. She hated the street and its inhabitants, their coarse humor and their impure speech. Once home, she would remove her veil, sink into a chair, and look about her at the treasures of my grandfather's day. Gradually peace would creep back into her face again. She lived always in the past, emerging unwillingly for the daily routine. Each night saw her tranquilly sewing in a deep chair, where the lamplight caught her hair, or tending her nails, the curtains drawn and her face composed, as though no hostile strangers lurked outside in the mean street. Her habit of going back to the past, of turning her mind ever inward would become perilous in later life; but none of us knew that then.

She lived in her memories, refusing to recognize the ever encroaching future of penury. Money was very scarce, but still she spent what we had like water. If she thought she was going to commence worrying about it, down came the shutter over her mind, and the thought was pushed into the uneasy background—along with all the other unpleasant thoughts she did not want to recognize. When my grandmother frequently remonstrated about the way money was slipping from our grasp, my mother would turn the subject aside, perhaps showing my grandmother some piece of embroidery she had just completed, and the discussion on money would be dropped almost as soon as it had started. And my mother would talk vivaciously about many things, eagerly switching the conversation if the subject of money threatened to crop up again.

She acted the part of a fashionable young woman of position, beginning to talk of my father's return from the war; after a time a disquieting note crept into her talk, for she began to forget that there was any war at all and took to mentioning names of men long dead. She would not accept defeat, but defeat crept up behind her like an assassin in the dark. She planned a visit to Sariyer, animatedly promising Mehmet and me a long holiday there; but now and then a little shadow would cross her face, as though she knew she was talking nonsense but preferred her nonsense to the unsavory truth. The more contact she had with the outside world, the more she turned her thoughts inward, the more extravagant became her plans.

I never remember her as demonstrative, clasping her children to her or kissing them in moments of nearness. We never had any moments of nearness to her, but nevertheless she remained our only bulwark against the world, our one security. The touch of her cool, remote hand, the rustle of her skirt, or the sound of her light, emotionless voice was enough for us. These things could still all our fears or soothe away pain. As time passed, she grew more cordial to the widow below us, although my grandmother did her best to discourage this. But my mother genuinely liked the widow. She had a sort of sure instinct for human nature, ignoring the outward pattern and swooping down, with a beautiful compassion, to discover the heart.

The rest of the street shunned the widow, hinting that she was no better than she should be. My mother, shunned and shunning, had a deep sympathy for her. She would invite the widow to come upstairs and drink coffee, ask her mature advice on the method of making clothes for Mehmet and me, or how to cook such and such a dish. The widow became very grateful for these little attentions from my mother, these subtle flatteries, and rapidly became the devoted slave of the family. She would sit with us and amuse us when my mother was out, wash us and feed us and dandle Muazzez for hours on her capacious knees. She was a sort of unpaid servant, an İnci and a lewd Hacer rolled into one, and was, no doubt, very useful to my mother. She even took to preparing all the food for us, but this my mother put a stop to, for the widow's hands were seldom clean and she had a habit of scratching her sparse gray hairs so

that some usually fell into whatever it was she was cooking. My
mother's passion for cleanliness was as great as her passion—an
odd one in the old, vanished Turkey—for fresh air.

One morning there was a great knocking at the door, and I
heard someone asking for my mother. I called out to her and she
ran down the stairs; then I heard her cry "Hasan!"

And while I was wondering who "Hasan" might be, she thanked
Bekci Baba for having directed her visitor here. Then I suddenly
recognized the voice of the mysterious "Hasan," and he was a mystery no longer: he was the gardener from Sariyer—the gardener
who must be commemorated for ever because he liked small boys.

My mother and he came up the narrow stairs and into the salon.
Hasan greeted Mehmet and me; then, with the privilege of a
very old family servant, he looked all about him and said querulously, "What is this dreadful place, hanim effendi?" And before
waiting for any answer, shook his old white head sadly. He peered
at my mother with his nearsighted eyes and said uncertainly:

"I went to your house first. Such a shock I got! I did not know
it was like that, hanim effendi: the news has not reached Sariyer."
He paused for a long minute, still grumbling into his beard, then
continued: "It was Bekci Baba who directed me to this house. Eh,
dear, dear! To think of you in a place like this!"

And to my acute embarrassment, large tears dropped from his
eyes, spilling down his ancient coat.

"Now, Hasan!" said my mother reprovingly, much as she would
speak to one of us children if we too easily gave way to tears.

Hasan wiped his eyes with the back of his hand.

"Ah!" he said deeply and darkly, "things are altering, hanim
effendi. Nobody knows from day to day what will happen next,
but to see *you* in a house like *this*—" and he paused, trying to find
the right words.

My mother covered the gap by asking swiftly, "And what news
of Sariyer, Hasan?"

The old man's eyes filled with tears again, the weak easy tears of
a very, very old man, but I could feel the laughter bubbling up in

my throat, like water from a spring well. My mother's eyes reproved my levity, which made me worse, so that I got quite red in the face with the effort to contain myself. But my laughter flew before Hasan's next words, which were so unexpected that they hit my brain like a little series of electric shocks.

"The master is believed dead, hanim effendi," he said, then broke off to cry bitterly, unable to contain himself any longer. My mother looked over his bent head, blindly, and with a face that might have been carved from stone.

"Dead!" she said. "Ahmet dead!"

Frightened by her white face, I began to cry too; Mehmet followed, and pandemonium was let loose in the room. I am sure I did not cry for Uncle Ahmet, being still young enough not to fully appreciate the meaning of the word "death." And I did not cry because I would never go to Sariyer again, for that I did not know. I cried, I suppose, because Hasan cried, because my mother had turned to stone and had gone far away from us and this still summer room. I cried on and on, bitterly, not knowing why I was crying but liking the noise I was making. Even when the tears had stopped flowing, I still cried on, broadcasting my woe to the house-tops and never wishing to stop. There is something so elemental, so primeval about human tears that the sound of them causes ripples and tremors to course up and down the spine and through the blood-stream; and my own tears, that day, had just that effect upon me. It was my mother's sharp, stinging hand on my cheek that made me cease, bringing me up short in the middle of a particularly heart-rending sob.

"Stop!" she cried so imperiously that stop I did immediately, my mouth still foolishly open but no sound emerging. Mehmet and I were sent to the sofa, in the far corner of the room, where we gulped and sniffled our way back to sanity.

"Hasan," I heard my mother say gently, "tell me all about it. How did your mistress discover?"

The old man made a valiant effort to recover himself and, after a moment or two, commenced to speak.

"My mistress has been worrying for many months; last week she sent me to the War Office to ask if they knew anything about my master. But they knew little there. At last a colonel was found who said my master was believed dead. They know nothing else about him. Nothing!"

"But that is terrible," said my mother in an odd sort of voice. Was my father's image in her eyes, I wonder?

Hasan continued: "My mistress took the news very hardly, hanim effendi. She has not eaten for three days now, and her cough does not get any better. Last night she had a haemorrhage."

"Poor Ayşe," said my mother. "Of course we guessed she had consumption—"

"Do not tell this news to the old lady," warned Hasan, the "old lady" being my respected grandmother, who would have been most indignant had she heard this term applied to herself.

"Certainly I shall not," said my mother. "But she is certain to find out. Oh, Hasan, the terrible things that are happening. All the doors are closing, one by one, and all the happy families dying. Oh, Hasan!" And she covered her face with her hands, but she did not cry. This was another thing to be bottled up, to be pushed into the back of her mind, not to be thought about, until one day the top would come flying off and all these fearsome things would leap out at her with a snarl.

"It is the will of God," said Hasan simply.

My mother uncovered her face and said,

"A hard will, Hasan."

"Do not say such things!" cried the old man, forgetting his sorrow, so thoroughly scandalized was he that a woman should question the will of God.

My mother ignored his remark and said instead:

"Do not tell your mistress of the fire, not just yet, anyway. She has enough trouble now, and the fire is over, and my house gone, and talking will not bring it back. We are comfortable enough here. . . ." Her eyes ranged round the room uncertainly, as though seeking reassurance of comfort. The old man got ready to leave, placing a basket of food on the table, and my mouth began to water as I saw the contents being emptied. My mother thanked him and he looked sad and doubtful, as though reluctant to leave. But he bowed to her and spoke a few more words, then went shuffling down the stairs, and we could hear him muttering to himself all the way down.

My mother sat back in a chair, looking as if she wanted to cry, but habit was too strong in her and she held back the treacherous tears. She sat looking into space, and presently a little smile touched her lips. I wondered what memory it was that had the power to override her sorrow for Uncle Ahmet, to bring light to her eyes and awareness of Mehmet and me, who sat watching her.

"You must not say anything to your grandmother," she warned sternly. We replied that we would not, and then she left us to continue with the work which Hasan's visit had interrupted. Mehmet immediately forgot why he had been so recently crying and went back to play, his thin brown face sharp with anxiety because a certain brick would not stand on top of another one. I watched him for a moment or two, then said, "Let me show you," and I took the bricks from his docile, clever fingers. "There!" I said, when I had finished. "That is the way you must build them." He looked at the edifice I had erected, then patiently, one by one, he pulled down all the bricks again and commenced to build them his own way. The gaily-painted bricks swayed in their insecure positions and fell to the floor. Mehmet sat thoughtfully back on his heels, jabbing at them with his fingers, his little face still sharp with anxiety.

I left him to it and went to examine the precious things that had been sent from Sariyer. There was a mountain of rice, a fat chicken, butter more golden than shop butter could ever be, large brown speckled eggs, and home-made bread. I pulled a brown crust from the bread and commenced to eat hungrily. Sorrows there might be in the world and in my family, but childhood's especial world revolves around a crust of fresh bread.

It was inconceivable that my mother should imagine my grandmother would not find out about Uncle Ahmet's death. I prefer to say "death" and not "supposed death" for two reasons. First, his death was afterward officially confirmed. Second, the War Office of that time was in such a state of flux, so confused and incapable, in fact, that alive but missing soldiers were frequently listed as dead, even though they might turn up afterward. But the War Office never rectified its mistakes, perhaps feeling that with the present state of things most of the so-called "missing" soldiers would eventually be dead anyway. It became fairly obvious to the people then that anyone listed as supposedly dead was as dead as he would ever be.

But, to return to my grandmother. Hasan had not long left us when she came angrily into the house, demanding coffee and the reason for Hasan's mysterious visit. My mother looked astonished and inquired how my grandmother could possibly know of his visit.

"I heard it," snapped my grandmother, furious because Hasan had not paid his respects to her and suspicious that my mother had been told something she had a right to know as well. My mother said, rather faintly, for her, that Hasan had merely brought a basket of food for us. And having said that much, she sat looking at my grandmother, as though the old lady was displaying almost supernatural powers in having known at all that anyone out of the usual had called at our house that day. My grandmother sat stiff as a ramrod in her chair and demanded what news there was of Sariyer.

"Oh, everything is very well there," said my mother rather hurriedly, but going red and white by turns with such rapidity that my grandmother must have wondered what on earth was wrong with her.

Mehmet strolled over to my grandmother and, with three-year-old unconcern, lisped "Sariyer." I was terrified that he would remember something of this morning's conversation, some isolated word perhaps, that would tell my grandmother everything. Perhaps I looked anxious, for she suddenly said to me, "What is wrong?"

I sulkily replied that nothing was wrong, but Mehmet, with infinite baby cunning, and perhaps scenting that something out of the ordinary was in the wind, plucked at her sleeve, reiterating in-

sistently: "Mehmet cried! Mehmet cried!" And when she would
not take any notice of him, he pulled at her skirt in a gust of temper.
"Cried!" he said to her, but she freed herself from his grasp, and my
mother's arrival with coffee distracted everyone's attention.

My grandmother drank her coffee as if it were poison and kept
making obscure references to Sariyer and Uncle Ahmet until I
thought my mother would faint with the effort to suppress the truth.
Once she almost gave herself away, for she indiscreetly mentioned
that she was thinking of going to the War Office to see if they could
give any news of my father. Naturally, my grandmother pounced
on this, demanding to know who had been putting such ideas into
my mother's head. The latter replied rather vaguely that nobody
had said anything, that she had just thought of the idea herself.
My grandmother looked at her fixedly. "Şevkiye," she accused, "you
are keeping something from me."

Her perception seemed to us uncanny; and though my mother
protested that she had nothing to keep back from anyone, she
warned me with her eyes to take Mehmet to a corner where we
could play and from where he would not be likely to give away any
secrets, for he was determined to attract her attention and would
not leave her side. When she was leaving, he beamed proudly at
her, saying very distinctly, "Dead! Dead!"

But my grandmother, strangely enough, had no idea of the
frightful thing he meant, and my mother interrupted Mehmet's
words so smoothly that his gruesome words were lost for the
moment.

But perhaps she remembered their message later, for we did not
see her for a few days and then, when she did come, there was
such a wailing and gnashing of teeth as there never has been in
the world before. Her visit did not start like that, of course. In fact
it started remarkably normally, with my grandmother sweeping in
to demand coffee, very controlled, though a little red about the eyes.
My mother just looked at her incredulously for a moment or two,
then said, "You have been to Sariyer."

And then everything happened at once. My grandmother's face

crumpled and she began to cry, not silently, as Hasan had done, but noisily and desperately, as though a great well were suddenly finding release. Her tears and her ugly working face frightened me, and I held tightly to my mother's hand, for never had the world seemed so full of tears as latterly. These last weeks had been steeped in tears. The world had become a grim place where people lost their homes and died in unknown places, where women struggled and grew irritable and wept, wept, wept. The appalling sorrows of the moment weighed me down, and I started to cry too. When peace had been more or less restored by the application of sharp words from my mother and still sharper slaps, Mehmet and I were sent to our corner and commanded to play! As if we could play when the pandemonium of my grandmother's tears filled the room! She wept unceasingly, as though she shed tears not only for her own son that day but for all humanity. After a long time she stopped, and my mother pressed cognac on her, forcing her to drink it. There was little affection in my mother's attitude toward her, for these two were never to know affection. Yet that day they clung very closely, each depending upon the other for strength to bear these blows from life.

"My son is dead and my daughter Ayşe is dead, and I have nobody left in the world."

"Ayşe?" asked my mother in a disbelieving voice, and perhaps feeling affronted that my grandmother had regarded her as nobody.

But my grandmother could not answer. She only rocked her body to and fro in an extremity of grief for her eldest born, who was dead. She was almost incoherent with her great grief, Aunt Ayşe's death appearing a mere incidental in the face of this larger, more suffocating grief.

But eventually my mother extracted the whole story. My grandmother had left our house dissatisfied with my mother's explanation of Hasan's visit. She had brooded over it all day, finally recollecting Mehmet's abortive attempts to tell her something, something, she became sure, that was connected with Sariyer. After a sleepless night she had arisen, determined to go to Sariyer immediately. She had informed her astonished husband of this, taken a maid as chaperone—for whereas she might visit us unescorted, to journey alone as far as Sariyer was quite another matter—and feverishly hurried to the boat.

Upon arrival at Sariyer she had been met by red-eyed servants, the sight of whom had further increased her alarm, and they had told her that Aunt Ayşe had died early that morning. My grandmother had borne up reasonably well under this news and thought her premonition had come from this. She had liked Aunt Ayşe, but, after all, she was only a daughter-in-law, and the women of old Turkey did not attach a great deal of importance to such a relationship. Nobody, at that time, mentioned my uncle; as a consequence, not knowing of the greater shock that lay before her, my grandmother, although feeling sorrow at Aunt Ayşe's untimely death, nevertheless was able to take charge of the situation competently. My aunt had died as the result of a violent haemorrhage, which a doctor, had he been available, would have been unable to check.

All this was explained to her by the doctor who had been afterward called by the terrified servants and who had waited in the house for my grandmother's arrival. He had been startled to hear that no message had been received by her from Sariyer and that her presence here now was pure chance, owing to her alarming premonition that something had been wrong. They had sat and talked in the silent, sun-drenched salon that looked out over the gardens of Sariyer, now at their most beautiful. The salon had affected my grandmother unbearably, for it looked so ready for occupation, as though it awaited the step of its mistress. Great jars of white lilac, gathered by Aunt Ayşe the day before, stood about on little tables, overpowering the still room with its cloying, sweet perfume.

Later in the morning a notary arrived, explaining that Sariyer and all its land and farms now reverted back to Aunt Ayşe's family, to a brother who was a cavalry officer away at the war. He had patiently explained to my grandmother's misunderstanding face that Aunt Ayşe had died intestate and *after* Uncle Ahmet; there-

fore, according to law, the property would go to any members remaining from her family. This was the first intimation my grandmother had received that her beloved son was dead, and she had
promptly fainted. But when she had been revived, although still
stunned by the terrible news, she had been able to arrange about
the burial of my aunt and dismiss the servants, all of them bewildered and wondering where to go, for they had preferred the servi-
tude of Sariyer to the doubtful freedom of being alone. She had
arranged that all the furniture should be shrouded and had, finally,
that same afternoon, seen Aunt Ayşe lowered into her lonely grave
—for burial is swift in Turkey, the summer climate being unkind to
the newly dead. Then she had bade farewell to Sariyer, lovely
under the June sun, but empty now and tenantless, with only the
fading memory of our laughter to echo now and then in ghostly
fashion. And my grandmother had returned to İstanbul, seeing no
beauty now in the lovely, sweeping line of the shores of the Bosporus, anxious only to come to my mother to cry her heart out.

So she sat in her chair all through the day and rocked herself to
and fro; and when the great tide of grief was exhausted, the sun
was far down the sky and the first evening yogurtcu was coming up
the street. My grandmother moved her stiffened, weary body and
prepared to go to her home. Her face was gray and brittle-looking,
and I do not think that anything else in life ever hurt her again
as much as this, the loss of her favorite, her best beloved.

12

Disillusionment of an Autocrat

DEATH.

The world seemed suddenly full of the word and the noise of women weeping. All down the street news had begun to arrive of sons and brothers and fathers who had been killed at the front. There were no heated arguments now with the street sellers. The women wearily bought what they could afford; the young boys went off to join their fathers in the fighting, and the street was given over to the dribbling babies and the dogs and the ever ravenous cats. Each waking day brought fresh news from the front, of the appalling casualties we were suffering; and the Red Crescent trains came faster and thicker than ever, bringing the wounded and dying to İstanbul. There was not a woman in the little street but had someone at the front, even the widow downstairs, whose only son was away. Food was scarcer than ever, even if one had the money to buy it; and the Bourse noir flourished unchecked, and people dropped in the streets for lack of nourishment. My grandmother had been in the habit of sending storable foods to us, but she stopped this practice. My mother would make soups for us from a handful of lentils or dried peas, or serve plain boiled haricot beans, conserving such precious items as rice and flour or olive oil for the leaner times just around the corner. Still she spent weary hours at the baker's, sometimes returning with bread, but more often empty-handed. And we were always hungry, always longing for fresh, crusty slices of the bread we could not get. During the mornings I would be left alone with Mehmet and Muazzez. Mehmet was docile enough, but Muazzez used to drive me into a frenzy of exasperation and fear, for she would cry so lustily that she became quite purple in the face with rage. She cried if I rocked the cradle; she cried if I did not, her eyes tearless and her screams shrill and unceasing. My mother would leave a bottle of milk for her, wrapped in a piece of material to keep it warm; this I would thrust exasperatedly at her, trying to quiet her, but it had no effect. One morning she was so terrible that by the time my mother returned, I was in tears myself. I told her what was wrong, and she lifted the now docile Muazzez, dandling her and calling me over to look at the pretty thing.

"I hate her!" I burst out passionately, stubbing my toe against the foot of the cradle, but the moment she heard my voice, Muazzez, the little tyrant, commenced to wail loudly again.

My mother was upset by my truculent attitude and, perhaps as some sort of reward, sent Mehmet and me into the street to play, telling us not to move from the front door. But when my grandmother, later in the day, came down the street, she was so scandalized to see us playing like street urchins, to quote her, that she was quite cool with my mother for the rest of the day, and accused her of bringing us up very badly.

She was in a gloomy mood that day, complaining that she could not remain long with us as the old man was not too well and had of late taken to demanding her at all impossible hours of the day and night, renewing his command that she should no longer visit us. She watched my mother's efforts to make clothes for us on the sewing machine and interfered so much that she quite upset my mother, who, in the end, was unable to do anything more while my grandmother remained.

That evening she made an odd sort of dummy for Muazzez. It was made of muslin and filled with cleaned sultanas, and she told

me to stick into her mouth when she commenced to cry and I
was alone with her. She also taught me an old Turkish nursery
rhyme, not only forcing me to sing it to her but called up the widow
to listen to my voice. I was sure the rhyme would be worse than
useless to quiet Muazzez, but my mother, lamenting for İnci,
looked so sad that I promised her I would try. This was the song:

> Dan dini dan dini das dana,
> Danalar grimiş bostana
> Kov bostançi danaye,
> Yemeşinler lahanye. . . .

which defies translation but means something to the effect that the
little water buffaloes are in the garden, with an injunction to the
gardener to push them out before they eat all the cabbages! The
soft, soothing words brought back memories of İnci crooning it
over Mehmet's cradle. So far as I could remember, the soporific
effect on Mehmet had been remarkable, and I hoped it would be
as successful with my sister. I had the opportunity of judging the
next day and was so relieved when it actually succeeded that I
did not know whether to laugh or cry and was afraid of doing
either for fear I should reawaken the sleeping angel. So the daily
round continued, with my grandmother continuing to supply money
and my mother growing accustomed to marketing. My father
seemed to have dropped entirely from our minds, so little was his
name mentioned; if my grandmother were to say his name, it hit
the senses like a little shock—as though she spoke of someone a
long time dead. He had become a dim, far figure, not easily remembered, and so sentimentalized by my grandmother that it was
not easy to recognize my flesh-and-blood father in the overdrawn
romantic figure she painted.

The street, too, had grown used to us and had even begun to
nod to my mother. Sometimes they would beg her to do some little
thing for them, perhaps decipher a letter from a Government office,
reply to one, or merely how to write one to their loved ones. Whatever it was they asked her, she did it with unfailing good humor

and tact. She became so well known for this latter characteristic that in the end Bekci Baba would ask her to impart the bad news that he had no heart to tell. He had had so much bad news, since the war had started, that the imparting of it should have inured him to the grief of the women; but he was old and tender-hearted and tears struck deep into his heart, and he never delivered a War Office message without inextricably entangling himself in the toils of the recipient's woe. So he ranged himself alongside my mother, often asking her advice before presenting himself fatefully before a door. She became greatly loved in the street. In time, as I grew older, I saw the women of that street showering kisses over her hands while they called from their hearts, Melek (Angel). If she suspected that a family was hungry, she would take something to them, presenting it in such a way that offense could not be taken.

She was generally the first to be found at the bedside of the sick or dying and received many last-minute instructions or confessions. She poured out whatever tenderness she had on the poor, and many died with her name on their lips. The halt and maimed who returned from the front aroused her especial pity, and she was never too tired to resist their appeals to her. I suppose that against the general social standards prevailing in our street, we were comparatively wealthy. The women automatically called her "hanim effendi," a title, in old Turkey, used only for the better classes. They would ask her opinion on everything concerning their family life, feeling no embarrassment in acquainting her with the more intimate details.

As that year drew to a close, she worried incessantly over my schooling, for I was almost seven and entirely ignorant. She had taught me the alphabet and kept my Turkish pure, but she only knew the barest rudiments of arithmetic and a little polite French, which could not equip me for the battle of life. Most of the district schools were closed through lack of teaching staff and were being used by the Red Crescent as military hospitals for the emergency treatment of casualties. So when my mother had taught me the little she knew herself, I languished both mentally and physically, learning instead how to peel potatoes and rock my sister to sleep.

Winter began early and coal was scarce, of poor quality, and very dear. My grandmother provided us with a winter's supply, which we supplemented with logs of firewood, huddling over the little stove in the salon, cold because of the lack of proper food and because of the poor quality of the wool with which our jerseys had been knitted.

There was much sickness in the street, and death weeded out the old and the infirm and the very young. My mother was kept busy going from one house to another, giving advice or consolation, or merely holding the hand of the one who was left. Then came a time when she herself fell sick and the fever came back to her. She cried out in her delirium, but this time there was no fashionable physician to visit her many times a day, for almost all the doctors had gone to the war, and the few who remained were too busy to visit badly paying patients in poor districts.

But the street surged in to help her. Thin old women, looking like crows in their black clothes, with black çarşafs tightly binding their foreheads, would sit beside her bed and give her sips of water or rub her forehead with eau de Cologne to cool the surface blood and so help reduce the fever. Loving and dirty hands washed and dressed and fed us children and laid us in our beds at night, then went back to the more serious business of tending my mother. Curious groping fingers sought for lice in our heads and drew back disappointed because none were to be found. They rocked Muazzez all day long, singing "Nini" to her when they wanted her to sleep, and she would lie regarding them with alert, bright eyes and was never known to cry in their presence. Other thin black crows would do the washing on the gloomy landing, silently and grimly, and I was so afraid of them that I used to creep past them and sit perched in my corner seat, longing for my mother to be well again. When my grandmother called, they would try to ingratiate themselves into her favor, reporting the progress or lack of progress of the patient, recite a long, interminable list of what they had done, bow deeply, and wait for further instructions. She was terribly, embarrassingly autocratic with them, treating them as her servants, but it was not she who kept them loyal to our house: they loved my mother and this was their only way of re-paying her kindnesses to themselves. Day and night the house was filled with them; and they were roughly kind to Mehmet and me, spending the money my grandmother gave them as honestly as she would have spent it herself. Their own children were blissfully permitted to go about the day long in dirt, but poor Mehmet and I were unmercifully scrubbed twenty times or more a day, for they felt that extraordinary cleanliness must be one of the peculiar at-tributes of the upper classes. They expended more time and energy over us than İnci had ever done. They would remove their shoes before entering the bedrooms or the sitting room, exclaiming over the softness of the carpets against their bare feet. They would ex-amine all my mother's table and bed linen with rough red hands, gloating over the silver and polishing it until the old treasures were in danger of snapping under their hurrying fingers. Inquisitive hands pried everywhere. Nothing was safe from them. Curtains were touched joyously and held against the cheek, china examined to see how fine and delicate it was, and then, in the midst of their wanderings through the three rooms in search of more treasures to gloat over, they would espy Mehmet and me and would sweep de-lightedly down on us, gathering us against their withered bosoms, and proceed to take the skin off us once more with yet another washing. The relief when at last my mother was able to get up again! Her illness had seemed like years and years to us, but when she saw our faces and hands and bodies shining from all the soap that had been used on us, she commenced to cry, saying we looked too clean.

We hastened to assure her that it was all a mistake and that left to ourselves it would never have occurred to us to be so clean. She commenced to laugh, the tears still shining in her eyes, and said that, anyway, the neighbors had been very kind. We could not agree wholeheartedly, feeling that there were limits to kindness.

One morning a few months later, when my mother was thoroughly well again, a servant called from my grandmother's house to say that the old man was dead. This was a great shock, for my mother had not heard he was ill. The servants explained that it was a heart attack and that my grandmother was overcome with shock, for it was she who had discovered him. She was asked to return with the servant, but this she strangely refused to do. She never spared herself for other people, and this reluctance to go to my grandmother's home was the opposite of her usual helpful attitude.

But perhaps she knew that genuine grief calls for every effort, whereas the grief manifested by my grandmother was a purely synthetic thing to impress outsiders. Whatever the true reason for my mother's refusal, she did not speak about it to us; and later that day, when the curtains were already drawn and the lamps were lit, my grandmother arrived. She looked tired and a little frightened, disposed to be short-tempered with my mother. For a long time she ignored my mother, talking to Mehmet and me, and my mother lay back in her long chair and refused to ask any questions. This attitude piqued my grandmother; and when at length she could no longer bear it, she burst out that my mother grew more and more callous and that she had expected her at least to have asked after the state of my grandmother's nerves, which were, she declared, simply shocking. She conventionally squeezed a few tears from her eyes and lamented her husband, but with so little enthusiasm that at last she gave up trying to deceive even herself. She was attempting to whip up a decorous picture of herself, the new widow, weeping for her husband, as if her marriage had been a normal, friendly, happy marriage. She said that she intended to spend the night with us, for she could not bear to go back to that dreaded house. My mother said nothing. Then my grandmother, all decorousness swept away, said with animation that now she was a very rich woman and that we would all go to live in her house.

She said we would never have to worry again about money or anything else, and waited for my mother's comments. She became more and more spry, and my mother began to laugh at her, but very soon she herself became infected with enthusiasm. There was only one small, rather insignificant fly in the ointment, but it was large enough to dampen happiness occasionally. After the old man's death, the notary who held his will had been summoned, also the nephew who controlled his various business concerns.

The nephew had said, "Well, Fatma hanim, what are we going to do with you, I wonder?"

And he had told her that this was not the time to discuss these things and that they would inform her later of the terms of the will.

"What do you think he meant by that?" my grandmother kept asking my mother, but the latter replied that everything would be all right, since she had been the old man's wife and had first rights of the property.

"Are you sure?" my grandmother wanted to know doubtfully, sinking her chin on her hands and going into a reverie. She got quite peevish because my mother suggested that we wait a few months before we move to her house, so that the neighbors would not be given any opportunity to talk unkindly behind us.

"Neighbors!" snapped my grandmother, and with that one word withered us all.

After Mehmet and I were sent to bed, we heard their argumentative voices rolling back and forth in battle for a long time, until finally we went to sleep.

A few days later my mother accompanied my grandmother to see the notary and the nephew, and we were left in the charge of the widow. I watched them walking down the street, my mother pulling black gloves over her hands, her step firm and confident, and my grandmother beside her, very upright and looking anything but a bereaved widow. Later that day they returned, looking no different, perhaps, to the uninitiated eye, but to Mehmet and me there was a certain grimness to be noted about the mouth and eyes, sufficient reason for us to keep angelically quiet and not ask questions. We heard no mention of going to live in my grandmother's house, and the next day a porter arrived with her remaining furniture from her old home. I was very curious and wondered where it was going to be put. An outsize in china cabinets ousted me from the door; and when a console table followed it, I retreated into the farthest corner of the salon, thinking that if any more furniture came in I should be buried under it. A covered ottoman was carried into my mother's room, Muazzez's cradle having to be moved to make room for it. Tin chests arrived, and the porters were told to leave them on the landing, since there was no room anywhere else. Every available inch of space seemed crowded, and our rooms looked dreadful. All the spacious gayety so carefully arranged by my mother had fled. Amid all the confusion she moved tight-lipped and uncompromising, yet with a contradictory air of serenity that I had not seen for a long time. I was aching to ask questions but was cowed into silence by my grandmother's attitude.

Soon after that the widow moved from the downstairs rooms, going to live farther down the street, and my grandmother moved in to take her place. Furniture was rearranged, but there was still far too much of it; the tin chests remained filled, and carpets were hung on the walls because there was no room for them on the floors. The rooms took on a dull, darkened look, looking ugly and overcrowded.

For many days my grandmother was very subdued and quarreled with my mother on the slightest provocation, reminding her frequently whose money was buying our food and the clothes we were wearing. This was so out of character that we could not but deduce that something very seriously was amiss. And indeed it was!

Her late husband had taken his revenge. He had cut her completely from his will, leaving her penniless. All his property and ready money had gone to his nephew—who today is to be found in America—and the old house in Bayazit was closed and shuttered. The house where we were living was left to my mother for her lifetime or for so long as she cared to live there, afterward reverting to his nephew. He had not even stipulated the use of one room for my grandmother, ignoring her existence as completely as if she had never been his wife.

All of this I learned from my mother when I was older, when we had lived in that house for many years. My grandmother always remained with us, but never docilely. She never mentioned the old man's name, but took to talking about my grandfather, as if the past year of marriage were only a dream. She became very religious suddenly, but remained autocratic to the end of her days, for that trait in her would never die until she did.

13

Ninety-nine Kuruş in Exchange for a Hero

WITH MY GRANDMOTHER'S ARRIVAL AT OUR house, life became easier for me, since she commenced to look after Muazzez whenever my mother was out. But the cramped communal life of a small house did not suit her temper, however, and she was more than ever uncertain and hard to please these days. She objected to Mehmet and me playing in the salon, regardless of the fact that there was no other place for us. So we took to accompanying my mother to the market place, in order to let my grandmother have the house to herself. We also depended upon her to get food, for my mother had long since exhausted her own meager supply of money. My grandmother kept all her money and valuables in a large tin chest in her bedroom, the keys of which she always carried with her. This habit annoyed my mother, and she ached to be independent. My grandmother continuously grumbled about expenses but would not forego her wine for dinner. In her especially bad times she would tell us that my father still owed her money from the sale of the business—which was totally untrue, since she had never been left any ready money by my grandfather. We ate food of poor quality and this, she complained, upset her stomach. She insisted on snowy table linen, despite the fact that soap was expensive and hard to obtain, but would not countenance the same tablecloth on two occasions. She sometimes bought little luxury foods and then said that we ate too much. She never forgot she had been a lady and would sit idle in the salon while my mother toiled in the kitchen, cooking the choice dishes she still demanded. Muazzez was the only one of us she seemed to like, and she spent a great deal of her time petting and spoiling her and then complaining to my mother that the child was unmanageable. News reached us that Orhan Bey, the husband of Madam Müjgan, had been killed; and the names of other men and boys who had died also ceased to be heard on our lips, for one did not like to talk too much about the peaceful dead.

One morning my mother excitedly returned from the market with news that a unit had returned from the Dardanelles to Yeşil-köy and that perhaps my father was with them.

This caused a great deal of speculation among us; but finally my grandmother declared it to be nonsense, since if my father had got as near to home as Yeşilköy, he would have somehow or other sent a message to us. But my mother was not to be so easily turned from the scent. The sons and husbands of other old neighbors had come back to Yeşilköy—why not my father? So off she set one early morning for Yeşilköy, taking me with her for company. We took the train from Sirkeci station, and I was very thrilled, for it was the first time I had ever been on a train. Despite my mother's warnings, I could not sit still but had to inspect thoroughly knobs and handles and the tattered upholstery of the seats. A dozen times or more I poked my head out of the window to watch the exciting country flying past us. I was in a seventh heaven of delight, for riding in this train was far more fun than it had been to ride behind Murat in the old days. I suppose I was not especially curious about meeting my father, being too thrilled with the noise the train was making and the shrill, almost continuous sound of the whistle. I was very disappointed when we at last reached our destination, and as my mother hurried me along the platform, I kept looking regretfully back at the great dark monster that had transported us here.

My mother inquired from the stationmaster how far it was to the military camp; he looked doubtfully at her thin, ladylike shoes and replied that it was a long walk. His tone implied doubt that she would ever make it, but he directed her the road to follow. We set out along the bare winter road, but that day there seemed to be just the littlest hint of spring in the air. Long before we reached the camp, however, our pace slackened. Many times we halted to get our breath back and to ease our aching feet, for the road was bad and our footwear light. At length we came to the top of the last hill, and there, at our feet, lay the camp with its camouflaged tents.

Excitement lent new wings to my mother, and in any case it was far easier to descend the hill than it had been to ascend it. We met only a peasant, with his mule, on the way down; everything was very still with that stillness especial to the country, only the caw-cawing of the crows now and then disturbed it. When we reached the camp we were breathless, and when an officer in a very ragged uniform came forward to ask our business, my mother had considerable difficulty in answering him at all. She explained, however, why she had come, and he looked vague for a moment or two, as though the name of my father perhaps struck a chord somewhere in his memory. With very great courtesy he begged my mother to wait a little, while he made inquiries. He walked away from us, and when I turned to say something to my mother, I was amazed to see that her eyes were filled with tears. A few spilled down her face and she said:

"Poor man! He looks so tired and shabby, and did you notice that he had his arm and his shoulder bandaged? That means he has been wounded and should be in hospital and not walking about this camp."

I had a horrible moment of remembering the first words of the song they had sung when they took my father to the war.

"*Ey, gaziler* . . ." they had sung, "O wounded ones . . ." and my heart began to beat unevenly for fear my mother would remember, too, or read the words in my eyes.

Presently two soldiers came toward us, and I held my breath expectantly as my mother gave a little gasp.

"Can it be your father?" she said in an unsteady sort of voice, and I commenced to run toward the soldiers, but she called me back. "Don't go," she said. "Neither of them is your father."

She sat down again to wait until they came up to us, and there was a dull, flat expression on her face that heightened the cheekbones and broadened the nostrils. As the soldiers came abreast of us, we saw that they were officers, although their uniforms, too, were so shabby that if it had not been for the insignia of rank on their shoulders, we could not have distinguished them from the soldiers.

"Ali Bey," she cried to one of the officers, and he saluted her, going red with some emotion that I could not understand. I looked at him curiously, wondering who he might be and how my mother knew him.

She asked eagerly for news of my father, and he looked uncertainly at her, as though perhaps weighing up her capabilities for shock. He said slowly, "We left him to his God a long time ago—" and paused, wondering what else there was to say to her. And although her face was whiter than I had ever seen it in my life, she said with swift impatience:

"Yes! Go on! I want to know whatever it is you have to tell me."

Then the man called Ali, who was a captain, plunged into conversation to tell her this story.

On the march to the Dardanelles, my father had suffered badly with foot trouble. He had to march day and night, night and day, and his feet commenced to swell; in the end they had to cut his torn boots off him. The two feet were found to be badly infected, right up to the ankles, and soaked in fresh bright blood. He had been left by the roadside, as was the custom, and they had called back down the lines that a wounded man lay under a tree. Eventually this message would reach the end of the marching lines, where a horse-drawn cart lumbered for the express purpose of picking up the sick and wounded. But if the cart were already full to overflowing with all the other sick soldiers who had dropped out on the way? Ah, well—in that case a man just lay there under the blazing sun and waited for the next lot of marching soldiers to take up the same old cry that a man lay wounded under the trees by the side of an alien road. Down, down the weary lines the cry would go, but perhaps by the time the sick-cart reached the spot, the man would be dead—and there was not much point in carrying a dead man when there were so many living who still might be saved. But, of course, Captain Ali hastened to assure my mother, my father was picked up and taken to a base hospital—where he died. As he told her all these things, his pale face flickered and his eyes were loath to meet hers, for how could he tell this white, courageous woman that neither he nor anyone else knew where her husband had died? But she persisted in subjecting herself to the useless agony, demanding the name of the hospital—as if the young captain could have told her, even supposing he knew. He was infinitely patient, holding himself stiffly to attention, assuring her that everything that could have been done had been done. And in the end she had to be content, for there was nothing else he could tell her. So she thanked him and he saluted her, as one brave soldier to another, and she took my hand and we began the long trudge back to the station.

She did not speak to me at all but walked as if mechanically propelled, never slackening or altering her pace, although my small legs were breaking under me. I begged her to sit down, to let me rest, crying in my tiredness and with cold, for the day had become overcast and all signs of spring had left the air. I tottered beside her and plucked at her skirt, but she looked at me as if she did not recognize me, as if I had brought her back from some far place; and I cried all the more bitterly in this new loneliness. Then I saw expression creep into her dead eyes, and she caught me to her and sat down with me in a ditch.

"Poor tired boy!" she said over and over again, as though she knew no other words, or as though this repetition would still remembrance of something else, something that lurked in the foreground of the mind and would not be pushed back, back with all those other memories that could not be looked upon because they were still too new. She put her arms around me and repeated her meaningless refrain, frightening me unendurably, for her arms held no security and her voice no comfort, and I did not know if she were speaking to me or to some image of my father that she held in her empty, rocking arms.

Back home, the wind of discontent blew coldly through the house. My mother became almost unapproachable and hard as we had never known her before. My grandmother forgot her grumblings and walked silently before such coldness and insensibility. Back to those days flies memory to feel again the soft breath of fear on the cheek, to feel the slow ice around the heart, and the feathery, barely perceptible insecurity that crept up on a child. I would catch sight of my mother sitting idly at her work in the kitchen, or looking steadily at some half-finished piece of sewing in her hands, her face expressing surprise that she should be holding anything, for she could not remember having picked it up. In her eyes would wander a gentle vagueness, its shadow flitting now and then across her face, darkening sanity—although a child's mind did not put it like that. A child was only conscious of strangeness, and she would not emerge from her dreams of the past, even though her children pulled at her arms and their cries beat on her brain. She shut herself away from them all, sat silent for long stretches, and became strange and odd and absent-minded. And fear flourished in the little house, in the unreasoning, illogical way fear will. Whatever she did she did with the heartless precision of an automaton and was never heard to mention my father or wonder about the future. My grandmother would try and rouse her out of this lethargic state, suggesting with intentional brutality that she should go to the War Office and find out what she could about my father. At these times my mother would look vaguely at my grandmother, and one could feel the difficulties she was having in focusing her attention on what had been said to her. Then she would turn her head away saying fretfully that she did not want to discuss the matter, and my grandmother would retire, defeated, helpless in the face of such implacability.

It was about this time, too, that my grandmother became almost totally deaf, and her thick, dark hair showed more and more gray and began to fall out. Decay and rot were setting in everywhere.

The day eventually came, of course, when my mother seemed to grow out of her morbidity, when her eyes showed alert awareness again and she took an interest in those about her. Just as she had been listless before, now she was teeming with energy, as though long sojourn with grief had revitalized her. She spoke of going to the War Office, and once she had made the decision, was impatient to be off at once. We were left to my grandmother, who nowadays seemed bowed and old, mumbling into the Koran most of the day, doling out money from her tin chest without murmur or protest. The day my mother went to the War Office, grandmother sat in the salon, reading from the Koran, talking to herself in a loud, grumbling voice, for she was so deaf that she did not realize she spoke aloud. By the time my mother returned, we were starving, for my grandmother could not be weaned from her prayers to get a meal for us. My mother looked tired herself and clicked her teeth exasperatedly when she saw that nothing had been prepared for her. She went to the kitchen, Mehmet and I excitedly running around her, the good smell of cooking that she was creating causing our mouths to water and our empty stomachs to ache. She was unusually patient with us, ignoring it when we snatched eagerly at the fresh, crusty outside of the bread she had brought home with her. When all was ready, we were told to call my grandmother. We bellowed loudly from the foot of the stairs, and she reluctantly put away her Koran and came down to eat.

My mother told us of her day. The War Office had been crowded with other black-clad, anxious women demanding news of their husbands. Harassed officials had bleated that no information could be given and had attempted to restore law and order and dignity to the War Office. But to have restored these that day would have required a Herculean effort, more than the few officials between them could manage, and one of them had retired to get more help. My mother had stood for hours in that smelling, angry queue of humanity, eventually learning that what she had been told by Captain Ali at Yeşilköy had been true. The records showed that my father had been dead for many months. Timidly, my mother had asked where he died, and the official dealing with her had snapped that he could not be expected to know everything. Surely it was enough for her to know that her husband was dead?

"But are your sure?" my mother had pleaded, impotent against such open, uncaring cruelty. "I have received no confirmation from you. Why did you not let me know before this, without my having to come here?"

The official had broken into her words brutally, saying:

"Hanim, your husband is dead; and with so many dead and dying, we *cannot* be expected to notify everyone!"

My mother, remembering, said that he had spoken with great petulance, as though she and all the other unhappy women waiting here were in some way responsible for the deaths of their menfolk, thereby causing this gallant young man a great deal of unnecessary trouble.

She had wanted to ask him something else, but he had forestalled her, slamming the wooden window shutter in her face, and she had been forced to retire. She said that all about her the women were being treated in the same way. Crying, wailing, beseeching for information, old ones and young ones with babies were unceremoniously pushed back from the inquiry windows. Then one woman, driven beyond endurance, commenced to shout insults while she held her startled baby above her head.

"Dogs!" she had shouted passionately, "my husband left five children behind him, and a mother to support. Are *you* going to support them, you miserable sons of bitches? Did my husband ask to be taken from his work and his family to fight for people like you? Will you give us food to put in our hungry stomachs? Do you care if we go hungry and naked, if strange men insult us in the streets, or if our children die of disease and starvation? Our husbands died to save their country, and then bastards like you shut the windows in our faces, because we ask for news—"

She had been roughly handled by the police and dragged, screaming further abuse, from the building. My mother, retelling her story, became heated for the injustice done to that woman and to all the women of Turkey.

"She was right, right!" she insisted passionately to my grandmother's disdainful face. "And she was no street woman either, and she would never have said what she did say without provocation. We didn't ask for this war. My poor wise Hüsnü was right when he once said that the conceit of a few men could ruin our country." She commenced to cry bitterly, my grandmother stirring uneasily in her chair. She was so deaf that she had only heard part of my mother's speech, and she did not know what to do to give comfort.

My mother raised her head to look at my grandmother.

"If we had not had your money," she said to her listening, straining face, "we could not have survived. There are thousands who have nothing, still the Government ignores them and leaves them to die in the streets. Is this what our men went to fight for? Did my husband leave me for this? If there is a God above, He must show mercy to the widows and orphans who are left! *If* there is a God above!"

My grandmother's half-deaf ears had caught some of the last words, and her lined face puckered with distress.

"No!" she protested gently. "Do not call upon God in that way. You will be punished, my child. It is not right for us to question His ways."

"Ach!" said my mother with disgust. "Will He feed us, Mother? Will He come down from His heaven and put food in my children's hungry stomachs?"

My grandmother strained pitifully to catch the angry words and shook her head protestingly.

"No, no!" she repeated. "It is not right to talk like this. Have you not had enough punishment? Do you want to see your children struck dead or blinded before your eyes?"

Her direful words made us shiver with horror.

My mother said: "You are old, Mother. You will never understand what it is to lose your husband when you are young, to know that never again will you be able to lie beside him at the end of the day or to feel his warm body close along the line of your back. Your day is finished, and you lost your husbands when all passion had gone from you long ago. But I lost mine before my body had time to wither. All the young and the brave are dying, and only the women and the helpless children are left. And our good sultan keeps to his palace and assesses the worth of a man in terms of money and will give me ninety-nine *kuruş* a month to compensate me for the loss of my husband—my husband who was young and strong and who rots in some grave we do not know where. Ninety-nine kuruş!"

"*What* is the ninety-nine kuruş?" asked my grandmother, bellowing in her anxiety so that Mehmet and I trembled.

"The pension I shall receive for myself and my three children," replied my mother.

"Pension?" queried my grandmother, not fully understanding anything, I think, but anxious to appear intelligent to the passionate young woman who faced her across the table.

My mother carefully kept her patience to explain.

"A pension is money you receive from the Government if you have lost your husband in the war. They have decided to give me ninety-nine kuruş because that is all that Hüsnü was worth to them. I have lost my home because we are at war. Ahmet is dead and Ayşe—and Sariyer will soon be less than a memory. My children grow and must be fed, and you and I cling to life because sometimes it is easier to live than to die. Bread is fifty kuruş a kilo and lasts us one day, two if we go hungry; and a man at the Treasury today congratulated me because I gave a man to the war. 'God has blessed you,' he said. 'Your husband died *sehit* [for his country] and his place is in heaven—and now, if you will just sign here, please—' and he gave me the paper which said I was willing to accept ninety-nine kuruş for my husband."

Her passionate voice broke and she sat staring into space, her eyes full of the saddest dreams, and curiously—but not frighteningly so—oblivious of her family about her. My grandmother noisily sipped her soup but spoke no word, for her deafness gave her a remoteness from life, and she could not always follow my mother's tripping tongue.

The first time my mother went to collect her pension, I went with her, to the building that is today the İstanbul College. Pushing, shouting women were everywhere, and the queues reached far down the street. But they were not the orderly, disciplined queues that I came to know so well in wartime England during the Second World War. No indeed! These queues could scarcely be called queues at all, since they consisted for the most part of women shrieking insults and imprecations at each other, pushing each other out of the way, and arguing spiritedly with the police, who, for a time, tried to instil some sense of decorum into the crowds. But the women, en masse, were too much for the police, so they left them to fight out their battles. My mother and I awaited our turn, she with considerable asperity, and if anyone attempted to take her place, she rounded on them so venomously that the attacker was forced to retire. Her sharp, uncompromising attitude brooked no interference, and I admired her for being able to defend herself against these rough women.

When it was our turn at the pay window, she took the money offered, handed it to me, and told me to buy sultanas for myself.

The official said sharply: "The Government gives you that money for food, sister, not to give it as pocket money to your children. Or are you too rich to need this money?"

My mother turned to him viciously, returning to where he stood at the little window, lightly pushing aside the woman who was awaiting her money.

"Your job," said my mother, with remarkable self-control, "is to attend to the people who come here, not to give them advice, for we none of us need your advice." A cheer went up from the other women. "I wonder how much your munificent sultan pays you in a month? Enough to feed your family well? I do not think so, for your suit, God help you, is a disgrace to you, and your thin body looks so weak that it is no wonder they did not send you to fight the English. If I give the money I receive here to my son for sweet-meats, it is all I consider it to be worth. I came here to collect a pension, not to listen to your uncalled-for advice."

"I'll have you arrested," spluttered the young man, very red in the face; and I shook with terror, for I thought perhaps he could really do this.

And my mother's clear voice rang out challengingly, "Try to have me arrested!"

And the voices of the other women rose threateningly, against the arrival of two policemen, who remained, however, at the edge of the crowd, not yet brave enough to wade through that angry milling crowd to lay hands on my mother.

The women shouted hoarsely, "Well spoken, sister!"

And they moved protectingly about her, ready to defend her if the police came too near. She stood staring at the hesitant police, her head thrown back proudly, but they made no move toward her. She moved through the ranks of women, her head still high. Some of the women caught her sleeve as she passed and cried, "God bless you, hanim effendi!"

And the police made no attempt to touch her, though the words she had spoken that morning were treacherous in old Turkey.

After that episode she did not ever go again to collect the meager pension but would let me go, for I used to buy nuts or sultanas for myself and Mehmet. But one morning I too had a never-to-be-forgotten experience, and after that the pension lay forgotten, for none of us bothered to claim it.

That last day I went, the crowds were as thick as ever, and I patiently awaited my turn. Although many people left the pay win-dows, still so many more were entering the hall that I never seemed to get any nearer to receiving money. I swallowed my fear of the fierce women and pushed my way between them, sometimes crawling under them, ignoring the threats of the angry men, and succeeded in almost reaching one of the windows. There was a tall man behind me who, seeing that I was not tall enough to reach up to the ledge with the pay book, lifted me up. Then, to my intense embarrassment, he quickly inserted his fingers into the crutch of my short pants, and I wriggled and shouted like a mad thing. My threshing legs hit a young woman on the side of the head and she angrily beat me. The man who held me continued with his investigations, and I screamed wildly and tried to hit out at him. There was an ominous muttering from the crowd, and I struggled to free myself; it was easier now, for the man had partially released me. I almost fell to the floor, hurt and bewildered that anyone should want to do such things, and I fled through the crowds, the pension book forgotten.

I ran home as fast as my legs could carry me, although they were trembling so much that I do not suppose I really made very much progress. When I got home, I sobbed out the whole story to my astonished mother. I saw her mouth tighten, then she bade me wash myself and to say nothing of this to Mehmet.

Afterward she explained: "When you are older, I shall tell you all these things, for now I am your father and your mother. But always remember that to certain men boys are more valuable than girls, especially a nice-looking boy like you."

She said no more beyond adding that I must try and put this day out of my head.

But it was hard to put the memory behind me. The shock had been so intense that for a long time afterward I flew like the wind from every man I met. And through childhood and youth the suspicion remained, and all men were potential enemies.

14

Poverty Makes a Bargain

MY GRANDMOTHER WAS AGING FAST.
She still read from the Koran each day and of late had taken to accusing my mother of trying to get another husband. She would mumble that nobody wanted her any more, that her money would soon be finished, and that once my mother had married again she would never be allowed to see her grandchildren. She wallowed in self-pity, refusing to listen when my mother explained that she had not the slightest intention of remarrying.

She shouted everything out in her loud voice for the whole neighborhood to hear. One day she bellowed to the widow, who was passing the door, to come up and drink coffee with her while she told all her troubles to her. The widow, being a kindly soul, forgot the many times my grandmother had snubbed her almost out of existence, and declared herself willing to drink coffee. She entered the house saying that she never drank good coffee unless she drank it in our house.

"Where you get the sugar—" she sighed, but my grandmother did not enlighten her and probably only heard part of the conversation in any case.

Although it was the widow who had been invited to partake of refreshment, it was she who made it, my grandmother roaring instructions at her, scarcely pausing for breath, insisting on the best cups being used. In a very short time the whole street knew that coffee was being brewed in our house, and very soon, they were also going to hear that the family was practically destitute.

Wood was added to the great white stove, and armchairs were drawn forward for the two women. I hovered uncertainly in the background and, no notice being taken of me, finally sat down on the soft warm carpet. The widow was delighted with her good luck and showed no inclination to leave this cozy room. My grandmother started to tell her that we had no money left, but the widow paid little attention to this, since she herself had never known anything else but a lack of money. When she finally got a chance to talk, she said cheerfully:

"But you have a sewing machine, hanim effendi, and with a sewing machine you can never be hungry. Why, I have eaten my bread from one for the last fifteen years!"

"Nonsense," said my grandmother. "How can I learn to use a sewing machine at my time of life?"

"What about your daughter-in-law?" yelled the widow, drawing closer to the crackling fire.

"Şevkiye?" said my grandmother, in great surprise. "Why she is as useless as I am!"

"No, she isn't," contradicted the widow. "Look how quickly she learned how to make the children's clothes."

"Yes," said my grandmother thoughtfully, "Of course she does the most exquisite embroidery—"

"Embroidery!" snorted the widow, with great disdain. "That's no use today in the world, hanim effendi. But machining—now that's quite another thing. Perhaps my patron in the Kapali çarşa would give her some work to do. I shall ask him tomorrow; if he is agreeable, I shall help her and show her how to do the things he wants."

The Kapali çarşa was a covered market, very famous in İstanbul.

"You are unusually kind," said my grandmother wonderingly, and the widow looked pleased.

In the midst of their talking, my mother came in, looking so odd, so disheveled, that my heart gave a lurch of fear.

"What is wrong?" cried the widow in dismay, and my mother replied in the new, hard voice that she always seemed to use nowadays.

"I am past wondering what is right and what is wrong. To live nowadays is to bear insults from everyone. At the Government departments they treat us like vermin, or tell us how fortunate we are that we have given a man to the war. I hunt bread every day, running from one baker's shop to another, and, in the end, what do I get? A piece of hard black bread that I would be ashamed to feed to the animals. The crowds push and kick and snarl with rage, and all decency seems to be gone from humanity—" Her voice broke and I thought she was going to cry, but she controlled herself, a faint furrow appearing between her delicate brows, almost as though she were wondering what she was talking about. She put out a hand to steady herself, and her face became very white, deadly white, so that the cheekbones were thrown into high relief, and the nose appeared sharper and more pinched.

"Did anything unusual happen this morning?" roared my grandmother.

"Plenty!" retorted my mother. "When you are a woman and alone in the world, you have to grow used to insults. This morning I tried several shops for bread; at last I found one open and joined the queue to take my chance with the rest. Just as I had handed my money and taken the bread offered to me, a woman beside me snatched it from my hand, saying that it was hers and that she had given her money first. I snatched it back again, and so the battle started. She was like a wild animal. She fought and kicked and screamed and pulled my veil from my face, saying only the rich wore veils and that I had no right to queue for bread when the poor needed it worse than I did. My veil!" my mother repeated, horrified. "Before all those people she pulled aside my veil, as if I were a prostitute, and then she called me one! Me! In front of all those people! I thought the world would fall on top of me. I tried to get away from her, but she had hold of my skirt and I was afraid she would tear that from me too. Two men interfered and gave me back the bread, and I ran away from that dreadful place with my veil all torn and the people shouting after me in the streets. They thought I was a bad woman and that I had been fighting with another bad woman! Oh, such disgrace! To think I should live to see the day that I should fight for such a thing—" She held up the piece of dry black bread. Then she swayed forward, and before I had time to realize what was happening she was lying across the sofa, lifted there by the strong, kindly arms of the widow. My grandmother, more agile than I ever remembered seeing her, was chafing her wrists, her own face almost as white as my mother's.

My mother commenced to grind her teeth. I was afraid that she was going to break them, but the widow jammed a spoon between her lips, raising her head to settle cushions more firmly behind it. After a while the awful grinding stopped, and my mother opened her eyes.

"Cognac!" shouted my grandmother, busying herself making strong coffee. She was almost crying to herself, calling upon the names of her dead sons to come back and defend their women. Her tears, long pent-up, rolled down her cheeks and fell into the hot ash of the mangal, making strange little sizzling sounds.

My mother opened her eyes and sat up, the color fast returning to her face. She stretched herself languidly, as though she were very tired and had come back from a long way off, then she accepted coffee and, presently, seemed perfectly normal again. The widow remained with us for the rest of the day; if she had work to do she gave no hint. Good soul that she was, she only wished to stay here with my mother, to serve her as best she could. Dusk came early and Ezzin was read from the little mosque, the signal for my grandmother to commence praying. Every evening she waited for the muezzin to climb into the minaret, for since her deafness this was the only way she could know the right time to pray. That evening she prayed in her loud, rumbling voice for her sons who were dead, for my grandfather, for my mother and us children. She put in a special little bit for herself at the end. Her voice filled the room, the old, liquid words falling softly on the ear. The widow had prepared the evening meal. Because my mother was still not really well enough to go downstairs, we had it in the salon. The fire blazed merrily and all the lamps—oh, rash extravagance—were brightly lit.

After dinner was over, my grandmother illogically expressed a desire to visit the little mosque to pray, saying that she wanted me with her. We started out into the black night, I pleasantly fearful and excited. My grandmother carried a lighted candle in a sort of storm lantern, and I could clearly see another candle glowing on the tomb of the holy man. We walked swiftly, for the night was bitterly cold, and when we came abreast of the window in which rested the tomb, my grandmother sternly bade me pray for the soul of the holy man. She opened her hands to the sky, palms upward in the Moslem fashion, and I did the same thing. I do not think I said much of a prayer, for my teeth were chattering with the cold and the wind had chosen just that moment to come whistling icily around the corner, cutting through my thin coat.When we went into the mosque, we sat down on the women's side. I was immediately acutely embarrassed, for my grandmother insisted on saying her prayers aloud. There were only a few other people there, but no peace was given to them, for, whether they wished it or not, they had to listen to my grandmother. Again and again she exhorted her God to be merciful to her dead ones and to make my mother well and strong again. I wriggled with impatience, trying to quiet her, but she refused to be quiet until she had finished what she had come here to say.

One day my mother and I went to Beşiktaş, some distance from our home. I have forgotten the reason we went but remember the occasion, for it was the first time I had ever seen the sultan, Mehmet Reşat. In the main street of Beşiktaş, soldiers were marching and a band played military music, while the police were roughly keeping back the curious crowds from the royal route.

We waited to see the sultan, and the cavalry came first, mounted on their high-stepping Arab horses. As far as I can accurately remember, they wore blue jackets with brightly shining brass buttons, scarlet trousers, and great tall calpacs on their heads, with flowing white plumes. They pranced toward us, their uniforms making a splash of welcome color in all that drab humanity, and their spurs clinked and jingled and gleamed in the watery sun. A carriage came after the cavalry, drawn by elegant, aristocratic horses, and dimly, through the windows, we caught a glimpse of a small old man with a little white beard. He was in uniform, many medals marching across his breast. A great loyal cry went up from the people, half of them in rags, a deep-throated rumbling roar of welcome. "Padişahim çok yaşa!" they roared, and then he was past us, and other voices took up the refrain. Even when the carriage had finally disappeared from sight, the echoes of the cheering crowds came back to us. Then the quiet streets grew quieter, for the people had dispersed, and my mother and I continued on our journey.

Mother had found work to do in these days. The widow, true to her word, had obtained sewing for her from her patron in the Kapali çarşa. The money was pitifully small, and nowadays the salon was eternally littered with made and unmade work: the never ceasing whirr of the sewing machine dominated all else. So the winter passed to the sound of my mother's machine and the merry, comforting, crackling sound of the logs in the china stove. Somehow or other life was readjusting itself: we had become used to bad food and not enough of it, and my grandmother did the marketing and I now hunted for bread. But the soft, early days of spring changed all that again. One had already learned that security was a fragile thing, sensitive to the first cold breath, yet one could not learn to accept this with finality. That spring of 1916 overrides all other memories and carries its scars to this day.

Sewing for my mother came to a sudden, abrupt end, for the patron of the Kapali çarşa explained that there was no more work for anyone, that the Government had bought all the available materials for the Army. He said that an Army sewing depot had been opened behind the Gülhane Parki and that anyone applying there would be given work to do. He had stretched his large, hairy hands to them, begging them to understand his position, and the women had looked at each other and wondered what to do. The widow said immediately that she, for one, would go to the Army depot, declaring that it was all the same to her where she worked as long as she got money for it. My mother and many of the other new poor were uncertain. They felt that to work in the privacy of their own homes was one thing but to expose themselves in a Government factory, quite another. When my mother came home, my grandmother looked with surprise at her empty hands and asked what was wrong.

"No more work," declared my mother. "The Army has bought all materials and opened a factory behind the Gülhane Parki. The widow has gone there today to look for work."

"Well, *you* will not!" roared my grandmother, so loudly that a pile of plates on the kitchen table vibrated slightly.

"What is the use of talking like that?" demanded my mother wearily. "We have so little money and the children must be fed. Can we see them going hungry because of our pride?"

My grandmother stood up and called to us to come with her. She led the way into the bedroom, produced a key from somewhere about her middle, and unlocked the tin chest where her valuables were stored.

"We have these five gold coins left to us," she said to my mother. "Take them. They will keep us for a little longer. And when they have gone, I still have my jewelry—my rings and my emerald pendant. I was keeping them for Muazzez."

She drew them out of their silk-lined box, and they glittered palely in her hands.

"No!" said my mother. "These rings will never be sold. The dealers will rob you nowadays because they know that people like us are selling our valuables, because we want money so desperately.

Why, only last week I heard from one of the women at the Kapali çarşa that she had sold a diamond and ruby chain, far finer than these, Mother, and all she got for the stones was a little gold. She did not know their value and she was so hungry that she let them go to the first dealer who offered to take them. No!" she said more softly, so softly that my grandmother could not catch her words. "These shall belong to Muazzez." And she touched the pretty trinkets, taking them from my grandmother and locking them up again. She put her hands on my grandmother's shoulders, lightly brushing her forehead with her lips.

"All our pretty things are gone," she said into the straining ears. "So let us keep Muazzez's pretty things. They will look very well one day on my daughter's neck!"

So the first crisis was averted and the little house grew silent again, without the whirr of the machine to disturb it. And gold in the pocket gave a temporary, transient gayety, for would it not buy good meals again—even for a brief while—and wine for my grandmother? Reckless and improvident and wildly extravagant were they, ignorant of the long years still to be lived. All through childhood their beauty and tears and gallantry pierced my heart. Their blood ran fiercely through my veins, and I have been as wildly improvident, but without the courage and wit and graciousness to face the sort of heartaches they faced.

Now and then the widow would come to visit us, amusing yet terrifying us with her coarse humor of what life was like in a factory. She had to stay there day and night, sleeping and eating with the others, doing different turns of duty, and she was only allowed one day off in a week. The pay, she said, was poor but sufficient for her, for the Army provided her food.

"Me," she said proudly, "I'm as strong as a lion, thank God! Only the strong can survive in a place like that."

She no longer pressed my mother to join her there, realizing my grandmother's fierce distate for such work, but since they talked openly to her, she could not help knowing that money was low again. Perhaps she knew, too, that it was only a matter of time before my mother joined her of her own free will. When has money not been low in my dear, idiotic family? They were excellent at spending but terrible at saving, and even life at its most cruel could not teach them anything else. One morning my grandmother went round all the rooms, ticking off on her fingers all the largest, and to my mind the ugliest, pieces of furniture we had. Several times she wondered aloud how much they would fetch if she sold them.

"It's good walnut furniture," she would mutter. "Not to be bought anywhere today. And Şevkiye was quite right when she said that these rooms are very overcrowded." Brave soul that she was, she was trying to convince herself that the sale of her furniture was a matter of no importance. She was hoping to defer the day when my mother would have to go to the factory.

She sent for a dealer, and it was I who ushered him into the transformed presence of my grandmother. She had dressed herself for the occasion and wore all her rings and her emerald pendant, defying him to guess she was desperate for money.

The dealer looked over the furniture with a cautious, jaundiced eye. Perhaps he did not know what to make of the situation, for though the house was small and in a bad district, the old lady wore diamonds that he could see were real enough. She was dressed in silk, too, the hall mark of respectability, and the furniture and carpets were the best that money could buy. He could be forgiven if he did not quite know how he stood in this place, before this indomitable, proud-faced old woman.

He ran his fingers over the smooth, polished wood, hemming and hawing. I trailed after him, a curious figure, no doubt, in my assortment of colors. I had been put into the best clothes that could be found to fit me, and I was afraid to sit down, for everything was uncomfortably tight, the seams in danger of giving way. The dealer rapped out a figure, and my grandmother's knuckles whitened over her ebony stick.

"Are you mad?" she demanded imperiously, her loud, self-conscious voice booming reverberatingly through the room. He looked doubtful again and ran his fingers over the wood for a second time, opening a few drawers as well.

"My offer stands," he said, and my grandmother drew herself up with great haughtiness.

"Then I think we have nothing further to discuss," she said, with an edge to her voice, and made a movement toward the door.

"Wait a moment," said the broker, adding "effendi" uncertainly, for he was still unsure of her status or, what was more important, her financial position. There was a long pause, each eyeing the other suspiciously, each trying to assess the obstinacy of the other. The dealer shifted his eyes first and slightly raised his figure—very slightly, mind you—but that was where he made his first mistake. My grandmother remained immovable, not a flicker of emotion crossing her poker face. I was entranced for I had not seen her like that since my grandfather's day. I had almost forgotten how she could look. She leaned on her stick and waited, the man slightly raising the figure, for he knew a good bargain when he saw one and was prepared to give way a little. But she just stood there like a statue and refused to give in. When at last he could bear it no longer, he burst out:

"I'm offering you the best price you will get anywhere. If you're in need of the money, I advise you to take it." And that was his second mistake, for it made my grandmother arrogant, and when she was arrogant she was at her most dangerous. Better people than the broker have been known to grow reckless under this danger.

"When I am in need of money," she said, "I shall no doubt be willing to let you cheat me. At the moment I am merely trying to get rid of the large furniture, for, as you can see, this house is far too small to house it. If, however, you do not wish to buy, then that is quite a different matter, and I can only regret that we have both wasted our time. Good morning."

And she walked determinedly toward the door, holding it open for the dealer to pass through. We heard him going down the stairs, and I wanted to cry with desperation, for perhaps my grandmother would never get such an offer again. I looked at her mutely, long-ing to cry; but then I heard his returning step on the stairs and I

again looked at my grandmother, who had not heard. I was afraid
she would make some false remark that he would overhear, a word
that would send him bounding out of the house or else cause him
to return with a lower offer. But she said nothing and showed no
trace of surprise when he came back into the salon. He sketched
a gesture on the air of desperation, of resignation, and took a deep
breath, saying: "You're ruining me, effendi, and I shall never be
able to get rid of such heavy, old-fashioned stuff as this; but here's
my final figure, take it or leave it—" He named a sum, and my
grandmother's mouth relaxed.

"Add twenty lire more," she said grandly, "and the furniture's
yours."

"Five!" said the dealer.

"Fifteen!" said my grandmother.

"Seven and a half!" shouted the dealer, perspiring by now and
looking as if he would like to discontinue but could not, because he
loved a good bargain too.

"Twelve and a half!" retorted my grandmother, indomitable
to the last.

"Ten!" said the dealer, passing his hand over his brow.

"Very well," conceded by grandmother, and he handed over a
greasy bundle of lire, and went to the window to call up his porters,
who had been waiting in case business was done.

He walked back to my grandmother.

"You drive a hard bargain," he said, "but if ever you want to sell
those diamonds and things of yours, I can put you on to a man
who will give you a good price for them."

"Thank you," said my grandmother, with distaste, anxious to be
rid of him now that the business was concluded. "But my jewelry
is never likely to be for sale."

And she sat down on the sofa and waited for the porters to clear
the rooms. She called out instructions to them, warning them to be
careful of her carpets and making them remove their footwear
before they entered the rooms. When at last they and the furniture
had gone, I saw that she was trembling violently.

"What is wrong, Grandmother?" I asked, going over to her.

"Nothing," she said. "Only happiness, that I, an old woman, have been able to get the price I wanted out of a broker!" She pulled me down beside her, and there was a great ripping, tearing sound from under me. We looked at each other in dismay, then suddenly burst out laughing, for the trousers, unable to bear the strain, had finally given way.

"Never mind!" comforted my grandmother. "We shall buy you some more. See! We have plenty of money again!" And she held up the greasy lire triumphantly, then carelessly threw them on a little inlaid table.

"After handling those," she shouted happily, "my hands need washing!"

She stumped downstairs to the kitchen, from where, presently, came the merry, splashing sound of water running. When she came up to the salon again, she took the eau de Cologne, sprinkling it fastidiously over her palms and saying to me as she did so:

"Always remember! Never let anyone know when you are desperate. Put your best clothes on and pride on your face and you can get anything in this world."

"Why?" I wanted to know.

"Because otherwise you will get nothing but kicks," she roared. "If that man had known how desperate I was, he would have succeeded in beating me down to his own price. As it was, I succeeded in beating him. Why," she continued complacently, "he even complimented me on my jewelry." And she patted the emerald pendant affectionately. "Your grandfather always had very good taste and only bought the best."

She took off the flashing, lovely pendant and all the rings from her fingers, and they lay gleaming in the palm of her hand with their lively, separate life.

"Now I shall lock them away again," she said to me, "and the next person to wear them will be your sister, who is going to be a great beauty one day."

My mother came in from market with Mehmet clinging to her.

"What are you dressed up for?" she asked my grandmother suspiciously.

"Look!" commanded my grandmother, pointing to the half-empty salon.

My mother's eyes flickered a little, then she turned back to my grandmother and said in an ordinary, conversational sort of voice:

"A great improvement. It was time to clear the room of all that heavy old furniture."

Her eyes met my grandmother's, held for a moment, and then they both smiled. My mother pushed a chair to a different position, standing back to see the effect.

"Oh, decidedly better!" she said merrily.

And I was immeasurably touched by her gallantry and by my grandmother's too, for neither of them broke down to weep that half their home had gone. Instead they stood in the salon and tried different arrangements with the furniture that was left, pretending that they had sold the other because the room was not big enough to house everything.

Young as I was, my heart swelled with pride.

Then my mother caught sight of my burst trousers and the bare skin showing through and she said, laughing at me, that she hoped that this had not happened while the dealer was there.

"No, indeed!" said my grandmother energetically. "If it had, I would have slapped his backside hard, for that bit of bare skin might have cost me fifty lire or so!"

And everyone laughed together; even Mehmet—that solemn little boy who rarely smiled—puckered his mouth into a grin and clasped my grandmother about the legs, deducing rightly that she was the cause of our happiness.

Life flew back to the little house again: there was much gayety and good food; my mother even sang for us, and my grandmother bellowed advice like the old autocrat she was. The neighbors marveled at her cleverness with the dealer and shook their heads in pity over the poor man, saying that if there were a few more of my grandmother's caliber, why the brokers of İstanbul would soon be bankrupt!

15

Charity School in Kadıköy

NO MATTER HOW THE WOMEN OF MY family tried to stave off poverty, it came eventually; and this time it was the real, unadulterated thing. There was either nothing left to be sold or, more correctly, what was left was unsalable, for though the carpets and furniture were very fine, the price they would have brought would only have been sufficient to keep us for a matter of months. And all prices had dropped considerably; all prices, that is, except the price of food. And this still continued to soar. Even had she been disposed to sell them, my grandmother's jewels were useless. The people wanted food, not jewelry, as the dealers took pains to point out when they offered a few lire for genuine stones worth hundreds. There seemed to be no way out of this impasse, and eventually my mother had to leave us and go to the Army depot behind the Gülhane Parki. It was the first time we had ever been separated from her, and we were overcome with a sense of loss. My grandmother did the marketing, leaving us three children to look after ourselves. She would return with the shopping bag pitifully empty, for the money she had bought only the most meager supplies. It seemed to us that we had lived forever on lentils and cabbage soup and the dry, black apology for bread. Yet although our stomachs revolted against this diet, we were always so hungry that we would wolf down the tasteless, insipid mixtures almost with relish.

Up and down the length of the street continued to come the fateful news of the dead or dying or wounded relatives. Fresh sickness broke out, for the people were starving; and they were likely to continue starving unless they bought from the Bourse noir, but who in that poor street was capable of raising sufficient money to buy from the Bourse noir? One day my grandmother took us to see my mother. I remember that it was a soft mild day, mild enough for us to dispense with our thin coats. We were very excited at the thought of seeing my mother, but when we reached the depot and a soldier halted us, inquiring our business there, we were afraid that perhaps he would not let us pass. My grandmother could not hear a word he said, but after I explained that we had come to visit our mother he stood aside for us to pass. The building was old and dirty, and we went up a long, tortuous flight of broken wooden stairs, making a great deal of noise. Another soldier stationed at the head, again inquired our business. I stammered why we were here, and he showed us into a large, gloomy room where many women sat working at their machines. There was a great silence in that room, as though the women were far too occupied to gossip together or as though the discipline were too severe. We stood uncertainly in the doorway, nobody taking any notice of us; presently Mehmet espied my mother and broke away from us, flying on his thin, brown sticks of legs down the busy ranks of the women. He reached my mother and flung himself into her arms, sobbing as though his heart would break. We followed him but there was no place to sit, so we stood around her table, our shadows blocking the light from a few of the other women sitting near her. It was the first time we had ever visited her here, and I was shocked by the dirt and the meanness and the poverty-stricken air of the place. My mother looked tired; her eyes were red-rimmed and her hands faintly soiled. All the fastidiousness in me was revolted, and I felt impotent, childish rage that my mother should have to work in a place like this. Perhaps my face spoke volumes to her, for she said to my grandmother:

"It would have been better not to have brought the children here."

My grandmother shrugged indifferently, shifting the weight of Muazzez to the other arm, then, in answer to my mother's outstretched arms, gave her over to her.

"What else could I do?" she grumbled loudly, all the other women momentarily pausing to listen to what she said. "There was nobody with whom I could leave them, and I need money."

My mother reached out for her purse, pushing the small contents across the table. My grandmother querulously asked if that was all. I saw my mother flush brilliantly; and the widow, who was sitting next to her, said—perhaps to create a diversion:

"We get all our food here, you know. Not much, but better than I could get at home. And they give me money and a place to sleep, and what more do I want?"

"Perhaps *you* are contented here," roared my grandmother pointedly. "But you have no family to depend upon you. I have these three children to try to feed, and this money will not buy very much for them."

Her lips folded obstinately, and as she looked with disdain at the few coins in her hand I saw the shadow of distress in my mother's eyes. She looked as though she wished to apologize for us children, and I ached to comfort her, to give some sort of assurance, but I did not know how. Then I saw her lift her hands in a little gesture of helplessness, and she said:

"I wish I knew what to do! I wish something could be done for the children."

My grandmother's face was cold and obstinate.

"They will die with hunger if they stay much longer with me," she declared. "I am old and I can do with little food if necessary, but these are young and keep demanding, demanding—"

My mother could not answer. She sat looking down at her roughened, soiled hands, and a few of the women threw sympathetic glances at her but nobody said anything. There was nothing that could be said.

After some minutes my grandmother retrieved Muazzez and prepared to depart. She looked anxious and mutinous and gray-faced and was probably as hungry as I, but in that moment I hated her with a passion that had nothing childish about it. She had humiliated my mother and spoken roughly to her and given her additional unhappiness.

"We are going now," she said.

My mother offered her cheek to be kissed, and there was no way of clasping her and telling her that one loved her and that she was not to worry. Her kiss was as distant and as cold as the waves that break on the seashore, her eyes looking past us to some torment we could not see but could perhaps dimly comprehend. In an effort to bring awareness of us back to her remote face, I wriggled against her shoulder, insinuating my warm face against her cold one.

"Yes, yes," she said absently to me, not thinking of me. I withdrew, rebuffed and helpless in my inarticulateness, feeling unwanted.

We left her and passed back through the ranks of the dissilusioned women. At the door we turned to wave to her, but she was not looking at us. She had her face cupped in her hands and perhaps she was crying. We did not know. We trudged home with my grandmother to the silent, cold house in Bayazit, all the world seeming dark, for my mother had appeared to renounce us that day and my grandmother had said she did not want us. There was nothing we could do, for we were children and our voices would not be heard amid the greater clamor of the world.

The next time my mother came home from the depot, it was earlier than usual, and we wondered what had brought her at this hour. She said she was home for three days, and my grandmother ladled the everlasting cabbage soup into her bowl silently, intimating perhaps that one more mouth to feed could make little difference to the food. My mother said she had received a letter from the depot commander, telling her that, if she wished, her children could be cared for at the school recently established in Kadıköy for the protection of children who had lost their fathers during the war. The idea appalled and frightened me, and the more my mother elaborated the theme, the more frightened did I become. It appeared from her conversation that she had made up her mind to send Mehmet and me to this school, and I felt as if everything of the old life were ending and that my mother no longer wanted us with her. My grandmother seemed relieved by the decision, saying she would keep Muazzez with her, but I ran to my mother, crying: "No, *Anne*, no! Don't leave us; don't send us away." And Mehmet took up the cry, but there was no softening in my mother's eyes as she looked at us. My grandmother snapped irritably:

"Stop crying, both of you! There is nothing to cry for. You will enjoy being at school and you will get plenty of good food to eat."

"I don't want good food," I sobbed, longing for some relaxation of my mother's hard, disinterested mood, some softening of expression that would let me run to her to be comforted. But there was none. There was only separation and school for us; there was no love, for there was nobody to give it to us. I wonder if my mother made her decision with tears and misgivings, or with relief that at last a place was found to house us, so that she need no longer feel responsibility for us? These are questions to which only she knew the answer, and she did not tell us these things. But it is not an idle thing to say that the heart and mind and spirit of a child can be broken, for the events of that melancholy day governed the whole of my future life.

Love can die as easily, if more bitterly, in the childish heart, as in the adult. Where the senses scream and beat helplessly against the ruthlessness of a decision, whether lightly made or not, and are forced to fall back, unrecognized, unheard, then love dies too, although a child would not call it that. Perhaps it is only fully realized afterward, when the child himself becomes adult and, looking back to that withered day, feels an old emnity.

So Mehmet and I went to bed that night knowing that rebellion was useless, that we were only children and would not be listened to, even if we had had the words to explain our agony of mind. My mother went to Kadıköy to register our names, and I asked my grandmother to explain why it was we must go. She gave me several very good cold material reasons but was further from understanding my distress than I was from knowing how ruthless she could be. She could not see that the poor food of home meant nothing to us, as long as we could remain there; that home meant security if nothing else. So I gave up futile questioning, for even one's flesh and blood can be most cruelly unaware of sorrow.

The next day Mehmet and I were taken to Galata Bridge by my mother, to cross the Bosporus for Kadıköy on the Anatolian side. On the boat she told us so many times how we would like the school that we became quite silent, no longer answering her. And she misunderstood the silence for sulkiness and set her lips tightly.

From the Kadıköy boat station we walked to the school—the building that is today the French Hospital. It was in a beauty spot, looking out across the sea, the school building so clean and fresh that it gleamed like gold in the mellow sun. We went up some wide stone steps, and still one of us hoped for some reprieve, some hitch in arrangements, for defeat is a difficult thing to accept. A uniformed porter in a cold, antiseptic-looking hall told us to sit down while he fetched someone to attend to us. I sat on the extreme edge of a rickety chair, my heart thumping so loudly that I expected everyone to hear it, and a big, white-faced clock on the wall ticked away the minutes in time with my heart. *Tick-tock, tick-tock, tick-tock,* it said unceasingly, uncaringly; and the big hand moved inexorably, not to be stopped by my silent pleading to stand still for ever. Several sisters in starched aprons passed through the hall, bending incurious eyes on us, but there were no children to be seen or heard.

Presently a woman dressed in a blue dress with a stiff white apron about her—we learned afterward that she was the matron—came across to my mother and they commenced to converse softly. She spoke appalling Turkish overlaid with a thick guttural accent, for she was a German matron with fair braided hair and blond skin.

After a little while she turned to Mehmet and me and said, "Say goodbye to your mother."

We started to cry, but she said sharply:

"Your mother will come to see you sometimes. Do not cry."

So we leaned toward our mother and brushed her hands with our lips. I longed for a kind word from her, for a look that held expression, but her face remained closed, empty, with nothing in it for us. We watched her go through the big glass door and saw her shadow preceding her down the glittering steps, but she did not look back or give any sign of her feelings. Was she distressed by having to leave us here? Or was she hard, harder than we had ever known her to be before? We could not know, we two little insignificant ones, as we stood beside the plump German matron, who told us to kiss each other goodbye, for Mehmet was to be taken to the kindergarten, a separate building from the one we were in.

Mehmet clung to my arm and would not let me go, his brown eyes asking what was happening to us. I whispered to him that everything would be all right, that I would soon be seeing him again. A red-haired nurse led him away, a small, silent boy of three and a half who did not know what to make of this topsy-turvy world. Another nurse took me from the matron's side, and I was bathed and put into a drab gray uniform—a charity-school uniform. Next I was taken to the dormitory and shown my bed, a narrow iron cot with a white coverlet. A low stool was placed beside it, and on it I laid my folded clothes each night. I was then shown the classroom and the place where I was to sit, the dining room, and the sister to whom I was responsible, a gimlet-eyed woman with no understanding of children. Big-boned she was and sadistic, with enormous red hands capable of chastisement. Timidly I asked her if I could see my brother. She snapped that I could not and that, furthermore, it would be as well for me to learn to speak only when spoken to. And during the whole of the time I remained in that school—some two years—I never once saw Mehmet, though at one time I heard my mother begging the matron to let him see me occasionally, as he was fretting for me. But the uncaring matron said that the rules of the school must be adhered to. It was *verboten* for the juniors to mix with the kindergarten, and the matron was not a German for nothing. *Verboten* was *verboten,* and that was all there was to it.

The food was very good at first, and everything in the school was very clean, always smelling of disinfectant. We had classes every day, and there was no chance of dreaming over the lessons, for the teachers would pull one back to attention in their excruciatingly bad Turkish, and the punishments even included going without meals. Twice a week we had singing lessons. One of the sisters would play the piano, and we would sing old Turkish and German folksongs, enjoying ourselves, for it was one of the few times we could really let ourselves go and shout as loudly as we wished. In the evenings we used to gather in the garden, that lovely wilderness that looked out across the Marmara, and the busy sisters would form us into martial lines about the Turkish flag. Lustily we would chant "Deutschland über Alles!" and, as an afterthought, "Padişahim çok yaşa!" We were all too young to see the irony of this.

Every two weeks my mother used to visit me, and, for many days beforehand, I looked forward to her coming.

Sometimes, during the play hour, I used to go to a corner of the garden, away from the others, and sit on the broken, low stone wall and look over the Marmara. I would think about my mother and wonder if she were missing me, or if she were relieved to have handed over the responsibility to someone else. Someone more impersonal. I would bury my face in the long grass and cry for her and for Mehmet, whom I never saw at all.

There was a small building to the left of the main school building, and in it was our cinema, such as it was. There was a little window just inside it, with a high step leading up to the operator's room. Sometimes I used to climb on this step, for from it I could see the large main gates; and I would remain there as many hours as I dared, waiting to see my mother's figure turn in at the gates, my heart pounding with excitement and the ever present fear that perhaps, after all, she would not come today. When I saw her, I would rush from the cinema and hurtle toward her like a small rocket, flinging myself into her arms, which never warmed, eternally begging the one thing:

"Am I coming home today, *Anne?*"

"Not today, my son. Perhaps soon."

Always the same question. always the same answer. Soon. Soon. Soon.

She would bring nuts and sultanas for me and tell me about my grandmother and my sister, but as the months flew by these things interested me less and less. They had all receded far into the background; even not seeing my brother had lost the first bitter poignancy. Only one thing remained real and bright and shining—my mother. Still I clung to my early image of her, trying to force her to show some love for me; and I would cry myself to sleep after she had gone, for her visits were never anything more than formal duty visits.

Time healed tears, too, even dimmed love; and as the months passed I grew taller and stronger, and good food filled out the hollows in my cheeks. New uniforms were given to me, and I went up two classes; the habit of school grew strong within me, and longings for my mother's love became fainter and fainter, until eventually they died altogether. I still watched for her visits, but without becoming excited, and I no longer asked when it was I would see my home again.

But the spring of 1918 saw the return for us to bad food and even worse conditions for my mother. The war was going badly for us, and food was becoming scarce in the whole country. At the school we had now begun to leave the dining room hungry after meals, and no more butter appeared on the tables. We went to sleep hungry, awoke hungry, and went through the day hungry. When my mother nowadays brought me precious nuts or dried fruits, I ate them so quickly that I was almost always sick after them. The German sisters disappeared and old Turkish women replaced them; the school began to smell less and less of disinfectant, and one missed the stiff crackle of the white aprons in the corridors. Lessons were rare and singing had stopped altogether, for how could we sing if we were hungry? But there still hung in the music room a large portrait of the sultan, Mehmet Reşat, and we used to shout "Padişahim çok yaşa!"—even on our empty stomachs. When the summer of that year was upon us, we did not even have dry bread in the school; and the old women used to take us to a place called Fenerbahçe, where grew many big *sakiz-agaci* (gum trees), on which small red, resinous berries grew in thick clusters. We used to throw stones into the trees, sometimes being lucky enough to knock down the berries into the long wild grass. These we would scramble madly for, knocking each other down to find the berries, eating them avidly, like little animals. They had a sour taste but were curiously satisfying, and we used to fill our pockets, taking them back with us to the school to eat during the night. At other times we would go to Fikir Tepesi, where we would pull and eat *kuzu-kulagi* (sorrel), helping the younger among us to choose the right grasses. We would search at Kalamiş for *bayir trupu,* small white radishes that gave us a raking thirst. And many times I remember eating the almond blossom from the trees, stuffing the blooms into my ever hungry mouth. Once, in a sea field bounding one side of our gardens, soldiers were pulling broad beans and throwing the green stalks to the edge of the field, the edge nearest our palings. We put our fingers through and took the stalks, sucking them afterward with great relish.

When my mother took to giving me a little pocket money, I, like the others, used to buy broad beans for myself, eating them raw, feverishly, stuffing them down me until, in the end, I would vomit —and then feel hungrier than ever. It became the custom among us to carry salt and red pepper in little bags concealed about our persons; and if we were ever lucky enough to find potato peelings or raw eggplant skins, we would wash them at the pump, expertly mix them with the contents of our little bags, and eat them when we were desperate with hunger. Our food-starved eyes overlooked nothing in the way of sustenance. But one day, in my hunger, I ate something unknown, something I had thought was bayir trupu. It made me so very ill that I was rushed to the school hospital. Here it was discovered that I had poisoned myself. Almost at the same time, scabies developed. I had been suffering from itchiness for weeks but had thought nothing of it; in any event the old women who had replaced the smart German sisters never paid any attention to things like that. Scabies spread over my body until I was almost mad with the red-hot prickling itch that would not let me rest. Every morning I was taken to the Turkish bath, and the scabby places were scrubbed with a hard brush until my body bled. It was torture, and I would scream continuously, but to no avail, for the scrubbing continued mercilessly.

The food in the hospital was a little better but not very much; however, we were not driven to the fields with hunger. We were given a little *lapa* (watery rice) in the middle of the day and a thin vegetable soup at night but no bread, for there simply was not any to be had. We were always hungry, and half an hour before a meal was due the children who were allowed up would gather impatiently under the big clock over the door. We used to count the seconds until sixty, then say triumphantly, "One minute!" and so on, thinking thereby to reduce the waiting time. It became a habit with me, and my right leg would jerk in time to the counting. Even today, automatically, when I am very tired or depressed, my right leg commences to jerk to the ticking of a clock.

During all the time that I was in the hospital, my mother had not been to see me and I was worrying for news of her, for never before had she failed in her two weekly visits. The long weeks passed and still there was no sign of her. I was released from the hospital, weak as a cat and very thin, for the last few months of starvation had taken all the roundness from my body and cheeks. When I got out of the hospital, I found that we were no longer allowed into the cinema to spy from the operator's window but that a blackboard had been erected in the garden instead. As the visitors arrived, the children's names were inscribed on the blackboard. Like all the others, I took to waiting beside the blackboard on visiting days, but my name never appeared. After a while I became alarmed for fear that I should never see my mother again, that she had at last deserted me for ever. I thought that I would have to remain in this frightful place for years, and vague, formless notions of escape began to take root in my mind. But then the lovely thing happened unexpectedly, as all miracles do. One summer day, in 1918, I saw my name being written on the blackboard. I walked slowly toward the reception hall, my heart ready to suffocate me and my right leg perilously inclined to jerk as I walked. When I reached the hall, I saw my mother sitting on one of the chairs, though indeed she was so changed that only the eye of love could have singled her out from the rest of the drab humanity about her. I ran to her, crying, and she clasped me in her arms, holding me tightly with hands that trembled.

She said to me: "But what is this, my son? You are so thin and white-looking. What have they been doing to you?"

So I cried again, in the unaccustomed luxury of sympathy, and told her that I had been in the hospital, how they had scrubbed my body until it bled, and that we had no food to eat. She looked horrified.

"Why," she said, "you would have been better off at home with me."

I asked her why she had not been to visit me, and she said that she had been ill, a return of the fever that would not entirely leave her. And then I realized that she too had become pitifully thin and gaunt; like a faintly animated skeleton she was, with her white face and her large eyes that never smiled. She had kept her beauty, largely because it was a beauty of bone and would never die: but now it was a mournful, disillusioned beauty that met the eye, with fine lines beside the mouth and sorrow etching the broad forehead with gossamer threads.

She ran her hand over my cropped head and said that I looked like a charity boy. I asked eagerly after my brother; but a troubled look ran across her face, and she said that he too was ill and that they had not let her visit him at all. Presently she stood up to go, and this time I did not ask when I would be coming home, for one had learned not to ask embarrassing questions. Home seemed remote as a dream nowadays: it was a word with no meaning.

She took my hand and said we were going to the matron's room

—not the same matron of two years ago, but a Turkish woman, more formidable, more unapproachable. We saw her without difficulty, and I could not believe that I was hearing aright when my mother said she was taking me home with her and that she would come for my brother in two weeks' time. The matron began to argue, but my mother was in no mood to be browbeaten. She said she would not move from this place without me and that my uniform would be returned when she came for Mehmet. She pressed for information regarding him, but the matron was vague and distant, either because she knew nothing or because she chose not to tell.

While they talked I stood by the door, my heart beating in a strange fashion. The day had come at last, the day I had longed for for over two years; but it had come too late, and now it did not matter whether my mother took me or not. It was true that I wished to be taken out of the place, but where I wanted to go I did not know. Home held no promise of heaven, and it was so remote, so difficult to remember, that it held in my mind even less security than did this mean charity school.

So we went home to the same sort of conditions I had left two years ago; and bitterness brooded within me because one had left this meanness for another kind of meanness and one had returned no better off. My mother was brave in 1918 to make such a decision; but childhood asked—perhaps unreasonably—why she had not been brave in 1916, when she banished two small boys to a school under German influence, killing all trust and love, then trying to win it back when it was too late. For that is how it seemed to us then and does today, even though she is long since dead and past all criticism.

Home was a strange and alien place, with my grandmother still serving the eternal vegetable soup and the rooms appearing smaller and darker after the large bare rooms of school. Muazzez was now three, a thin little creature with blue eyes and hair that had lightened to brown. She was fretful and listless, for she was hungry too —like the rest of us. I would try to play with her, but she seemed uninterested, as if playing were something strange for her. She could not talk plainly either, stammering and flushing and running away from me, preferring to be alone, for she had never known anything else. She was an odd, nervous, sensitive child, always hungry and always inclined to tears. I could not feel as close to her as I had once felt to Mehmet, that little brown-eyed, silent brother who had known my father and Sariyer and shared my toys.

My mother was still at the Army sewing depot, and my grandmother looked after the little house. One day I went with her to market, but we could not buy anything. The shops were shuttered and closed, the few that remained open having only a little Indian corn for sale and rotten vegetables. Flour was treble its normal price, black and sour-looking, giving off an acrid smell. My grandmother looked at what she had bought and at the few remaining coins in her hands, then said in amazement:

"This is the first time I have ever come back from market with money still left in my hand!"

And that day we ate sour bread and soup that tasted like salt water. Then came a succession of days when only olive oil, much adulterated, could be poured over our ration of bread and I became so weak I was even unable to walk. I remember that I lay most of the day in the salon, faint with hunger and unable so much as to move a limb. Muazzez was with me, sitting on the carpet and whimpering that she was hungry, but I was far too lightheaded to pay much attention to her. Not until dusk did my grandmother return from some long trek she had made into the hills. She gave us bread, fresh, almost white bread, and quartered raw onions, and butter that was rank, but it made no difference to our appetites. We ate until we could eat no more, and Muazzez went to sleep where she was, stretched out on the carpet, and no one cared because she was not in bed.

My grandmother sat by the window, crying and talking to herself, as was her habit nowadays.

"There is no food anywhere," she said. "For the first time in years I have money in my pocket, and there is nothing to buy with it."

Where she had got the money, I do not know. Perhaps she had sold some small thing for less than half its worth in order to buy food from the hoarding, greedy peasants, who would never be too hungry.

I think she sat by the window all night, for when I awoke the next morning she was still there, her old eyes rimmed and strained from tiredness, and Muazzez still lay sleeping on the hard floor.

16

Ending with the Barber's Apprentice

I SHALL NOT EASILY FORGET THE DAY WE went to Bebek, to the hospital where Mehmet lay dying.

It was a fine, warm summer day, and from Galata Bridge the green hills of Anatolia shone fair and peaceful under the light-filled sky. Sea gulls cried in the wake of the boats, the big and little boats that rode the Bosporus, which was so divinely blue that day that the heart expanded with happiness. Hunger was momentarily forgotten in this translucent illusion of peacefulness, and when we arrived at Eminönü, to board the tram, I was giddy and slightly lightheaded from the shine and sparkle of the new day and the crisp salt tang blown from the sea. The tram hurtled through the streets in the heart-lurching way of all İstanbul trams. Up hills we flew and down again, faster and faster, with a constant *clang-clang-clang-clang*, as though the driver and the tram together were impatient of these mean, secretive streets and were wishful to reach the clean, breathtaking sweep of Bebek as soon as they could. So deserted was Beşiktaş that day that we might have been alone there. On, on we flew exhilaratingly, past Ortaköy, catching a glimpse of its white, shining mosque with the two tall minarets piercing the heavens, the mosque itself looking over the Bosporus. Down to Kuru Çeşme, with its tumble-down wooden houses over which lay a black film of

*   191   *

coal dust from the innumerable depots. Still down, until we reached Arnavutköy—the word spelling romance in itself, since it means "Albanian Village." All along the low sea wall we ran now, looking across to Anatolia, Çengelköy like a jewel in its wooded hills, the long white military school of Kuleli skirting the Bosporus, until finally the tall granite walls of the Summer Palace of the Khedive of Egypt hid the view and we spun furiously down the single-track line that led to Bebek and the glorious sweep of the bay.

Bebek catches the heart with its fragile, fadeless beauty, a beauty that is composed chiefly, I think, of the blue waters that lap the shores, the tall, white-masted ships that seem to lie there eternally at anchor, and the old narrow houses that rise high behind the town, marching up the steep hills, up to the forests that brood greenly all the year long. That summer morning in 1918 I had my first glimpse of Bebek, and I was transported with joy that such subtle, pictorial beauty should meet my starved eyes at last.

From the tram terminal my mother inquired the way to the Children's Hospital, but when we found it we had to wait in the cold tiled hall until a sister was free to see us. She came at last, efficient and rustling in her starched skirts, the traditional white veil bound low over her forehead, hiding all trace of hair, so that today she would resemble, were she still alive, a surgeon ready for the operating theater. There was difficulty in finding Mehmet. In those days in Turkey, there were no surnames, consequently there was quite often the greatest confusion in identifying people. The formula went something like this: Mehmet, the son of Hüsnü and Şevkiye of Bayazit. Clumsy as this method was, people could usually be safely identified in the end, as there were rarely two or more parents with exactly the same set of names or a child with the same name.

When the sister discovered who Mehmet was, she informed my mother that we could not see him because he was too ill. But my mother was obstinate and pressed hard for details. The sister hinted at malnutrition; my mother thought about this for a moment or two and then said she wished to take him home with her. The sister

raised horrified eyebrows, saying that Mehmet would certainly die
if he were moved from the hospital. My mother insisted, and the
sister doubtfully went to find a doctor. While she was gone, my
mother opened the package of clothes she had brought for Mehmet,
fretting that they would be too small for him; but there had been
nothing else to bring.

A doctor, old and untidy-looking, came back with the sister and
proceeded to bully my mother, but she replied in kind, saying that
she wished only to remove her son from this place.

"I want my child," she insisted stubbornly. "If he is to die, he
can die at home as easily as here. I am prepared to take all the responsibility."

The doctor shrugged with superb indifference, turned to the
sister, and told her to have Mehmet got ready. My mother handed
over the bundle of clothing and signed a paper which the doctor
handed to her. We sat back to wait for Mehmet.

When the sister returned, she was carrying across her arm a
small, lifeless-looking child. She handed the child to my mother,
who glanced briefly at it, saying:

"This is not my son. This is a baby, and my child is five years
old. There is some mistake . . ." but her voice trailed away uncertainly, for now she was looking more closely at the child across
her arms. And indeed it was Mehmet. Even I could see the like-
ness.

"He is as light as a bird," said my mother wonderingly.

"He is very ill," said the sister severely. "It is wrong of you to
take him home."

I peeped at Mehmet in awe, at the little brown closed face with
the jawbones sticking pitifully out from the fleshless cheeks, the
faint dark lines of eyebrow, so delicately traced, like my mother's,
the skeleton arms and wrists, and the poor, wasted body that was
dying with hunger. I saw swift tears prick my mother's eyes, but
she thanked the sister and we came away.

Back to İstanbul again, in the hurtling tram, Mehmet held close
against my mother so that the jolting would be minimized for him.

With my nose pressed against the window, I was conscious of my mother's sorrow and the shadow that surrounded my brother. The bright day was dimmed for me; the Bosporus had lost some of its blueness.

For several days Mehmet lay in a sort of stupor, with my grandmother constantly reading the Koran over him and Muazzez and I now and then going to look at him, silenced in the face of such tremendous silence. After a while they tried to spoon-feed him with condensed milk my mother had obtained through the sewing depot, and sometimes he would sip a little boiled water, moving his head plaintively from side to side, as though in pain. If he did not seem to get any better at home, he certainly became no worse. And then a day came when two important things happened to me. The first concerned Mehmet, for he opened his eyes and looked at me. He looked first at me unrecognizingly, but after a while awareness crept back to him and he smiled and he held out his small hand.

"Brother" he said to me in a weak, wondering voice, a voice that was not voice but a thin thread of sound on the air. I flew over to him, held tightly to his hand, and asked him if he wanted anything. He said that he was hungry, and I went to the kitchen for a spoon and the half-empty tin of condensed milk. I spooned it into his avid, greedy mouth until the tin was shining and empty. He begged for a glass of water. Muazzez staggered to him with the carafe, spilling a few drops over his sheet, and we laughed uproariously, as though it were a great joke. Presently Mehmet turned on his side and went to sleep. I stayed by his bed until my grandmother returned from the market. As she came into the house, I could hear Muazzez's excited, high-pitched voice telling her the joyful news. Upstairs rushed my grandmother like the wind, and in a loud roar, which she thought was a whisper, asked me what had happened. When I told her, she threw up her hands in delight and commenced to recite a prayer of thanksgiving from the Koran. She crept across to Mehmet and listened for a few moments to his still, even breathing. Then she said simply, with great faith, that he would get better now, and took us with her from the room, leaving him to his good sleep.

She had brought back a few uninspiring things with her from the market, and presently she told me to go to the Sewing depot, whence my mother would be returning that day. She instructed me to tell my mother about Mehmet and to ask her to come home by way of Sirkeçi, where the shops might have something other than the eternal Indian corn which my grandmother always bought in Bayazit.

She could not get me out of the house quickly enough, so great was her desire to prepare something appetizing for my brother, and she grumbled that her legs would not carry her as far as Sirkeçi these days.

The second thing of importance that happened to me that day occurred when I went to meet my mother. I delivered my message and we walked toward Sirkeçi. She was very excited that her son had chosen to live.

I remember that we managed to get some haricot beans, dried peas, and a little sugar, a rare luxury nowadays. We were on our way home, just behind the station at the time, and making slow progress along the narrow, cobbled street, for this was one of the busiest spots in the city. We sidestepped out of the path of horses and of men pushing barrows. Presently, above all the street cries, there came another sound, a sound more insistent on the ear. My mother paused and looked at the sky. I followed her eyes, and there, coming in across the Golden Horn, were three airplanes.

"English 'planes!" a man shouted, dashing past us into a shop doorway.

My mother and I stood looking at them, both of us unaware of the load of destruction they carried. People were hurrying by us into shops, into Sirkeçi Station, into doorways, but I think my mother was too paralyzed to move very swiftly. I remember that she eventually pulled me under a shop awning and that we cowered there. It was only in after years that I learned that she had been convinced the awning would save us, that if the pilots could not see us they could not hurt us!

The airplanes flew into İstanbul with a roar, and then came a dull explosion that shook the earth.

I thought the noise would never cease. Clouds of dust billowed toward us, and I discovered that my legs were in danger of giving way.

They bombed Mahmut Paşa Street that day, İstanbul's busiest market place, and there was scarcely a gun to defend the city.

Soon the sound of hurtling ambulances came piercingly from all directions, and the airplanes were gone.

We started home, having to pass Mahmut Paşa Street on the way, and already flames licked the little shops and the mean houses. A horse lay on its side, neighing horribly, its cart overturned across its broken body and the driver perched high above the debris, with his face blown in. There were not enough ambulances, so lorries were commandeered. They passed us with their loads of wounded, some unconscious, some crying out in agony, their flapping stumps of arms flaying the air sickeningly.

Carts piled with the dead passed near by, and I was almost sick with horror when I saw the gory, exposed contents—heads lolling fearfully without their bodies, hands and legs jumbled together indecently, all bundled in together—for these were the dead and were no longer important when there were still the living to be saved.

"They meant to bomb the War Office," someone was saying, "but the bombs went wide and fell here."

The people who heard him commenced to boo him, and he was suddenly in danger of his life, for the people were convinced that Mahmut Paşa Street had been deliberately bombed because it was a crowded district.

I still remember that day and the murmurings of the people and the crying of the bereaved, and none of us will ever know whether the pilots went wide of their target or not.

All the way home my mother's eyes were blinded by the tears she shed for the innocent ones who had suffered and even for the unaware, surprised ones who had died. And that bombing lived in my mind for many years. Even recently, when I had occasion to pass through Mahmut Paşa Street, still with its ugly, unconcealed scars, I relived that day again and wondered if anyone else in the still overcrowded street sometimes remembered too.

Mehmet continued to thrive, though slowly. I would take him out each day as far as the wall that bounded for us the Sea of Marmara, and his brown face became browner under the friendly sun. He had become more than ever a quiet, thoughtful little boy, not talking overmuch and flinching if one made a too sudden gesture. To this day he is the same, preferring to listen rather than contribute, rarely expressing an opinion, as if the two years in the school at Kadiköy had taken all initiative from him.

Summer passed, and the first leaves began to fall, choking the dirty gutters and scurrying along the pavements like prim, frightened old ladies. As the weather grew chillier, we went less to the sea wall. My tenth birthday loomed, but birthdays were no longer important. Then suddenly the war was over for Turkey.

One night we went to bed still at war, and the next day we heard that our country had had enough and was quitting.

But for us who were left it mattered little: we had lost everything. But then there were many families like us, so we had no right to complain either.

My mother left the sewing depot, and we wondered what would become of us now. Gold, we heard, was bringing fabulous prices, but we had long since spent all our gold—those gleaming, chinking coins that had rattled merrily in my grandmother's trunk—many years ago now, it seemed. But stay! Had we not an old salver that my great-grandfather had given to my grandmother on her wedding day? A golden salver that shone like the sun and was never used because it was such a clumsy size? We had indeed! And my grandmother took little time in remembering where she had last seen it: lying at the bottom of the ottoman in my mother's room, among all the china and glass that was never used nowadays. Out it came to be polished and talked about, for it was dull and lackluster, and whoever would have thought that such a useless thing might now bring us money? My grandmother was given the job of getting rid of it, for none of us could ever forget how she had once bested the dealer.

When she was ready to go to the gold market, she was dressed with great care. Once again her jewels sparkled on her hands and her bosom; and the whole street turned out to see her and admire the giant salver that bloomed by itself in a corner, a little self-consciously, for it had always been a despised thing, even in my grandfather's day.

"Now you know the market price per gram," reminded my mother sternly, "and do not sell it at all if you do not get the right price!"

"Certainly not!" snapped my grandmother importantly, just as though the house were filled with money and we had no further need of any.

Off she went, the tray hastily and shamefully wrapped in brown paper but so eager to show itself off that bits of it peeped through and winked and sparkled at us as it was carried down the street. And all the neighbors gasped with admiration and said that it was a beautiful tray and that we were blessed by God to have such a thing to sell in these hard times.

All morning we and the neighbors waited for my grandmother to return, they speculating on the price the tray would bring and I almost dizzy with disbelief as I heard the lire mounting by the hundred. In those days the sum of 100 lire was worth a thousand or more today. The old men, the young women, and even the children counted up how much she would get, and once I ran in to my mother, gasping with the piles of lire ringing in my ears.

"I know *exactly* how much she will get," said my mother severely. "Or nearly," she amended. "We had it weighed on the bakkal's scales yesterday, so run off now and do not listen to the neighbors' nonsense!"

And off I went, disappointed by my mother's matter-of-fact tone of voice.

When my grandmother was sighted, slowly ascending the hilly street, the crowd surged forward to meet her, but I was fleetest of all and reached her first. I knew the moment I saw her that she had been successful, for she carried her head proudly again—a sure sign of triumph in my family. There were many packages in her hands and, tucked under her arm, of all things, was a bottle of wine!

She handed some of the packages to me but refused to surrender the wine, and home we marched with the excited, talkative neighbors, who were much too polite to ask how much she had got yet knew her well enough by now to recognize victory in her step.

"Well!" said my mother's voice at the door. "Well, you are a disgrace, Mother! Did you carry a bottle of wine through the streets like a drunkard?"

"I missed my wine with dinner," roared my grandmother, for all the world as though dinner was still a habit in our house. "And what is more," she added, "I have fresh coffee here and sugar from the Bourse noir, so let us invite our good neighbors to drink to our good fortune."

In surged the ready neighbors, up the stairs and into the salon, all of them politely removing their shoes before they trod the precious Sparta carpets. They were as happy as if the good luck of this day had been theirs. They helped my mother dispense coffee and cognac and lifted their cups and glasses to shout:

"Güle-Güle! Mahşallah hanim effendi!" (Good luck! God bless you!)

We were all overcome with emotion, and the easy tears of old age started to the eyes of some of the older ones.

"Now we can buy plenty of good food," shouted my grandmother, waving her coffee cup in the air excitedly. "And clothes for the children," she added, her eye catching mine.

I dreamed of bright picture books and scrapbooks and a box of paints to carry me through the autumn days.

I do not know how much my grandmother got for that old salver, but I think it was more than she and my mother had anticipated, mathematics not being their strong point. And strangely enough, when we had enough money in the house again, so that we did not need to worry for a long time to come, more came in unexpectedly. From appalling poverty we jumped to comparative riches in the space of a few weeks. This happened because my mother started to embroider again, supplying orders to the bigger shops in Beyoğlu.

Traycloths, tablecloths, pillowcases, babies' dresses: all passed through her nimble fingers. She used to design and trace her own patterns, giving a touch of uniqueness to her work, an individuality that was liked by the discriminating foreign customers of the big shops.

So the machine lay idle again, relegated to the kitchen, where it was forgotten for months on end, until my grandmother suddenly conceived a passion for making new clothes for us. Muazzez began to look like a little doll, usually dressed all in white, with exquisite embroidery done by my mother and two white bows atop her brown hair. She was developing into a winning and imperious little girl, very like my grandmother in temperament, ruthlessly bullying Mehmet and me into performing small duties for her. My grandmother was very proud of her and spent hours each day on her clustering curls.

"She is really going to be a great beauty," she would say to a bored Mehmet and to me, "and one day she will marry a very rich man. You will see!"

And Muazzez, already vain, became vainer.

I had become very restless at home and was often insubordinate. My mother worried incessantly about my education, but all the schools were still disorganized and many teachers had never come back from the war. I used to haunt the streets, playing a corrupt version of football near the gardens of the mosque, but I had nothing to keep my mind constantly occupied. My mother and I used to have fierce and bitter quarrels; and because I could not bear being confined to the house, I took to roaming farther and farther away from home. No doubt had I had a father to discipline me, I should never have dared to do these things; but I would not listen to my mother or grandmother, flying into a passion if they attempted to interfere with me.

My mother was rebelling against life too—but for a different reason. Her rebellion, unexpectedly enough, was against wearing the veil, for she had noticed that none of the foreign women wore them and that even a few of the more daring Turkish women from good families had ceased the practice also. She used to complain about it to my grandmother, declaring that she was sick and tired of keeping her face covered. I would interrupt from the lofty perch of my ten years, saying that I would not have her going about the streets with her face open. I would chastise her, too, for her many goings-out.

"You are never at home," I would declare; and although usually I was told to mind my own affairs, one day I was very surprised when my grandmother actually agreed with me.

"It is quite true," she said heatedly. "You are always out these days. And it is not right for you to complain that you have to wear the veil. Why, many women are still behind the kafes, and they never see the color of the sky, except from behind their veils. But at least you cannot complain of that, for you tore the kafes from here; and it is a wonder to me that you were ever accepted in this street, for you behaved exactly like a fast woman looking for another husband, or like a prostitute. Yes, you did!" she assured my mother's astonished face. "And now you talk of leaving aside your veil. Why, I lived for thirty years with my husband, and I never went out without his permission and I had to keep my face covered all the time. If I went out in the carriage with Murat, immediately all the windows were closed and sometimes the blinds were drawn too. I say it is a scandal that women today are revealing their faces. God will punish them! Do not let me hear another word from you, my daughter, for surely the sky will open on you for such impiety."

Never had I heard my grandmother talk at such length or with such obvious passion.

My mother replied: "You are talking a great deal of old-fashioned nonsense, Mother! My place is not in the home these days. If I were to sit at home all day, or you either for that matter, who would go to market for us? Do you expect me to stay here all day, reading the Koran and wearing my veil for fear the passers-by should see me from the street? I tell you again: from now on I shall go without my veil!"

She angrily tore the pretty veil from her face and threw it petulantly on the floor.

My grandmother lifted her hands to heaven.

"I never thought I should live to see this day," she said.

"Ach! Times are changing," said my mother.

"They will say you are a prostitute!" wailed my grandmother, genuinely distressed and totally incapable of accepting such a fierce gesture as the opening of the face.

"If they do, it will not worry me," retorted my mother. "Their words will not bring bread to me. And from now on, you will throw aside your veil too, Mother."

"Oh, no, no, no!" said my grandmother in superstitious horror. "God forbid that I should invite punishment upon myself!"

But the next morning, when my mother went into Beyoğlu with a box of embroidered articles under her arm and her lovely face naked to the world, she was stoned by some children near Bayazit and received a nasty cut on the side of her head.

After that she was cautious about going anywhere alone; but she was obstinate about reveiling herself, and Mehmet or I would go with her to Beyoğlu, my grandmother steadfastly refusing to be seen with her. The reaction to her in the street was mixed. The older ones were stricken with horror, more especially since they had always recognized my mother as a good woman; now their faith in her was badly shaken. She was still young and attractive—she was twenty-five—and despite the shadows that lingered now and then in her eyes, she was so unusually beautiful that people could not help staring at her. Certain sections of the street wondered if she were trying to catch a husband. They came in droves, the old men as well, to remonstrate with my grandmother, urging her to put a stop to this terrible thing; and my grandmother, thoroughly enjoying herself, would groan to them that she had no authority left in this wayward family of hers. But the younger women sided with my mother, and some of them even began to follow her example. Their fathers, however, in the absence of dead husbands, took a stick to them, muttering piously that no woman in their families would so disgrace themselves. So they put their veils on again in a hurry.

Not a few wished to apply the chastening stick to my mother

also. They gave my grandmother sympathy until she was sick of it, prophesying gloomily—but with a little bit of anticipatory relish too, I think—that my mother would come to a bad end.

And indeed she very nearly did!

For one day in Bayazit, when she was alone, an impressionable Frenchman attempted to flirt with her. She tried walking hurriedly on, but this had no effect at all; or, if anything, it had a worse effect, for the gallant Frenchman became more than ever aware of the swing of her silk skirts and the little dark curls that twined so coquettishly at the nape of her neck. Naturally, he followed her. All the little boys of the district became aware, as is the way of all little boys, of the one-sided flirtation that was in progress. And naturally enough, they followed the tall Frenchman, so there was that day in Bayazit the very, very unusual sight of a young Turkish woman, with open face, followed by a foreigner and innumerable small, dirty-nosed boys. When my mother made the mistake of stopping, trying to explain in her entirely inadequate French that the gentleman was making a great mistake, he took off his hat, bowed elegantly, and declared with obvious feeling, "Vous êtes ravissante!"

The small boys, who could not understand a word of what he said, cheered or jeered, according to their several temperaments, and my mother—very properly—hurried on, blushing and breathless and perhaps wishing a little for the security of her veil.

When she came down our street, with her procession behind her, the neighbors were more scandalized than ever and ran into their houses to tell the ones inside. But when my mother called out to them in Turkish that she was being followed, and very much against her will, they set to with a vengeance and brought out sticks and brooms, shooing off the gallant representative of Gallicism in no uncertain manner. Mehmet and I, who were watching the whole proceedings from the window, were bursting with laughter, but my poor grandmother was quite ready to die with shame.

"Such a disgrace!" she kept saying. "We shall never be able to live in this street again."

But in this she was wrong, for when the street had finally disposed of the amorous Frenchman, and a few old men had, in fact, chased him halfway to Bayazit with tin buckets in their hands, to break his head, the street settled down again to lethargy, exonerating my mother from all blame—all except the old women, that is.

Still the problem of my schooling was unsettled. It was eventually decided that I should be sent to a private school. When my mother inquired about these, however, she found that Turkish was excluded from the curriculum, and this made her so cross that she said she would rather keep me at home. While she continued the search, I roamed the streets, usually with boys older than myself, defiant of all discipline, impatient of the slightest restraint. A few of the old men attempted to advise me, but their outworn, futile shibboleths so infuriated me that I threatened to run away somewhere if my grandmother did not cease to enlist the aid of these doddering, antiquated people. Then my mother had a talk with the local imam. The decision they reached was very unpleasant for me, although I did not know that at the time.

They decided that as schooling was, for the moment, impossible, the next best thing to keep me out of mischief was to put me somewhere as an apprentice. Actually, "apprentice" is far too grand a word to apply in the circumstances, since I was only to remain "apprenticed" until a school could be found for me.

They chose a barbershop.

I was incoherent with ten-year-old rage when they told me. Point-blank, I refused to go. But the imam, with indescribable cunning, painted such a rosy picture of my independence, of the tips I would get, of the fascination of perhaps one day owning my *own* barbershop, that he talked me into enthusiasm. My mother and grandmother for once had the wisdom to remain silent, though I suspect that their silence had something to do with previous warnings from the imam, a capable man who liked to take matters into his own hands. By whatever hypnotism was employed, I found myself the next day being taken to the barbershop, which was only a few streets from our house.

The barber greeted me with an oily effusiveness that I instantly mistrusted. He said in a hissing whisper to my mother that he would train me well and see that I did not get into any mischief.

"You do understand," said my mother insistently, "that he is not here to earn money but to remain occupied until a suitable school can be found for him."

"Of course!" said the barber in a perfectly indescribable voice. He bowed to my mother, hiding his eyes from her open face, and his enormous shoulders shrugged under his soiled, patched shirt.

"I shall look after him like a father," he added. "Like a father!" he repeated, flicking his eyes over me rapidly, as though wondering just what sort of father he ought to be to me.

My mother looked terribly doubtful now that we were here, but nevertheless she left me in his care and went home, perhaps feeling thankful that at any rate I was not roaming the streets that day. I had terrible doubts too. Looking about me, I could not recognize the glowing picture that had formed in my mind. The shop was very small, with only two chairs for customers, and it was primitive in the extreme. A copper mangal that was used for heating and at the same time for brewing coffee stood in one corner. The window was draped with some sort of muslin, much in need of washing, and the glasses were all fly-blown and bluish with the haze of dirt and smoke and dust. I no longer believed in the romantic aspect of such a job, but the thought of the tips still lured me on.

After my mother departed, the barber lost all of his oily civility and said to me:

"This is a good job, my boy. If you are clever and keep your eyes open, you will learn much and then you will pray for me all your life, yes?"

His little eyes snapped at me, and as he bent his face closer I could smell dirt and perspiration. The blue tassel of his greasy fez waggled with a separate life of its own.

"Over here," said he, waving his hand, "is the box where you will put all the tips. When I shave a customer or cut his hair, you will stand beside me and you will watch what I am doing. At the same

time you will watch in my eyes, and when I want soap or a towel
you will get them immediately. You will make coffee and take it to
the neighboring shops, and they will pay you for it. You will *not*
come back without the money. You understand, yes?"

"Yes," I muttered sulkily, already in a mild state of rebellion
against this dirty saloon and the dirtier old barber.

"Smile when you say 'Yes,'" he snarled, pulling back his upper
lip from his broken teeth and giving an imitation of a smile.

"You gotta learn to smile in this job," he continued, "and if you
break any coffee cups, I take the money from your tips; if you
haven't any tips, I break your God-damned head, yes?"

"No," I said, and fled from his upraised hand.

All the morning I spent beside him while he shaved and cut hair
and passed rough jokes with the customers, all of them street sellers
or small shopkeepers, curious about me and inclined to jeer at my
accent. My eyes became tired with the strain of watching what the
barber did and at the same time trying to watch his eyes for signals,
although I never brought the right things for him. My head was
constantly twisting and turning, until finally I thought it would
twist itself off my neck altogether.

At midday I was sent across the street to a delicatessen store and
ordered to bring back one and a half portions of haricot beans,
already cooked in oil and onions. I got bread too, great hunks cut by
unclean fingers. The half-portion was for me, and we ate in the
customers' chairs, washing down the meal with water from smeared
glasses. The afternoon passed quietly enough until suddenly an
order came from a shop across the way for five coffees. I was ordered
to make it, but the fire had died in the mangal, so I tried to light it
again with charcoal. This is not nearly so simple as it sounds. The
barber swore at me and threatened to break my bones, but I had
learned to ignore him and placed pieces of wood on the mangal,
afterward building up with charcoal. Then I poured oil generously
over the whole, to the consternation of the barber, who said that I
would set the place on fire. A match was applied and *Wouf* went
the contents of the mangal. A yellow sheet of flame almost enveloped

me, and dust flew everywhere. The barber chattered with rage. Just at that awkward moment a customer came in, and the dirty remains of the haricot beans had to be removed from the chairs before he could sit down. The barber was forced to bring water and towels for himself, and he alternated between bright, pleasant conversation with his customer and brief, pithy asides to me. I lay stretched full length along the stone floor, going *pouf-pouf* at intervals at the reluctant mangal, red in the face with my labors and oblivious of the fumes and dust I was creating. Finally the barber lost his patience, left the customer half-shaved, lay down beside me on the floor, and blew with tremendous energy. His fat, pendulous belly wobbled under him, and I watched it with fascination. The customer came over to us, one side of his face still white with lather, and gave encouraging advice to the barber, who did not want it.

When the charcoal was eventually persuaded to burn, the barber was tired from all the puffing and blowing he had done, and black streaks ran down his face, the charcoal dust and perspiration mingling. The customer began to lose his patience, and within a very short time they had nearly come to blows. I quickly brewed coffee, preferring to keep out of their way until their tempers were cooler. When the five coffees were ready, I placed them on a brass tray suspended from a chain and went over to the shop that had called for them. I served the coffees and asked for the money, but they all laughed at me and said between spasms of laughter, "Tell Ali Bey he has our compliments." Ali Bey was the name of the barber.

When I got back to the shop and delivered this message, the barber tore at his sparse gray hair, pulled me by the ear to the box for tips, and emptied the meager contents into the palm of his hand.

"This is for me," he said grimly, and I was sad, reflecting that it was not easy to earn money—even tips.

"You will learn the job like this," said the sadistic old barber grimly. "If you are such a fool that you let them drink coffee without paying for it, then you must pay for it. You see?"

I commenced to argue with him, calling him a son of a donkey and many other choice expressions I had picked up in the streets.

"*Pezevenk!*" I yelled indignantly, which even to this day in Turkey is a deadly insult, and he danced around me, threatening to break my bloody head if he got at me. I continued to dance with him, but in the opposite direction, feeling that closer acquaintance would not be beneficial, and I searched my vocabulary for more insults.

Were it not for the fact that a customer walked in, he would have probably half killed me. As it was, he collected himself sufficiently to attend to the customer. But his temper had suffered so badly that he nicked a piece out of the customer's cheek, and heated words flared up immediately. I crouched sulkily in a corner, refusing to hand towels or anything else. Another order came in for coffees and I made them, anxious to be out of the saloon for as long as possible before some harm befell me. Unfortunately, in my haste to get out, I collided with two more customers in the doorway. The tray with the coffees lurched dangerously and deposited all the contents over the legs of the prospective customers. I yelped with dismay, dropped the wet tray with a clatter, and streaked through their coffee-stained legs. Their threats and curses filled the air after me. One man even gave chase, but I was fleeter than he and continued to run like the wind until I arrived home. Even there all I could do was to choke and gurgle with aching laughter, for the brief glance I had had of the barber's face—after I had upset the tray—was excruciatingly funny.

Thus, ignominiously, ended my first and last day as a barber's apprentice. '

17

Kuleli

I<small>T WAS</small> 1919, <small>THE WAR WAS OVER, AND</small> İstanbul was studded with Allied commissioners and officers in their khaki uniforms. The sibilant twittering of the English language filled the air, and the English, with the French and the Italians, supervised the police and the ports. They were everywhere, advising and ordering and suggesting.

One day my mother came home from Beyoğlu with two items of exciting news. The one concerned herself, for her designs in needlework were attracting attention and she had taken so many orders that morning that she wanted my grandmother to help her to complete them. This my grandmother was perfectly willing to do, for although she perhaps lacked true creative skill, she was an expert needlewoman, quite frequently paying more attention to detail than my mother. My mother had great sensibility, and when she was working out her patterns she could lose herself to the exclusion of her family and the world.

Her designs were most vivid and appealing. They lived in bold colorings and outline, as though painted on the materials. A number of foreign women had asked for repetitions of her work, but she refused to repeat, even if the sum offered were high. Instead she would work out some new design for them, intricate or simple, according to her mood of the moment, offering it casually, as though it did not matter whether they accepted or not. I often wonder what they thought of her, so slim and haughty, with the flaring wing of nose and the delicate eyebrows that seemed painted on, with her unveiled face and her halting French. Today all women in İstanbul and the other cities and towns go unveiled, but in 1919 she must have been a rare sight. Many of the shops in Beyoğlu suggested that she open an atelier, but she laughed at them, saying she had no head for business. My grandmother, excited by the demand created by my mother's designs, also nagged that an atelier was becoming essential. She even wanted to turn her bedroom into one, declaring that she would sleep somewhere else, but my mother held out against this for a long time.

The year 1919 saw my family on its feet again, my mother being the breadwinner.

The second item of news that spring day concerned Mehmet and me. Mother had met, in Beyoğlu, the wife of the colonel in whose house I had been circumcised, but he was a general now and an important person in the War Office. His wife had been so delighted to see my mother after the lapse of years that she had insisted upon her returning home with her to partake of coffee and to gossip about all that had happened in the years they had not met. She had hustled my unveiled mother into her husband's motor car, driven by his batman. My mother, never having been in a motor car before, was too terrified to speak during the journey to Bayazit. She told us that the sense of speed was terrible, that her heart had been perpetually in her mouth, and that every time another motor car had whizzed past in the opposite direction she had closed her eyes and left herself entirely to God's mercy.

This feminine attitude annoyed Mehmet and me, who would have given much to have been in her place.

"But you are not afraid of trams," Mehmet said in great contempt; and she replied that trams ran on rails and were, in consequence, perfectly safe, and did not go so fast as a motor car. During coffee the general's wife had asked about us children. When she heard of

the difficulties of having us suitably schooled, she suggested that
we be sent to the Military School.

"The what?" roared my grandmother, perhaps feeling, like us,
that she had not heard aright, and a queer little excited feeling
began to pull at my heart.

"The Military School," repeated my mother with some impatience. "She told me that a very close friend of her husband's is
in the War Office and can use his influence to enter the boys.
Apparently the Government intends to establish a junior school,
which will be attached to the academy. They will only accept pure
Turkish children so that eventually only Turkish officers will be in
the Army."

"I shall be a general," I said boastfully, and Mehmet said gently,
"I shall be a doctor, and then I can help the wounded soldiers to
get better. . . ."

And if I may digress a little, of the two of us he got his wish.

"But what sort of education will they get in a military school?"
demanded my grandmother, who knew nothing about schools but
who always liked to put in her opinion.

"How can I know?" demanded my mother, displeased that her
startling news had not had a better reception. "And I do not suppose
it matters very much," she added. "For if they are going to be
officers, they need to know very little, except how to kill each other,
of course."

"I shall not kill anyone," interposed the seven-year-old Mehmet
in his soft voice, taking her words literally.

"Do you really think the general can do anything?" I asked,
thrilled by the idea of life in a military school, picturing it to be
anything but what it turned out to be.

"Let us see," returned my mother. "Anyway, the general's wife
is going to see her husband's friend this afternoon to discuss it
for me."

"Shameless woman!" interjected my grandmother in horror, still
firmly entrenched in the past; and we commenced to laugh at the
bewilderment on her face, for she was half inclined to believe that

the general's wife was conducting a clandestine affair with her husband's friend.

That evening the general's batman arrived with a letter from the great man himself which said that he had talked over matters with the general in charge of the scheme, that he was willing to see us at the War Office the following afternoon, that he himself had given some information about the family and its present difficulties, that he hoped my mother would take advantage of the good life offered to her sons, and so forth.

My mother thoughtfully folded the letter, and the widow, who was spending the evening with us, declared that good luck was returning to the family.

"Perhaps you are right," said my mother. "But of course I was told this afternoon that everything at the school is still very disorganized after the war, that it will take a long time before it settles back to normal. Still, it is a great opportunity."

I commenced to laugh, remembering the barbershop. My mother, with remarkable intuition, looked across at me, saying, "Well, at least there will be no more coffee cups to break!"

The following afternoon Mehmet and I were taken to the War Office, excitement and fear gnawing at our vitals, and hunger, too, for we had been unable to eat any luncheon. My mother also seemed nervous, but she tried to put this behind her when we arrived at the War Office. A soldier showed us into the office of a very beautiful young officer, the general's adjutant, and he blushed when he spoke to my mother, asking her name and her business. She gave him this information. He asked her to be seated for a moment and then dashed gracefully into an adjoining room where, presumably, lurked his general. Mehmet and I stood awkwardly, while my mother sat stiff as a ramrod on a hard chair, a bright spot of color in either cheek. The adjutant returned, saying that the general would see us at once. He held the door open, keeping his eyes respectfully on the ground as my mother passed him. I passed through the door last of all and looked back to see the beautiful young adjutant staring at my mother's back, an unreadable expression in his eyes. Perhaps he thought it strange for a Turkish woman to go with open face.

The general was tall and lean, with silvery hair and a kind, intelligent face. Or did he only seem kind as he looked at my mother with that especial look that even old men reserve for lovely women?

He pushed forward an armchair for her, hard ones for Mehmet and me, and said with an affectation of joviality, "What! Are these young lions yours?"

My mother replied that this was so.

"Well, well!" said the general, as though this were a great surprise. "Our old friend General X has told me all about you. I once knew your father-in-law, in my youth, you know. A very fine man. I was sorry to hear that you lost your husband during the war. I am afraid things cannot have been easy for you."

"I lost my brother-in-law too," said my mother.

"Very sad," said the general, painting sympathy on his face, and he fiddled with papers on his desk and for a few moments they talked of family affairs. Then the general turned to me and said:

"So you are İrfan! How old are you, my boy?"

"Ten, sir," I replied in a weak voice.

"This war! This war!" he sighed to my mother. "This child should have been at school three years ago. However, he looks intelligent; let us see what we can make of him. So you would like to be an officer?" he demanded, turning suddenly back to me.

"Yes, sir," I said, adding boldly, "I should like to be a general like you!"

He laughed.

"And perhaps you will," he retorted. "It is something, at least, to know what one wants from life. And what about the little one?" he asked, chucking Mehmet under the chin, then saying thoughtfully to my mother: "Yes, he is like his grandfather. I can see the resemblance quite plainly." He mused over Mehmet's small, shut-away face, then asked, "What is your name?"

"Mehmet, sir," stammered my brother, very red in the face with such close, unwelcome scrutiny.

"And what do you want to be, Mehmet? A general too?"

"No, sir," said Mehmet. "I want to be a doctor."

"Two young gentlemen who know their minds!" declared the general. "I remember that when I was their age I wanted to be a street seller, for they seemed to be the only people who ever had horses. But the only way I ever got a horse was by becoming a cavalry officer, so perhaps to all of us Fate gives our desires in a roundabout way. Well," he declared, turning his attention back to my mother, "you appear to be a fortunate mother, for here you have, in embryo, a future general and a future doctor."

He patted our heads and rang for his adjutant.

"I shall leave you in my adjutant's hands," he said to my mother, adding in a conspiratorial whisper, "He knows far more about this business than I do!"

We went out to the office of the adjutant, who said, "You understand, hanim effendi, that you have to sign a contract for the military education of these two boys?"

"No," said my mother.

The adjutant grew red and could scarcely bear to look at her.

"But did not the general explain?" he said in astonishment.

"No," replied my mother.

"Dear, dear!" said the adjutant fussily, clearing his throat and tapping a piece of parchment with a finger.

"This contract," he began, "states that your two sons shall be educated at the Military School in Kuleli and afterward at the Military College—providing they pass their examinations—entirely at the expense of the Government. In return for this, they will serve in the Turkish Army for fifteen years; but if they fail in their final examinations they will serve as sergeants for the same number of years, without any chances of promotion. There is no promotion from the ranks."

"That seems very hard," murmured my mother doubtfully. "If I sign this contract, I sign my sons' lives away for twenty-five years, and how can I tell if they will be able to pass their examinations or not? How can I tell?" she said again, looking up at the young

officer. He smiled a little, perhaps remembering his own years in the
military institutions.

"It is generally found, hanim effendi, that if a boy wants to become an officer he passes his examinations."

My mother smiled too.

"I think that perhaps you are right," she said. "Nevertheless, I
should like a little time to think this over before I take their freedom
from them with a stroke of the pen. How long will it be before
these contracts are ready for my signature?"

"There are many formalities to complete first," replied the adjutant. "Perhaps in fifteen days' time."

"That surely gives me time enough to decide," answered my
mother, and I was in an agony that she, with her feminine prejudices, was going to take this chance from my hands. I dared not
interrupt their conversation, but I felt sick with apprehension that
my bright and shining dream of becoming an officer, a general,
would end in nothing.

The adjutant explained that he required certain documents from
the local police, from the muktar, a certificate of good health from
the proper authorities, and twelve photographs of each of us.

"References are not needed," said he with some embarrassment.
"For General X has already given them."

"Thank you," said my mother with a faint ironical inflection in
her cool voice, and the adjutant bowed us out of his office, his eyes
once more on the floor, his attitude beautifully restrained.

For the next few days there was a great deal of argument at
home, for my mother was extremely obstinate, refusing to be advised or guided by anyone. My grandmother said that she could
not understand why so much fuss was being made, since nothing
very serious could go amiss with our lives while we were in the
hands of the military authorities.

"But can you not see that other schools can be soon found again?
Civil schools with as sound an education but without the tie of
signing away their lives for twenty-five years?"

"I do not want to go to any other school," I wept, impotent and unable to stand up against my mother's reasoning. "I want to be an officer! Please!" I begged, as a last sop to politeness.

The battle rolled back and forth, now in favor of, now against, the Military School; and the neighbors animatedly joined the discussion. My mother did not listen to what they said, however, for she mistrusted everyone else's opinion. In the meantime, however, she took us to the Bayazit police for the necessary papers. We went to the muktar's office and to the hospital for examination. Having obtained all the relevant documents, we went to be photographed, and still no final decision was forthcoming from my mother.

I took to going to the mosque, praying fervently in that cool, quiet place. I prayed no prescribed prayers, for I was unable to concentrate on anything but: "Please God, let me go to the Military School. Please God let me go to the Military School!" saying the same thing over and over again, with feverish intensity. And perhaps a benevolent God heard my anxious prayers, for the evening the finished photographs arrived my mother announced that she had carefully thought everything over and that she was convinced she was doing the right thing in allowing us to go to Kuleli.

Once again we visited the War Office, my mother leaving us in the adjutant's room while she went to speak to the general in private. As she was leaving, he said:

"Personally, I think you have made a wise decision. Good luck to you and your sons."

The contracts were signed at last, and only then did I feel able to breathe properly. It was done now and could not be undone! Oh, proud and lovely moment! We had been given to Kuleli Military School, that long white rambling building that I was to know so well.

The adjutant solemnly shook our hands.

"Report to Kuleli on the 15th of May," he said crisply, in a man-to-man tone of voice, and I grew scarlet with pleasure.

May 15th, 1919, is a date in Turkish history, for, on that day, Kemal Atatürk sailed toward Samsun. It was the date on which the admiral of the British Mediterranean Fleet declared that the Greeks would occupy İzmir; it was also the date that I entered Kuleli. Young and insignificant and as yet untried by life, yet could I also claim a share in the date that was making Turkish history.

The morning dawned fair and promising, and Mehmet and I were taken by my grandmother to the mosque to pray. We prayed for different things, we three. My grandmother prayed for our health and our success in school life. I know, for I heard her loud rumbling voice intoning, intoning. . . . Perhaps Mehmet prayed to become a doctor, but who can say? for Mehmet could be as secretive as the grave. And I prayed one little prayer only. I gave thanks because I was going to Kuleli at last. Over and over again I prayed: "Thank you, God. Thank you, God." And I felt His invisible presence all around me.

Goodbyes were said to the street, for we did not know when we would be returning again; and the old women cried over us, and the old men sighed and wished they were young again. Eventually we got away for Galata Bridge and the boat that would take us down the Bosporus, to the beginning of our youthful dreams.

Were we nervous, I wonder, that May morning, just the littlest bit reluctant to leave home and familiar faces so far behind us? I do not think so, although, looking back from this distance, it is no longer possible to judge that with any accuracy. We went to the boat dressed stiffly in our best, our faces and hands so clean and shining that all who saw us must have realized that this was a great occasion. And in my case, whenever we passed a French or British officer—and the way to Galata Bridge was thick with them—I felt proud of the future my mother had chosen for me, telling myself that I too should one day walk like that, in uniform, the badges of rank on my collar.

My mother allowed me to buy the boat tickets and I felt very important, as though the humble clerk who attended to me should know that I was bound for Kuleli and adventure. When I requested three tickets for Çengelköy, he paid no attention to me at all, as if

I were the merest passenger and not a potential general. But my inflated ego was not jolted, and I talked loudly to my mother and Mehmet about Kuleli and what I would do there. Once my mother said:

"Hush! It is very vulgar to boast, you know."

But she did not speak sharply.

We bought simit on the boat, and I dimly remembered Sariyer. My father came back fleetingly, for less than a second, to tantalize with his shut-away face, and Aunt Ayşe smiled welcome; but Uncle Ahmet stayed maddeningly just outside the line of mental vision, refusing to show his face.

But Sariyer was more than just an hour down the Bosporus: Sariyer was four years away, and deader for us than its dead owners. I asked Mehmet if he remembered Sariyer and Uncle Ahmet, but he looked vague and said he did not. I tried to paint a picture for him, there on the boat, of that old red-roofed house we had visited before the war. The pictures poured through my brain like pictures shaken up in a kaleidoscope: I talked of the magnolia trees that had stood on the lawn; of the shine on the grass when the sun came out to dry the rain; of the dogs, Fidèle and Joly; of the grapes on the house vine of which my aunt had been so proud. And as I talked, I was in Sariyer again.

"I used to fish in the Bosporus with Uncle Ahmet," I told Mehmet's listening face. "We never used to catch very much, but it was fun rowing home under the moon and sometimes hearing the voices coming across the water from İstanbul side."

"I did not know you would remember so much," said my mother. "And you have a gift for words, my son. You have brought Sariyer back to me again too. I hope I have not done the wrong thing in entering you for a military school. Perhaps you would have been better somewhere else."

"Of course not, Mother," I said indignantly. "I wanted to come to Kuleli and I should have hated any other school. I am going to be an officer, and one day I shall be a general: you will see! I shall carry you everywhere on my arm; all the people will say that you look young enough to be my wife, and the women will be jealous of you."

My mother laughed merrily.

"Your imagination is too vivid," she said. "And misplaced at that."

We reached the boat station of Çengelköy and disembarked, feeling less important now that we were so near our goal.

"Kuleli?" my mother asked the ticket collector. "The Military School?"

"Turn to the left," replied the ticket collector briefly, barely glancing at Mehmet and me. "It is only a few minutes' walk from here, and the school is so big you cannot miss it."

So out to the quiet dusty roads of Çengelköy and along the sea road, tree-lined and white in the noonday sun. The school loomed on our right, like a palace, I thought, so white it was against the cloudless summer sky that 15th of May, 1919, the day Atatürk's little boat rode the waters to Samsun.

We mounted the stone steps to the main door, and my heart commenced to thump furiously. A porter on sentry duty asked my mother's business. She said that she had come to leave us at the school, as arranged with the War Office.

"This is the Military College," he informed her coldly, "the school is on the hill, along this road and up. It is a big gray building, and you will find it quite easily."

Up the hill road we toiled, hot and uncomfortable, disappointed that the white shining palace was not for us after all. We arrived at the school panting and out of breath, and a great iron-barred gate prevented our entering. There was the sound of boys' voices, and a few of them came near to the gate to look at us. There was a sentry box near the gate, and a soldier on guard there shouted, "Huseyin Aga!"

Down toward the gate came an old, old man with a flowing white beard and a bent back. He grumblingly withdrew the bolts of the gates and asked our business. My mother told him, but this time impatience made her imperious and she tossed her piled-up curls. The old man grew civil and eyed her unveiled face with open curiosity. He allowed us to enter the garden, motioned to my mother to take a seat under the cool shade of the trees, and said that he was going to look for the captain, muttering a bit to himself, as though uncertain where to find the captain.

My mother sat down gratefully, for the heat had tired her, and while she was resting I strolled away to explore. I went near the gate, and there I saw two men unloading lamb carcasses from a cart. Another man was carrying a sack of something that from the partially opened top looked like spinach. An old man who might have been a cook or a kitchen servant was haggling over the lamb, and several mangy curs snarling under the horse's legs were kicked away by the men. I heard Mehmet's voice calling for me, and I ran back to where I had left him with my mother. Huseyin Aga was back again and waiting to lead us to the captain. We came near the main school building, and to our left there was a long, one-storied hut which, judging from the noise of cutlery, was the dining room. The din coming from there was appalling, and several big boys were entering. Most of them had very dark skins, and one was, to my horror, quite black. They were shabbily dressed, but they looked jeeringly at Mehmet and me and talked among themselves. One of them said something aloud to us, but I could not understand what language he was speaking. He is not Turkish, I said to myself, wondering how many different nationalities might be housed in this place.

The captain met us at the door of his office with a big stick in his hands. He seemed to be a very nervous type of man and was quite pale. He clutched his stick fiercely, as though he were accustomed quite frequently to defend himself from the hordes of young savages in the school. Taking us into his room, he gave us rickety chairs to sit on. The room was indescribably dirty and untidy, and the captain stuttered so badly every time he spoke that I felt a sort of hysteria beginning to bubble inside me. He thumbed through a pile of papers on his desk and finally extracted two that evidently concerned us.

"İrfan and Mehmet?" he asked, and my mother replied that this was so.

"Turkish and Moslem. Thank God for that!" he said, stuttering very badly. "Two more Turks in the school!"

He looked at my mother.

"We are, unfortunately, not yet organized here. There is still a great deal to do, and we have been saddled with many Kurds and Armenians from eastern Anatolia. There are, as yet, only a few Turks. No doubt one day the authorities will make up their minds which are to remain and which are to be sent elsewhere. Our intention, hanim effendi, is to bring up a new generation of purely Turkish officers."

It was odd, but when he commenced to speak in sentences he forgot his stutter and poured out a lot of irrelevant detail to my mother, as if that now at last he had begun to unburden himself he could not cease.

When he had tired himself with talking, he stood up and said, with the stutter back again and his mouth twitching nervously:

"Well, hanim effendi, you may safely leave the boys in my hands. You may visit them once a week if you wish, but they will not be permitted to go home until they have had several months' training."

My mother thanked him and we kissed her hands. Huseyin Aga shuffled out into the garden to escort her to the main gates, and Mehmet and I were left alone with the captain. He looked at us quizzically and we solemnly stared back at him; then I remembered all the things he had told my mother. Suddenly twenty-five years seemed a very long time, a lifetime surely; and as I looked through the unclean windows into the rank, untidy gardens where the hordes of boys were streaming from the dining room, my heart began to beat nervously.

The gilt had worn off the gingerbread a bit. It was still true that this was the Military School, to which I had passionately wanted to come; but where was the glamour I had expected, the pomp, and the military splendor?

18

The New Republic

WHEN I THINK BACK TO THAT DAY IN Kuleli, in that gray, dilapidated building on the hill, I cannot help being glad that it has been abolished, that the present generation of cadet officers are better housed and study under better conditions than obtained when we were there.

Sometimes when I see them in the İstanbul streets, with their smart, dark-blue uniforms, the dashing red line running down the trouser legs to show that they belong to the military caste, I cannot help remembering my generation's early years as cadets.

That morning in May, 1919, when my mother left us and we stood there in the captain's forbidding room awaiting his instructions, all the romance of soldiering left me.

Mehmet and I stood there uncertainly while the captain rustled papers on his desk and ignored us.

I suppose I cried myself to sleep that night. A bugler commenced to play from the garden, and the sound was low, mournful and sad in its isolated loneliness. It was the one thing needed to make me feel conscious of being far away from home, and I buried my head in the pillow and started to cry.

My mother visited us every few weeks, and when she first saw us in our baggy uniforms she looked as if she did not know whether to laugh or cry. She asked many questions about our lessons, the sort of food we were being given, and was disposed to lump all Kurds and Armenians as murderers. Impetuously, she wanted to take us home again. She complained to the captain that the place was dirty and that she did not wish to leave us here any longer. The captain, it appeared, spread his hands expressively and repeated the same old refrain that everything was, of course, still very disorganized. He then gently reminded her that she had signed contracts for us, and said that if we were taken home he would be most regretfully compelled to send the Military Police after us! This really frightened her, for it had never occurred to her that the contracts would be used against her in this fashion. Not to be entirely thwarted, however, she furiously told the captain, with more spirit than accuracy, that she would use her influence at the War Office to have us removed. The captain, no doubt having heard this before, remained unimpressed.

My mother would come to the school unveiled; but when several of the older boys said she was a *tango* (tart), I became involved in many fights and begged her to cover her face. Although she indignantly refused at first, she nevertheless soon gave in. One day she complained that Mehmet and I smelled, and the next time she visited us she brought perfumed soap with her. This we refused in horror, declaring that life was already sufficiently difficult for us without adding to the burden with scented soaps.

It was a popular belief amongst the Moslems of İstanbul that if they prayed in the same mosque as their sultan, and at the same hour, God would listen with greater intensity to their supplications. Consequently the Shadow of God, as the sultan was called, was everywhere followed by admiring crowds who yearned for Paradise. I remember a morning in the Bayazit Mosque when I was in the middle of such a crush that it was not possible to do anything but remain in a cramped, semiupright position, in imminent danger from the movement of arms or legs all about me. When the prayers began, I was in an even greater quandary, for the person in front of me, who was a porter, had a pair of evil-smelling feet, and when I attempted to make my obeisance, impelled forward and downward by the pressure from behind, I was almost drowned in the odor of dirt and perspiration so perilously close to my nose. It was an odor sufficient, I swear, to kill even the rats who sported in the mosque's lavatories. But fear of the Lord held me in my place securely, and I stifled my squeamishness and eventually escaped from the mosque to lave my hands and face in the water basins in the gardens. I gulped the clean sweet air as avidly as a man newly rescued from a gaseous mine.

In those days during Ramazan there were no lessons in the schools, and we were allowed home on leave. Twenty-seven years ago the streets at Ramazan time were crowded as they have not been since and perhaps never will be again. Not only the Moslems who were keeping the fast were in the streets, but the British, French, and American soldiers were also there to watch the ceremonies. And on the last night of Ramazan, in the year of which I write, Bayazit Square and its mosque were places not to be forgotten by those who saw them.

The tall, slender minarets of the mosque were ringed with gleaming electric candles, and between the minarets, silhouetted brilliantly against the dark sky, stretched electric lettering spelling Elveda, Ramazan. (Goodbye Ramazan). The nostalgia of the words and the effect of so much nocturnal beauty caught at the heart in a strange sadness, even though this was meant to be a happy occasion. On both minarets were the muezzins, their chanting, lovely voices busily calling the people to prayer, and the square and the gardens of the mosque were thronged with silent, listening people—like an army of the dead. High above them swayed the muezzins, their voices the only sound in that vast silence.

I edged my way to the mosque cautiously, for one felt oddly guilty to be moving in that dead sea of silence. The interior was ablaze with light. Light poured down from the great chandeliers, and the arched dome itself was ringed with light that glittered as the glasses swayed. On the walls gigantic branching candelabra threw a blinding glare over everything. Many muezzins were here too, reading from the Koran; and the faithful bowed and moved in unison and beat their breasts. I remember that I was aflame that night with the pomp, the splendor, and the majesty, and that all my senses reeled.

The day eventually came when we, who had now become seniors, left the ancient gray building on the hill and moved into the white palace fronting the Bosporus. Great was our joy to be there at last.

Kuleli's rooms were large and bright, for, as a welcome change from oil lamps, we had our own electrical plant. The classrooms were on the ground floor, facing the dusty, quiet road, and there was silence all the day long, for none came to Kuleli except the students and the officers stationed there.

A mosque was established in the basement, and on our first evening in the school we were all herded there for prayers of thanksgiving. Whether we wished it or not, religion was forced down our throats. I had lost some of my early adolescent fervor, but I needed no forcing. Many of the older boys, however, resented the interference of the officers—especially when they used large sticks as a better means of persuasion. In those days in Turkey, when the Moslem religion was a national institution, a fixed habit of the centuries, the Kuleli gardens would be full of sullen, protesting boys washing their hands and faces under the fountains, balancing against a tree while they pulled socks over newly cleaned feet, rushing at the last moment to the lavatories for more private ablutions, with everyone in a panic for fear of being late. The muezzin would start to read, and groans would rend the air, for that meant that we were late already. Irate officers would be stationed at the mosque door, their sticks ready in their hands to whack the backsides of the latecomers smartly.

When Kemal Atatürk formally declared, on October 29th, 1923, that our country was now a Republic, everything slowly began to change its face. Orders were sent to Kuleli that it would no longer be necessary to force the students to go to the mosque. Religion was to be a matter of choice. So the sticks were temporarily abandoned, and only the merest handful of boys now attended the mosque. But now the sticks were brought out for quite a different purpose, for we who still visited the mosque were frequently late for lessons. Whereas before the sticks had soundly whacked the backsides of reluctant devotees, now they whacked the backsides of reluctant scholars.

Atatürk and his Government decided that religion and public affairs must be separated, and the new Constitution read, "The language of the Turkish Republic is Turkish and the capital, Ankara." Whereas formerly it had read, "The religion of the Turkish Republic is Moslem; the language, Turkish, and the capital, Ankara."

The change was far greater than perhaps it would appear to European eyes. Religion was practically abolished, since, although the mosques remained places of worship, the people no longer had time to pray the prescribed five times in a day—except the old and perhaps the infirm who had no public duties to perform. The majority of the Turks simply had no time. The work of the Government offices could no longer wait on the prayers of the officials. Religious teachings were abolished in all schools, Moslem or Christian, and religious sects were no longer permitted to appear in the streets in the clothes of their particular religious orders.

Nowadays when the muezzin called, there were few to listen and fewer still to respond. The week end was changed also, and we observed the Christian Saturday and Sunday in place of the old Moslem Thursday and Friday.

The mosque at Kuleli was abandoned and given over to broken chairs and tables in need of repair.

Our uniform changed and became the familiar navy blue of today's students, with the smart red line down the seams of the trousers. A cap with the smallest suspicion of a peak was issued, for the fez had been abolished by law.

On week ends Mehmet and I would go proudly home, my grandmother being convinced that there were not two better-looking boys in all Turkey.

Muazzez was nine now and attending a girls' day school in Bayazit. A pert, conceited little thing she was, with her long twinkling legs in their demure black-silk stockings, her brief skirts flying out jauntily. She was incredibly pretty, and her hair had still further lightened with the years, so that by now it was almost blond. My grandmother spoiled her as she had never spoiled Mehmet or me, but perhaps she had softened with age. Nevertheless, she was as autocratic as ever and quite frequently had long, bitter quarrels with my mother.

After a time week ends spent at home were no longer a novelty, and I spent more and more of my free time at Kuleli. We would swim together whole summer days in the Bosporus afterward lazing in the school gardens, pleasantly conscious that this was the week end and that no lessons loomed before us for two whole days.

Just prior to Atatürk's abolishment of the fez, the military were issued the cap with a small peak mentioned previously. The peak, we were told, was to guard the eyes against the sun. It was so small, however, that the idea of it being able to guard against anything, let alone the sun, was laughable. We had always previously worn a fez with the Turkish moon and stars woven into the front, and we were now very much ashamed to be seen with our new headgear, which we thought was too much like the hat the Christians wore. So we carried the offensive hat in our hands as often as we dared, and the few boys who were brave enough to keep it on were called ğavur, an epithet relating to a Christian in an unsavory way.

When I used to pass through Bayazit, all the old men in the coffeehouses, and those sitting at the tables in the streets, would look at the cap with the apology of a peak and shake their gray heads.

"What is this?" they would mutter in dismay. "Where is this country going to?"

One day the district barber—not the barber of the earlier episode in my childhood—came up to me in the street and solemnly advised me never to put this terrible Christian thing on my head.

"It is a Christian hat," he warned. "If a Moslem puts such a shocking thing on his head, the good God will surely punish him."

When I laughed at him, he grew angry and later complained to my grandmother about my lack of piety.

It was in 1925 that Atatürk ordered that from henceforth all men in Turkey must wear the Christian hat. What consternation there was throughout the nation. Was Atatürk playing with them? Was he sitting in his château in Ankara devising new things to disturb and break their habits of centuries?

The men indignantly refused to throw away the fez, and it became a common sight to see fighting taking place between the supporters of the new order and the die-hards of the old. Government officials were the first to give way to Atatürk. They were forced into this position by reason of their work, and the streets were dotted with men wearing bowler hats with a self-conscious air. The children used to throw stones after them, and the police arrested men who still persisted in wearing the fez. In desperation the street sellers put fancy paper hats on their heads, adding a note of unusual gayety to the market places; and in the country towns and villages the men even wore women's hats to evade arrest. The old men took to tying handkerchiefs on their heads, placing the offending Christian hat over this; but the police became wise to this ruse and promptly arrested them. Arrested men were hauled to the police stations in such great numbers that they could not be dealt with, and the white handkerchiefs were pulled off the bald pates, the insulting headgear being firmly clamped over the naked, uneasy heads.

Sometimes I and a few others would take our textbooks into the country on week ends, asking farmers on the way if we could buy cucumbers or tomatoes from them.

Usually they permitted us to take as much as we wished, refusing to accept payment from us. Well laden, we would go to the top of the hill above Kuleli, a quiet, lovely spot where a little spring trickled icily, and there we washed our vegetables or fruits before finding a comfortable place to study. Time passed swiftly in that tranquil place; and when we were hungry we would feast royally, feeling at peace in the lonely, silent hills.

Sometimes, tiring of study, I would lean against my particular fir tree and look down upon the Bosporus shining coolly below me. There was a good view from that tree, I remember, right down the Bosporus to the Black Sea. Little Bebek was in front of me in all its shimmering morning beauty. If I turned my head a little to the right, I could see the famous fortress walls on the Asiatic side. Turning it back again to İstanbul, I could see that other fortress, the old crumbling fortress built in 1452. The parts of it that were visible from my tree were the narrowest parts of all, being a little over 649 meters. In connection with this there is a story which says that the Sultan Mehmet once approached the Emperor Constantine and asked to be granted a piece of land on the European side. Constantine, it appears, acceded to this request, stipulating that the land be only the size of a cow's skin. So the Sultan Mehmet took a cow's skin, had it cut into narrow strips, and then laid them end to end, building his fortress according to those measurements. And no matter how the emperor protested, he was always told the one thing: that the land only measured just so much as a cow's skin.

And all down the Bosporus, down, down to the Black Sea, ran the tall trees and the old wooden houses that suited the skyline so well. If I turned my head to the left, there on the hilltop I could see the Dolmabahçe Saray, white and artificial as a wedding cake in its peaceful setting. Miniature mosques fronted the water's edge, and at the end of all the shining palaces lay İstanbul—my İstanbul, which will forever hold something of my heart. Gray it appeared from the hill, and the smoke from the boats lay over it like a soft veil. The minarets that enchanted the skyline were tall and tapering, and from my hill I could see, behind the mosques, the Marmara like a faint line of thread.

I would turn back to my books reluctantly, only half aware of the printed word.

Toward evening, when the sun grew kinder, we would put away our books and stroll down the hill to Anadolu Hissari, where we would play football—for we never forgot to bring the football, whatever else we might forget.

Later, in the soft green dusk, the hot day behind us only a memory, we would return to Kuleli; and there was none to notice our coming, except perhaps the fishermen in their rowboats, and to them we were no novelty.

19

A Bayram Morning and
a Journey into Bleakness

A BAYRAM WAS APPROACHING, AND MEH-
met and I hurried into İstanbul for three days' holiday. We had
money in our pockets with which to buy presents for the family, as
was the custom at Bayram.

When we got off the boat at Galata Bridge, we automatically
made for the Kapali çarşa. Most of the traders were Armenian or
Greek, with a sprinkling of Turks among them, and I do not know
which had the greatest aptitude for cheating—the Greeks, the
Armenians, or the Turks. Mehmet insisted on separating from me,
telling me fussily that we would meet at a certain place at a certain
time. He then went off by himself, his hands thrust into his pockets,
his shut-away face oddly like the image my mind still held of my
father's face.

He never liked to shop with me. My methods bored him pro-
foundly, for I would pore over something for a very long time, until
I was finally persuaded into buying it by a weary trader. Mehmet
bought everything with great care and never afterward regretted a
purchase, as I frequently did.

I went to the antiques section, where I immediately lost my heart
to an old samovar—a shining, elegant thing—a reminder of lost days.
I stood admiring it for so long that the owner became quite nervous

as to my intentions and was too apprehensive to even cry out his wares in the usual wheedling tone.

In the end I bought a brass candlestick for my grandmother, for she had a passion for old things and knew about them in a way I could never hope to imitate. When I had paid the price demanded, there was an absurdly small amount of money left in my pocket. I hastily tore myself from the lovely old treasures in search of something that would please my mother and at the same time cause no heartburnings over the candlestick. I searched wildly for something to fill these requirements and finally, in sheer despair, bought some sort of a sachet which looked absurdly small in relation to the price asked for it. However, I felt I could not bargain for a present for my mother, so I bought it resignedly. A red hair ribbon was purchased for my sister, on which I saved ten kuruş, for I had no qualms about bargaining for a present for my sister. A solid-looking comb was bought for Mehmet, which might be a useless present since he had no hair to comb, but nevertheless the price of it was just right for the amount of money I had left in my pocket.

Well pleased with myself, I sauntered to the spot we had arranged for meeting, to find him already there. He accused me of tardiness and was so put out that he did not utter a word to me all the way home. Sulkily he stalked along beside me, his parcels under his arm, and at Bayazit Square he left me on some mysterious, highly secret errand.

The square was crowded with late shoppers, men jauntily carrying diminutive parcels and big parcels with exciting shapes, and women stepping sedately on their high heels, hurrying past the moon-faced men almost as though they feared assault.

I stood at the corner of the square, looking at the crowds and the great old arch of the university, which twinkled with electric lights. The twin minarets of the Bayazit Mosque shone with electric candles too; but though it was the hour for prayer, only a few oldish people were going inside. I could not help remembering the old days and the crowds who had answered the call of the muezzins.

From everywhere came their lost, mournful cry, half drowned

under the roar of the traffic, the Klaxons of the cars, and the never ceasing clanging of the busy trams. The guns boomed out to proclaim that now the fast could be broken, and I, like the rest of the crowd, hurried homeward for feasting and merrymaking.

I caught up with Mehmet again at the corner of the street. He was loitering there, waiting for me; and Muazzez met us at the door of the friendly little house. She pulled us into the narrow hall, which smelled like a garden, so full was it of flowers put there by my mother to welcome the Bayram.

We went together to the kitchen, where my mother was heating soup, an apron protecting her silk dress.

We kissed her hands and handed her our presents. She looked very youthful and gay, with her face heated from the fire and tendrils of hair falling across her forehead. Then she opened my present to her and said that the sachet was really very pretty indeed. Muazzez, however, was less tactful. She resentfully examined her hair ribbon and remarked on the poor quality of the satin. "Red does not suit me," she said pettishly, throwing the gay ribbon on the ground; and Mehmet said in disgust, when he saw the comb, "What am I expected to do with a comb?"

Altogether, there was no pleasing them. I hoped to fare better with my grandmother. We judged it time for her to have finished with her praying, for no loud rumbling noises were coming from the salon. We went upstairs to find her.

She was just rising stiffly and her first words were, "Now my heart is comfortable, for I have just prayed for all our dead."

We kissed her hands, and I noticed that for this Bayram all her rings sparkled and the great emerald lay winking across her breast. We gave her our presents, and when she saw the candlestick she said to me, "You have a very rare genius of knowing how to please people."

We all burst out laughing. Mehmet showed his comb, and my sister thrust forward the offensive hair ribbon; but my grandmother's eyes twinkled and she said that some were very hard to please, but that for herself she was happy only in being alive.

She set Muazzez to prepare the table, handing out snowy damask and silver that shone brighter than the lighted lamps. Crystal glasses were set on the damask and wine in a carafe. I teased my grandmother, telling her that no good Moslem would drink wine. She shook her head sadly and said she knew well enough she was not a good person but that nevertheless, surely the good God did not begrudge her a glass of wine with her dinner.

I looked about the room, at the high gleam on old furniture, at the flowers massed droopingly in dark corners, at the silver bowl of early roses which hung their tender heads in the center of the table, and I was glad to be home for this Bayram, proud that the spirit of my family had not died.

The next morning Mehmet and I were sent to the mosque to pray. We went to the little mosque my father and my grandfather had attended when we were children, the mosque that stood near the burned, blackened skeleton of our old house. And, too, we went there from custom, for that mosque was associated with my family, and on a Bayram morning it was unthinkable to go elsewhere.

After the prayers were over, we stood on the steps of the mosque. The little garden was thick with wild flowers and people, and the tall trees shadowed the lush green grass. The imam issued the traditional bonbons and Turkish delight, and Mehmet and I respectfully saluted the old men. One of them came over to me and said, "Are you Hüsnü's son?"

I replied that this was so. He looked at Mehmet and me, and I saw memory slipping a long way back.

"I remember your father," he said, "but you are not like him. This one here," touching Mehmet. "Now he is very like him indeed. Very like."

He paused a moment, struggling with the memories that crowded the old brain.

"Your father," he said heavily, "used to come to this mosque to pray. I remember him when he was quite a small boy. He used to come here with your grandfather. Ah, well," he sighed, "that was a long time ago: you could not know of that."

He patted my shoulder with a frail, gentle hand.

"You are a fine boy," he said. "God bless you."

He pottered away from us, muttering to himself; and I saw him young again and upstanding, with perhaps a child on either hand, watching the small boy who was to become my father approach with the young man who was to become my grandfather. And I clearly heard their voices and felt the tug of the impatient small boy. I thought how sad a thing is age; I wondered if that old, old man and all other old people felt this same sadness. What did they think when they saw their withered cheeks that were once smooth, their dimmed eyes that were once bright? Did they sometimes wish for death to carry them swiftly from the ancient bodies before they could see the further cruel encroachment Time would surely make?

We went home to feasting and merrymaking, but before the feasting a certain ritual had to be observed.

My grandmother had to seat herself, my mother going to her to kiss her hands as a sign of her respect for her greater age. My grandmother would respond by kissing my mother's cheeks, then motioning to her to sit beside her. Now it was my turn to pay my respects to the women of the family, next Mehmet, and last of all Muazzez, for she was the youngest.

Only at the conclusion of the little ceremony could the serious business of the day begin. Muazzez handed sweets on the tray that had never known any other duty; my mother served liqueurs to each one to drink to the others' health, and everyone sat a little stiffly in his new clothes.

Later in the morning Bekci Baba came to the street. He was accompanied by the man who played the big drum and another who played the clarinet. The man with the drum had gaily colored handkerchiefs tied all about the instrument as evidence of all the tips Bekci Baba had received from the various houses in the district. My mother handed a small blue handkerchief to me with money tied in one corner, and I handed this in turn to Bekci Baba in appreciation of his care of us throughout the year. It was tied on the drum with the other handkerchiefs, and the little group then called at the house next door. A crowd of children flew after them, shouting ribaldry. Then it was the turn of the famous local firemen. The dustmen came too, and money was given to all of them. To children of the neighborhood who played near the house we tossed out exotically wrapped sweets, watching them eagerly scrambling for them.

After luncheon neighbors called, and Mehmet and I decided to take Muazzez to Yeşilköy, to the sea. Yeşilköy (green village) is a pretty suburb of Istanbul, and very popular in the summer months. The little local trains were packed to capacity; and although Muazzez protested of discomfort, Mehmet and I were perfectly satisfied to stand in the corridor among the dribbling, crying babies and the hot, sticky children.

At Yeşilköy we hired a rowboat; but the Marmara was rough, and when Muazzez began suddenly to look white about the nostrils, we took her to land again, where she soon recovered. We climbed the hilly village street, quiet and cool, with birds singing behind high garden walls. The old gray houses stood back coolly amid their flower beds, and the striped blinds mocked the early heat of the spring sunlight. We walked down a wide gravel road that was tree-lined and tranquil, and up the hill to the Casino, which was less than a hundred feet above sea level. We chose a table overlooking the sweep of the Marmara, a table with a bare hot top, partially shaded by acacia trees. Because it was Bayram, Turkish music was played by the orchestra and a singer sang sadly of her love who was gone. When the waiter came, I ordered pastries and sickly chocolate cakes and iced coffee topped with mouth-melting *crème santé*. I ordered recklessly, for my mother had slipped money into my pocket before we left home.

Muazzez, in her soft white dress and with gay blue ribbons in her hair, was in a seventh heaven of delight, trying to pretend that she was older than her meager eleven years. Still I see that day before my eyes and remember the moment I realized that my sister was beautiful. For her eyes that day were the mad, mad blue of the Marmara, catching and matching the gayety about her, and her elfin laughter tinkled joyously.

We returned late from the Casino, glad to rest weary young limbs in easy chairs, and there was a languor, a pallor about my sister that was half childish, half sensual. I realized, with a little wondering shock, that she was growing up.

With the Bayram over, we went back to Kuleli again and the surging happiness of meeting old friends. On May 4 of that year, however, certain of us were transferred to the Military School at Tokat, in the north of Anatolia, for a year and a half, and great was our regret to leave Kuleli for such a long time.

Mehmet was given permission to see me off, and he waved madly, growing smaller and smaller as the boat pulled away from the shore. We slid past Kuleli, and I looked nostalgically back at it. Soon we had reached Galata, and this time it was İstanbul, mysterious under the evening haze, to which I looked back. It was hard to say goodbye to İstanbul, my own city, for it seemed most fair against the sky, like a lovely jewel in the Bosporus. Down the darkening strait we sailed, and still I looked back to the dim face of the city. Presently a friend pulled me by the arm.

"Stop dreaming!" he laughed. "Come and eat something. I packed extra things for you because I knew you would not remember."

I laughed too, for it was true that I had not remembered, and I gladly accepted the bread, black olives, and hard-boiled eggs which he proffered.

Soon we slid into the long length of the Black Sea, and the Bosporus with all its memories lay far behind. One bade it adieu, as regretful, as sentimental an adieu as though one would never again return to its blue waters.

That night we slept on deck, only our seniors being privileged to sleep in the comparative half-comfort of below. We huddled beneath our overcoats, trying to sleep to the roll and lurch of the uneasy boat, conscious of the keen winds that blew from Russia, even though it was May and we had left summer behind in Kuleli.

The next day we arrived at Zonguldak, a dirty, dusty coal-mining city, its outline drab and depressing. Everything was covered with a fine thin pall of coal dust. The buildings beside the wharf looked infinitely dreary, all of them coal-begrimed, a few yellow houses on the hill adding the only note of relief. There was something infinitely sorrowful in the sight of their gray roofs against the skyline, and we were desolate to think that we had to spend twelve hours here while the captain of the ship took on supplies of coal, water, and other commodities.

Our next port of call was İnebolu. We stopped about a mile off shore, for İnebolu has no harbor. It stood like a picture in its green frame of trees, with the high mountain forests behind it. Many rowboats were coming out to us; the soft day was still and calm; and a brilliant sun shone on the pink and white houses of the little town, perhaps giving it a false beauty, a beauty that would, nevertheless, sparkle in the memory. The rowboats came up to us and we leaned over the rails and watched.

First came a fussy little Customs boat, flying the Turkish flag, and a man jumped out and ran with remarkable agility up the ladder of our boat. Other rowboats either carried more passengers for us or had come to collect passengers wishing to disembark. Many of the little craft sold bread, olives, hard-boiled eggs, and cream cheese. Their shouts mingled with the talk and the laughter of the passengers and struck gayety from that still summer sea that lay as quiet as glass. Far away, on the shore, we could hear the morning noises of İnebolu.

Some of the passengers let down large handkerchiefs on strings and bought foodstuffs from the boats. The seller would make a deft package of the handkerchief, the passenger hauling it up, and money would be flung to the grinning boatman. Sometimes arguments would arise, the hoarse bellowing voice of the boatman swearing by Allah that the price he asked was under the price he himself had paid.

We left İnebolu to the cries of the vendors and the ribald songs of the boatmen. Gradually the voices grew fainter and our view of pretty İnebolu dimmer, until after a while it was just a green blur many miles behind us. Because we had not been ashore we grew sentimental about the town and wondered what romantic things lay concealed behind the pink and white façades of the houses, the formal green pattern of trees.

Now the scenery was sheer beauty. For a long time after İnebolu, we hugged the shore line, the big mountains of Anatolia smiling and frowning upon us according to the changing position of the sun. The mountains, which were covered with thick foliage, are the natural fortresses of Anatolia against her Black Sea neighbors.

Sometimes we saw a tiny shore village, a huddle of small mud houses only, and we wondered how it was possible to live so remote from civilization of any kind. Sometimes a village clung to the rocky slopes of the mountains, and then we tried to imagine the rough, primitive life of the inhabitants. Presently the shore line curved away from us, the following, crying sea gulls left us, and we were out in the open sea again.

That night the sea was rough and cold, and many of us were sick. The journey through the dark became a nightmare, with the hiss of the foaming water in our wake and torrents of rain driving those of us on deck to seek shelter.

When we arrived at Samsun the rain had ceased, but the weather was still cold, the gray, angry sea still choppy under a leaden sky.

Samsun is a big city, the most important Turkish city on the Black Sea coast, and it reminded me in a vague sort of way of Kadıköy, on the Asiatic side of İstanbul. Again our boat stopped a mile or so off shore, and motorboats chugged and battled across the huge waves; but they could not reach us, and our captain roared through a megaphone, telling them to go back until the sea was calmer.

. Five hours we waited, cold and sick and longing for the nightmare journey to end. Finally the motorboats were able to reach us, and they rocked like toys in the grip of the breakers, which now and then threatened to submerge them entirely.

I was one of the first down the swaying, greasy ladder, jumping dizzily into the motorboat to await the others. The waves tossed us furiously up and down; the horizon reeled and wavered, and was sometimes lost from sight altogether. I was sick continuously, and that night I slept like a log in the narrow bed in the Samsun military hospital.

The next morning we left for Tokat and the end of our journey. Busses appeared and we piled in, starting off with a great roar and a cloud of dust. We rushed at a terrifying pace out of the city, the busses swaying and the drivers leaning over the wheels like fanatics in a team of racing cars.

In the early afternoon we came to a small village, halting at the communal pump to wash the dust off our faces and to drink avidly of the bitter-tasting water.

We sat down to eat the bread and cheese the hospital authorities had given us that morning. The mongrel curs of the village sniffed at us curiously, and the shy wild children came to stare, their fingers in their mouths, ready to fly from our slightest movement.

On again we went, refreshed after our food and the rest, and once again ready to brave the perils of the eccentric bus. For hours we ran by the banks of a cool brown river, the fir forests climbing steeply up on either side of us. Occasionally we met a cowherd leading his cows to his village. Dour and dark-skinned, with sullen eyes, he would look curiously at us, and the cows would bellow fearfully at the frightful apparition of the snorting bus.

Evening fell, tender and green, and presently the moon rose behind the hills, climbing steadily up the sky, high and silvery and remote. Shadows stole out on the blanched roads and the fir forests were bathed in radiance. We arrived at Amasya, an old, historic city famous for its luscious apples that have a smell like no other apples in all the world and are red and shining and delicate to the taste. The apple orchards commenced about an hour before we reached the city itself, and the moon shone tenderly on the young curled petals of the blossom. We might have been on an enchanted road, so fairylike it was, so unreal with the never ending foam of pink beauty. We reached the big rock fortress of Amasya; the slender charm of minarets came into view; and we halted by the wooden bridge on the Yeşil Irmak, a river that flows through the center of the city. Once again we went to the military hospital, where we were fed and given beds for the night. Our number, however, very seriously disorganized their resources and almost had the same effect upon their hospitality.

We left Amasya the following morning, the apple orchards continuing to flank the road for some time. When they abruptly ended, we were in a wilderness of dusty road again, with flat, uninteresting, desolate meadows on either side of us. "Tokat soon," shouted our driver encouragingly, and I, who was nearest to the door, leaned out and saw the gray stone of a fortress appearing over the tops of some trees. Over a bridge that forded a shallow river we ran, and now houses began to appear, little houses set in wild gardens. The road had narrowed and the dust rose from it like a cloud, invading the bus and covering us with a film of white. We turned into the main street, a few straggling houses marking its beginning; some small shops also came into view, and children and dogs strayed in the street. Our Klaxon made a great noise as we tore past, with no regard for life, human or otherwise, and the dogs yelped in terror. On to a newly built stone road we ran, and ahead of us loomed a big dark huddle of buildings on a hill. It was the military school: we had reached our journey's end at last. We sighed at the unrelieved bleakness and thought of Kuleli fronting the Bosporus.

20

Return to İstanbul

I HATED MY FIFTEEN MONTHS IN TOKAT. I had stifled under a sense of frustration and had missed the sight and sound of the sea from Kuleli's wide windows. I had fretted in the stony, bleak mountains of Tokat, many a time longing for the bustle and splendor and squalid romance of old İstanbul, the splash of shadow caused by a sudden, unexpected tree in a lonely corner of the city. I had hated the dust and bareness of Tokat; I had missed the green of trees and the cool sweet look of grass; I had starved for all these things, yet I never fully realized it until that morning when we were told we were being sent back to Kuleli again, three months sooner than anticipated.

The same old weary busses came to take us to Samsun, where we would board the boat for home; but twenty miles or so before we reached the city, they broke down, one after the other, and we had no alternative but to walk the distance to Samsun.

We started off well enough through the clear night and walked swiftly at first, then slower and slower as the night wore by. Before many miles had been covered, we were footsore and weary and our throats ached with thirst. We became almost stupid with tiredness and began to see the vague shapes of houses or mosques before us—rather like the sort of mirage a traveler may see in the desert.

The vague, indistinct shapes were always a little ahead of us, but we could never catch up with them. Sometimes they disappeared altogether as we marched along, sleeping as we marched; and all our uneasy dreams were colored by the sight of brown tumbling rivers, and we could clearly hear the sound of their soft rushing waters. Our parched mouths burned like fire, and we leaned against each other dazedly, trying to snatch sleep, not even knowing whether we were walking in the right direction or not.

Sometimes one of us would shout "Samsun! Samsun!" Our tired eyelids would part; and because of the intensity of our desires, for a moment we would indeed see the morning silhouette of Samsun lying before us—though it was still night. But the illusion would fade, and the lights we thought we had seen became the lights of the hot, glittering stars.

Once we passed the first of the derelict busses lying at the side of the road. Shouting to the sleeping driver, we asked where the rest of the students were; he told us drowsily that, like us, they were walking to Samsun. We envied them the start they had had.

"How much farther?" we asked, and the driver replied that it was another ten miles. Our spirits and bodies groaned as we thought of the hard stretch of road that still lay before us and of the boat that would take us to İstanbul. We wondered how we would ever have the strength to reach that waiting boat in time.

"Water?" we asked him. "Do you know where we can find water?"

And the driver, already half-asleep again, told us that a little stream ran from the mountains, just a short way down the road in front of us. And the coolness and the freshness of his words made us mad to find it. On we went, looking everywhere for the little stream that ran from the mountains, torturing ourselves with thoughts of the sweet sound it would make in our ears, of the coldness of the water against our lips. But we never found the little stream: either the driver had lied or our stupid, sleep-laden bodies had missed it. We wept on each other's shoulders for the little stream that we had lost, saying that if we could get a drink of water we should be all right. We said we could walk to İstanbul—if we had only a drop of water.

By dawn we had reached the suburbs of Samsun. We went into the gardens of a cool gray mosque, where water gushed from a fountain. We were gasping with thirst, and our swollen tongues had made a little hillock in our mouths. I flung myself on the fountain, and the icy water trickled into my mouth and over my face and hair. I felt faint with relief. We drank until we could drink no more, until the water ran down our chins and we were tired of it.

On we stumbled to Samsun, this time complaining that our feet hurt, for we had had no time to notice the aching of our feet while the greater need for water held us.

Kuleli lay coolly under the painted sky, and many students stood on the steps; but we were too far away to see them clearly, for our boat swung a course in the middle of the Bosporus. Long-distance boats did not stop at so insignificant a boat station as Çengelköy; therefore it was necessary for us to go to the Galata docks again in order to board another, smaller boat to take us back to Kuleli.

It was good to see old friends, to see Mehmet waiting to greet me —a tall brown Mehmet suddenly grown good-looking.

We went home together, and I was very excited as we walked toward Bayazit. Landmarks stood out all the more clearly because I had been absent for more than a year.

After the bare aridity of Tokat, the trees of İstanbul looked greener than they ever had before. The colorful flowers in the quiet old gardens made a splash of cool beauty.

The little house behind whose crumbling walls my family sheltered looked smaller than ever and more dingy than I had remembered, but the windows stood wide to the summer air and the soft sound of singing floated out to us. We looked at each other, Mehmet and I, and smiled in that rare moment of understanding, for it was my mother's voice that sang for us that morning. Peeping in through the downstairs window, we saw her at her eternal tracing of designs, her figure bent over the sloping board, her face tranquil, as though some intricate piece of work had come right for her. She was unaware of us, for we peeped slyly, wanting to surprise her. Then Mehmet pulled the old-fashioned bell rope, and the creaking, heavy footsteps of my grandmother were heard on the stairs.

She opened the door a fraction, a milk pot in her hands, not immediately comprehending that two tall grandsons awaited entry.

"I thought it was the sütcü," she grumbled to Mehmet; then her glance fell on me, standing there beside him. Awareness leaped into her old eyes, the milk pot went rattling to the floor, and she held out her arms to me.

She called my name in a happy shout that shook the street and the foundations of the old house; it brought my mother from the workroom, joy and disbelief struggling for supremacy in her face.

They folded me to them, those two, and the familiar childhood smell of eau de Cologne tickled my nostrils. It was then that I really knew that I was home again.

While they extravagantly praised my looks and my height, in the way families do, I noticed little things I should not have noticed a year ago. I saw that now my mother's black hair no longer curled, but hung lankly, heavily streaked with gray. I noticed the dull look in her eyes and that they now and then slid away disconcertingly from the person to whom she was talking. It was as though only part of her were aware of the things going on about her. For the first time in my life, perhaps, I wondered what her life had been in all the years we had been away from her. I wondered if she had forgotten the quiet young man who had been my father and the gay, pretty young woman that she herself had been in my childhood, with her fashionable silk dresses. I thought of the young wife who had sat in my grandmother's salon and sipped coffee with the neighbors, never raising her voice above a whisper, never putting forward an opinion for fear she should be frowned upon. I looked at the changed face and wondered about her. The fastidious

young woman she had been would never have permitted her hair
to lose its luster, its springy curl, or her figure to thicken—no matter
how faintly perceptible.

I suppose the years of grinding poverty had taken their toll.
Though money no longer appeared to be a problem, yet she looked
as if she dared not sit back, dared not relax, lest poverty come leaping back through the window again.

She looked tired and worn that summer morning, despite the
seeming tranquillity of her face and the smile that had momentarily
lightened her eyes when first she saw us. Her smiles were so brief
that I could not help wondering whether half the time she were
aware of her children or not.

I looked back down the years to the day she had heard of my
father's death. I remembered the night our house burned, the fever
that had held her captive for weeks, and I thought that had she not
had my grandmother with her through those weary days she could
not have kept her sanity. My grandmother was so essentially sane
that her mere presence was a sort of staff for my mother to rest
upon.

Few of us know the dreams or the longings of those nearest us;
and on that long-ago morning when Mehmet and I stood together
in the little house that has now gone, taking our secrets with it, I
was unaware of the dark menace the future held.

Muazzez, with her long legs, was on holiday too, her thirteen-
year-old self as delicious, as refreshing as iced water on a hot day.
She brought a note of youthful innocence into the house and
seemed very close to my grandmother.

One day when the sunlight poured into the salon and the piled-
up flowers were touched to brief glory, my mother, looking unexpectedly like a young girl again, confessed to her longing to
possess a garden once more. I wished then that I could satisfy that
longing, that I had finished with schooling and the indignity of
having to accept pocket money from her.

On May 29th, 1929, I said goodbye to Kuleli and the bits of my
life that would live there for ever. There was a rousing send-off from

the boat station for us lucky ones; but I think we were all of us
reluctant to say goodbye, regretful that we were not to sleep again
under its tall roof.

The boat was gaily decorated with flags, and as we sailed down
the Bosporus I leaned over the rail, taking my last long look at
Kuleli, which still seemed as beautiful to me as it had that first long-
ago morning in 1919, when I had gone there for the first time and
the cross old porter had directed my mother to the inferior gray
school on the hill. The Military College band and a unit of the
college students were at Galata Bridge to greet us. We marched
proudly with them through the İstanbul streets.

The watching crowds cheered and cheered until they were
hoarse, and the stirring martial music of the band held triumph
and victory, as well as the heartache of all marching soldiers.

On, on with the band we marched, our shoulders squared in
military fashion, our dark-blue-trousered legs one unbroken line.
Past Beyoğlu we went, and all the shopkeepers stood in their doors
to watch us. We marched to Taksim Square, and then the great
yellow building of the Military College came into view, with its
back to the Bosporus, its close high trees shading the gardens with
their stiff pale flowers in formal patterns. On the other side of the
Bosporus lay Kuleli, but it could not be seen from Harbiye, however hard one looked, for it was too far down the Bosporus and
hidden by an elbow of land. But we who had so recently left it
knew that it was there, that it would always be there, shining bravely
to the skies, throwing its white reflection on the blue waters.

Up the wide steps of Harbiye we marched, feeling raw and new
in this alien atmosphere, and the crowds in the street sent up their
cheers and their blessings to us. Soldiers guarded the doors, but we
passed through, for we belonged here now. We went into a marble
hall where marble corridors ran to right and to left; let into the walls
were plaques to commemorate the officers of Harbiye who had died
in the war of 1914–1918.

Before us stood a door that opened on wide green lawns at the
bottom of which glimmered the eternal Bosporus. Great intricacies
of electric globes lined the high ceilings, and I was awed by the

splendor and majesty of Harbiye, proud to belong to this ancient place. For here I walked hand in hand with history, where many more famous than I had walked, where Kemal Atatürk had once walked long ago.

The band had ceased playing; there was silence in the cool white hall; and we newcomers stood awkwardly, ill at ease, longing for Time to merge our separate identities into the one great identity that was Harbiye.

Sixteen cadets, myself included, were to be sent to train for six months in an infantry regiment. We went to Mudanya, four hours' journey down the Marmara from İstanbul. When we arrived there, the commanding officer—quite a different type, incidentally, from any we had ever met in the military establishments—divided us into various units.

The officers treated us like dogs and the soldiers treated us like dogs, for this was the only opportunity to do so the soldiers would ever get in their lives.

We used to sleep in a large tent, the roof of which had hundreds of holes in it. At night, when we lay down, we could see the stars peeping through the holes; and sometimes mulberries used to drop from the trees on our sleeping faces, so that one would come awake with a tiny shock of surprise to find an overripe, succulent mulberry just rolling off one's nose.

Our uniforms soon lost their crisp, conceited look, and I never remember coming back to the garrison from training with a dry jacket. Mud and rain and perspiration all combined to give our uniforms a greenish, indeterminate hue, so that we sixteen cadets soon began to look like well seasoned soldiers.

There was a young lieutenant who used to give us physical training. He would walk up and down, up and down the field, toying with a whistle in his hand, his face sharp with the tortures he was thinking up for us. Suddenly he would blow smartly on the whistle and we would jump to attention.

"Lie down," he would say. Obediently, like dogs, we would lie down.

"Get up," he would snarl, and we would scramble to our feet with more alacrity than dignity. We had no time for dignity.

"Again!" he would command. "Get up quicker the next time, you lazy young swine."

Thirty minutes of it: up, down, up, down. Fling yourself on the stony ground; drag yourself erect again. Pant for breath and feel your jacket dampening with perspiration; pick the jagged stones from your bleeding, lily-white hands. Listen for the whistle that will reprieve you for less time than it takes to tell; pause for the breath that comes painfully, chokingly. Wait for a change of command. Run! Lie down! Get up! Run! Lie down! Get up! On, on cowardly body! Shake off the betraying puppy fat and grow as slim as the sardonic young lieutenant who is enjoying your misery, who is taking it out of you all the time because he is young enough to remember his own despair.

Hours and hours of training every day for months, until our abraded knees through our torn trousers became immune, until our ladylike hands were tough and brown and insensitive and our waists were clipped in to imitate the young lieutenant who had become our model.

Then we went to Bursa area for the biggest maneuver the new Republic had ever staged, where the reserve officers had already poured in and we would really see field action. March, march, march; on under the blinding sun and over the hot roads that scorch your feet. Never mind if your ill fitting boots hurt you. This is the Army. This is the life.

We marched those days until we were ready to drop, and the forty-year-old reservists felt it worse than we did. Sometimes we slept in the fields and were not aware of the heavy rain that soaked us, that ran into the tents and turned the heavy ground to mud. We would wake in the mornings stiff and aching, with our jackets wet through; but the sun would presently come up again to dry us and burn us and parch us with thirst. And we marched all the time. Sometimes we walked through the long chilly nights, leaning against each other and sleeping, or against the necks of our mules, and even the mules would plod wearily too. Many times we started to march before dawn, our clothes chill with dew, our limbs stiff and heavy, not belonging to us any more. We would march on through the new day and continue beneath the torrid sun of afternoon. Soldiers would start to fall out, and down the lines of weary men would pass the never ending cry: "Sick soldier fallen out. Sick soldier fallen out."

When we came up with the sick soldier—or perhaps there would be more than one—he would be lying on his side, too exhausted to care if he never lived again. Perhaps some of them would have their boots off their torn and bleeding feet, which looked frightful under the glare of the sun, with the flies already gathering to feast. Then I would remember the stories I had heard of my father and imagine him in that soldier's uniform, waiting patiently for the sick-cart that might never have come, for that was war and this was only a maneuver.

May 1st, 1931, dawned quite differently from any other day, for that day I became an officer, school life lying forever behind me.

On that proud morning I was handed a smart new uniform, a clanking sword, and white gloves, and my shoes shone like mirrors. I tilted my cap to an angle and thought that there was nobody like me in all the world.

After a ceremony at Taksim Square, we went back to Harbiye and were handed our diplomas, the commanding officer wishing us the customary good luck and telling us we were on leave until our postings came through.

The rest of that day seemed to be filled with the dashing sight of the new officers strutting a trifle self-consciously through the corridors and the wide gardens of the college. We were all awaiting the arrival of our families to take us home, for none of us, as usual, had any money. Taxis constantly arrived to depart again with a very important-looking new lieutenant seated in the center of his admiring family, like a precious jewel in a casket. As the afternoon wore on, I became fearful that nobody would come for me. Awful visions of sudden deaths or taxi crashes began to obsess me.

I remember that I felt the one kuruş in my pocket and started to laugh at myself—the new young officer, with but one kuruş to his name.

I drew it out and looked at it; then I placed it in my sword, where it still rests to this day, a souvenir of that time.

Up and down I walked impatiently, and sometimes, no doubt, I stared at myself in the mirrors and thought what a very fine fellow I was to be sure. I thrust out my chest, squared my shoulders under the new khaki jacket, and then slowly, pompously, strolled out to the garden, my head in the clouds, already a general. My sword clanked rudely against the stone steps; I heard the one kuruş rattling, and I came out of my daydream.

At last a taxi arrived for me with a giggling, excited Muazzez within, and we set off for home with a great fanfare from the Klaxon.

At home I was surrounded by excitement and congratulations, for half the street had crowded into the little rooms and old friends had arrived. Strange old women kept kissing me, and senile men I had never seen in my life before kept crying over me, telling me they had known my father. Drinks were distributed, but through all the ·merriment I noticed my mother's proud cold face, keeping its secrets; yet I, who knew her, knew that she was happy, for a red rose was tucked into her hair and her eyes smiled each time she looked at me.

Pretty Muazzez was there in a brief blue dress, seeming to be eternally handing bonbons on a silver dish. My grandmother wore black, her diamonds flashing scintillatingly, brought from their resting place for this occasion. Her high old voice talked arrogantly, praising, always praising. . . . I saw the widow, fatter now than the day I had first seen her as a child, and I caught her worn hand and held it tightly, for she was shy of approaching me in all my splendor. My head grew giddy and light as air with all the liqueurs I had consumed, so that I laughed without reason and flirted with all the pretty girls.

Mehmet arrived from Kuleli with the news that he had passed the examinations into Harbiye. The laughter and the excitement grew more intense, the kissing more indiscriminate, and all the time the tray of liqueurs circulated nonstop. My head was dizzy, but what of that? Float, stupid wooden head, and care nothing for tomorrow. It is not often an officer comes out of famous Harbiye!

I loosened my jacket and sought fresh air, turning my back on the chattering, merry crowd. I looked at the stars in the sky, remembering that Kuleli was lying under these stars, and I heard the faint sigh of the Bosporus as it lapped the shores where none walked by night. They broke into my dreaming and called me back to the merry throng, for the neighbors were departing and they wanted, once more, to wish me good luck.

"Long life to you, my friends!" I said, and tossed off yet another fiery, sickly liqueur.

21

*My Batman Averts a Crisis and
Muazzez Finds a Beau*

IN DECEMBER, 1931, I TRANSFERRED FROM an infantry regiment to the Air Force, since volunteers had been asked for. I left Istanbul on January 20th, 1932, for two years' training at the Air College in Eskişehir.

After a short time I decided to bring my family to Eskişehir, for the small, improvised Officers' Club on the banks of the river Porsuk was far too expensive for a very junior officer to patronize for very long.

My batman was sent to look for a house, and after a week of searching he told me he had discovered an empty one on the newly built station road. He said it was a "good" house. By that he meant "new," for to him the two were synonymous.

"Is there water in the house?" I demanded, and he replied enthusiastically that indeed there was water—lovely boiling water that spouted from a natural geyser in the back garden.

"And what about cold water, drinking water?" I wanted to know.

He looked shocked that I did not know there was no drinking water in Eskişehir and said pointedly that we should have to do the same as everyone else—that is, fill vessels with the boiling water and leave it to grow cold. I was very dubious as to my mother's reactions to such an arrangement; but since there was no alternative, I accordingly went with my batman to view this remarkable house that could not provide cold water but gave us as much hot water as we required. It turned out to be a newish villa, looking extremely small in the very large garden surrounding it. When we rang the doorbell, a thin, wispy little woman opened the door, wiping her hands hurriedly on her apron when she saw the magnificent sight of an Air Force uniform confronting her.

I explained that I understood that the house was to be let, and she said that this was so, offering to show me it.

I was quite incapable of knowing what things my mother and grandmother would look for in a house, but I manfully plunged through the small rooms, foreseeing storms over the accommodations for our cumbersome furniture. There seemed to be many unnecessary cupboards, but knowing the contrary ways of women, I could not be sure that even this would not please my womenfolk. There was no bath at all—the woman looked surprised that I should want such a thing—and the toilet was so small that the customary fittings, together with the bidet, left barely room to close the door behind one.

In the garden spouted the famous geyser. I was just on the point of asking what happened in the sudden event of one requiring cold water, when my eye lit on what looked undoubtedly like a pump. I turned accusingly to my batman and he grinned sheepishly, saying that he had not noticed this on his first visit. The wispy little woman explained proudly that from this pump came ice-cold water the year round, but that it was not for drinking purposes. At this my batman's face lit up triumphantly, with an "I-told-you-so" expression. But it fell again several centimeters when she explained that a man called once a week with fresh water for drinking. This, she said, could be stored in an earthenware *küp*, a sort of barrel with a covered top and a tap.

I was delighted to hear that civilization had not entirely by-passed the city, and afterward told my batman that he was a blockhead. I arranged to rent the house, and the batman was sent to find people to redecorate it for me. A few days later I discovered him lording it over two bearded, wild-looking painters who slashed the paint on with a reckless disregard for where it might eventually land. He was directing and instructing them in a very knowing way, lounging grandly beside them, but when he saw me he deflated like a pricked balloon. From then on I took care to keep out of his way, entirely leaving the workmen in his hands. Heaven knew he had little enough chance in his military life to feel important.

The day arrived for the great move. The furniture had already come from İstanbul, and a lorry from the airdrome deposited it at the house.

Next came my mother, my grandmother, and Muazzez, carrying many hampers and parcels and looking overdressed for their new place of residence. My batman and I proudly showed them the house. Their faces remained unitedly detached, as though they had already planned to make all the difficulties they could. In an effort to arouse their enthusiasm, I eagerly pointed out the obvious advantages of our unique hot-and-cold-water system. It failed to impress them. Then when they saw the way we had haphazardly arranged their precious furniture, they ran clucking around, like three distraught hens, examining everything for scratches or other damage. When they had finished, they firmly declared their intention of returning by the next train to İstanbul.

"But you can't!" I appealed frantically, darting the most furious glances at my open-mouthed, gaping batman, who had never bargained for three obstinate women with whom to deal.

Do something you great dolt! I implored him silently. He correctly interpreted my distress signals and put himself forward to quiet the three disillusioned ladies. He told my grandmother that he would arrange all her furniture wherever she wished, guessing that this would be the best line of approach with her. To my mother he explained that the house was beautifully clean, that he himself had seen to this. He was completely carried away by the signs of mollification in the faces before him and recklessly promised to do everything they wished. I could see that he was fast getting my mother on his side—which in the circumstances was just as well, since he would be more often under her orders than he would mine.

My grandmother planted herself firmly on a packing case and remarked that she had never expected one day to find herself living in a hen coop. This inspired the batman to say that we could keep hens in the back garden, and he quite dazzled my town-bred mother with the number of eggs we should be able to produce. Enthusiastically he said he would build a chicken run for her—not even looking in my direction for permission. It was painfully obvious that already he knew which was the safest side to be on. He then told my grandmother that he would find for her the best washerwoman in all Eskişehir, and that he himself would guard her like a child.

My grandmother cheered up somewhat at this, her face implying that she and the batman would get on very well together after all. I left them to it and hurried back to the Air College, breathing with relief, for it looked as if they might settle down after all.

Life was far pleasanter with my family in Eskişehir. My life became regularized, and sometimes I would invite friends to dine with me or to play poker. And always on these occasions the women would vacate the salon, leaving it for us, for my grandmother still felt that it was not seemly for the ladies of the house to remain in the same room as the gentlemen. This was especially the case where Muazzez was concerned, and my grandmother would whip her off swiftly, for fear the eyes of the men would alight on her. Poor Muazzez never dared to protest; but years later she told me that had it been left to us to acquire a husband for her she would have remained single all her days, since we all seemed to combine to shut her off from masculine company.

During the same year, though, she acquired a beau.

There was a young officer who lived almost next door to us, and he had an elder brother who was in the Foreign Office in Ankara. This brother was what is known as a smart young man about town, invariably to be seen in striped trousers and impeccable morning coat. He took to visiting his brother in Eskişehir with such great

regularity that even I, not always observant, became suspiciously
aware of his pompous figure walking the streets frequently. The
mother of this elegant young man developed a rapid friendship with
my mother, and the result was that the gentleman from Ankara
proposed marriage to my gratified sister. He professed, so I gathered,
undying love for her and waived all notion of a large dowry. In fact
he went further. He declared with great passion and feeling that he
required no dowry at all, that my sister was sufficient dowry in herself. This attitude delighted me, but my mother was shocked by
such callowness on my part and said that her daughter could not be
allowed to go penniless to such a proper, such an upright young
man. She was quite firm on this point, and I gloomily had to prepare myself to spend much money. I had no great affection for the
prospective bridegroom, but Muazzez and my mother insisted that
he was very good-looking and a model of propriety. My sister was
determined to marry him, flooding the house with tears if one so
much as criticized him.

A trousseau was bought and we clad her in bridal white with
trailing flowers. My grandmother parted with her long-treasured
jewels, and my sister was married with great ceremony to the dapper
young intruder from Ankara.

Muazzez shone brightly that day, and a big reception was given—
for which I had to pay. This did nothing to improve my general out-
look upon the alliance. The loving looks frequently exchanged
between the newly-wed pair began to fill me with boredom; and
when playful, frolicsome ladies coyly suggested that it would be my
turn next, I fled from them. I was able to return to normal, however,
after the party was over and the bridal pair had departed for Ankara.
There they still live to this day, in great state and elegance, as befits
their nobility. And either the years have mellowed me or Ali has
lost some of his unreal suavity, for nowadays, on the rare occasions
when we meet, we find much in common. Muazzez has retained her
wearable beauty, but her figure has prodigiously thickened and
sophistication has overlaid the earlier charm of her girlhood
years.

The excitement of the wedding over, the house seemed strangely quiet. After a time my mother started to complain that she disliked the house and its prominent position on the station road.

I found another house on the south side of the city, on the crest of a hill, and I transferred my family there. For a long time my mother had been uneasy in the other house, for the funerals of Air Force victims who had crashed wound their way past—sometimes as many as two in a week. She had always lived with the fear that one day I too would be carried past her windows.

Then, too, in summer, the dust was choking. Even with the windows tightly sealed, the dust would seep in, getting into food and between the sheets on the beds, leaving its fine white mark everywhere. But up on the hill there was no dust and no sound of the Funeral March, and I hoped that in time my mother would lose this morbid dread she had of my crashing.

On the hill, too, it was cooler, and in the evenings one could sit on the old wooden vine-clad balcony and look down to Eskişehir, lying below amid hazy dust clouds, the heat, and the flies.

22

Feminine Affairs

UP ON THE HILL, ALONGSIDE OUR HOUSE, lived the regimental paymaster, who soon became very friendly with my mother. They both loved everything to do with food and spent a great deal of their time exchanging recipes or sending succulent dishes to each other, all of which my grandmother viewed with the gravest suspicion.

He was a strange person, living an eccentric, lonely life in his big house on the hill, with only his batman to look after him. He did all his cooking himself, devoting hours to it. Sometimes I would drop in on a winter's evening to find several stray guests lounging in the salon, officers, perhaps, merely passing through Eskişehir and wanting a bed for the night. Because he was noted for keeping open house, they naturally and automatically made for his home. More often than not he would himself be in the kitchen, a large apron enveloping him and his shortsighted eyes peering anxiously into whatever savory dishes he was concocting by way of surprise for his guests. Sometimes he would let me stay in the kitchen; but at other times he would send me away from him, telling me that tonight's dish was a secret, that I must not see what he was doing, since I might tell my mother and he did not want her stealing his recipes before he was ready to part with them.

I would go up the stairs to the salon to stretch unmolested on a divan until a shout from below would tell me that the meal was ready.

There was a very ornate, rococo dining room opening off the salon, and he would have dinner served there when he wanted to show off; but dinner in the tasteless dining room was a somber affair, for he would not let us forget our politeness, chiding us severely if a drop of wine was spilled over his elaborate tablecloth, losing his familiar identity as our contemporary, becoming the paymaster, a senior officer. We liked it best when he allowed us to eat in the unrefined atmosphere of the kitchen. Perhaps half a dozen of us would squat ungracefully over the huge open fire while he slowly roasted a whole lamb, cutting strips for us as they cooked. His batman would place glasses and raki on the bare wooden table, and oil lamps would glow kindly, for there was no electricity in the kitchen. The lamb finished, he would produce stuffed tomatoes or some such delicacy. Occasionally there would be freshly grilled fish, and then he would furiously exhort us to eat it immediately and not to wait for each other, for grilled foods should be eaten directly they are cooked.

We would stuff ourselves to repletion, glad for once of the lack of women to curtail our gossip and our purely masculine jokes. When we could eat no more, we would stagger up to the salon, throwing ourselves inelegantly on divans and loosening our belts. Our host would turn on the lights in the domed ceiling and draw the curtains against the night, feeding more logs to the already bright fire in the china stove. Presently the batman would appear with Turkish coffee to take the taste of grease from our mouths and with a choice of cigarettes for the smokers. One of us would start up an old Turkish song, and soon everyone would join in, well content with the world in that coarse atmosphere of unashamed belchings and loosened trousers. Disreputable and unglamorous we might be tonight, but the girls of Eskişehir would not know that tomorrow, when they met us strutting through the city streets.

Muazzez arrived on a visit, her husband having been sent to Rome on duty. The house suddenly became like a private hospital, with my mother in bed with one of her innumerable headaches and my sister, looking for sympathy, complaining of pains in the most unlikely places.

My grandmother and my batman ran the ménage—one as autocratic as the other—both of them driving the hired servant into constant outbreaks of semihysteria. Once, long ago, a far-away Hacer had had to put up with similar treatment.

One morning a doctor was called to the house and I was telephoned at the airdrome, the doctor testily telling me that both patients were to go to the hospital. Muazzez, he said, needed an immediate operation. My mother, he said, was a very obstinate woman indeed. She had refused to listen to any suggestion of hospitals. He ended by telling me that, furthermore, all her teeth needed to be removed.

When I arrived home, there was bedlam in the house, with my sister having the most terrible premonitions of her death and begging my grandmother to look after her baby for her. My mother was sitting up in her bed crying and declaring that never, never would she go into a hospital, nor would her teeth be removed either. This was the direst blow to her, that her strong, white, even teeth should be removed. We managed to calm her, telling her that they would probably never have to come out, anyway. Muazzez was our most immediate problem, and we had her rushed to a hospital, where she was operated upon with outstanding success, recovering with remarkable speed. She returned to my home for convalescence, cried constantly for her husband and her child, and wrote reams of letters daily to all her friends, recounting the most horrific details of her operation.

Dislike sprang up between us.

It was she who eventually persuaded my mother to have her teeth removed. When in the course of time my mother received her new ones, my grandmother examined them with great suspicion, then handed them back, saying piously that thank God *she* did not have to wear them.

This caused my mother to cry and declare that she would rather be dead than put such monstrous things in her mouth. Maliciously, my grandmother encouraged this attitude. But one evening I lost my temper to such an extent that my mother nervously promised to do whatever she had to do with the confounded teeth if only I would quiet down before the neighbors came in to investigate a possible murder.

Not very long after this I was walking home one sunny afternoon from the airdrome when I saw two fighter planes taking off from the field. They were flying very close to each other, and I stood and watched them for a few moments, mentally criticizing them. They commenced to attack each other in mock battle, flying under and over each other—and they flew just that much too close. I walked on toward the town, remembering the crazy things we had done, too, when we had first become pilots. When I reached the center of the city, I became aware that the sound of the engines above me had ceased, and I turned my face skyward. Hundreds of pieces of plane were hurtling down.

I turned about and hurried toward home, suddenly sure that my mother had witnessed or heard of the accident, and I wanted desperately to reassure her that I was all right.

The streets had become crowded with people, with the wives and the children and the mothers of airmen. Their faces were white and frightened-looking, all of them wondering if it were their turn to become widows, orphans, or the mothers of the dead.

An ambulance tore by, clanging with feverish urgency, and I had a fleeting thought that if the one pilot who had jumped by parachute were not already dead, he most certainly would be by the time that jolting ambulance had got him to hospital over these uneven roads.

The pale, trembling wives and mothers rushed on me like an army of mad things, begging me to tell them the names of the pilots who had crashed. When I replied that I did not know, they held tightly to me, crying into my face that I *did* know, that I *must* know who was on duty. Still I said I did not know, and they wailed that I would not tell them, beating my arms with their soft, impotent fists, begging the one question over and over again.

"Please!" they said. "Please, Lieutenant, tell us the names. Please, please, please . . ."

I tore myself out of their grasp, and their tormented cries pierced my ears all the way down the crowded street.

Suddenly I saw my mother running on bare feet, and for an incredible, unbelievable moment, I was a child again, our house was burning, and I saw her running thus down the desolate garden on her bare feet.

She was only partially dressed, having run out in the middle of changing, and my batman was running after her with a cloak in his hand. I was numbed with shock and felt coldness creep all over my body. When she saw me, she stood still. The batman caught up with her and threw the protective cloak over her bare white shoulders.

I cannot forget her eyes, those wandering eyes that told their own story, only we were still too blind to read their message correctly, though fear stirred somewhere, warning. . . .

We none of us knew then that the madness would one day leap out at us, when all the repressed thoughts and memories of a quarter of a century would darken the overtired brain, dim the bright, mournful eyes.

"Take that uniform off," she said to me, her voice so low and hoarse that involuntarily I backed away from her. "You will send me to my death!" she said. "You will make me lose my mind!"

Her voice died away in a great strangled sob, and she half collapsed into my batman's arms.

He picked her up as if she were a baby, carrying her home through the oblivious streets, and I walked beside him. My mind was numb and cold and drained of all thought. I could only see before me, imprinted forever on the summer air, the gentle madness that had looked out of her eyes.

23

The Wise Woman of Eskişehir

I SUPPOSE THE MEMORY OF THAT DAY NEVER quite left me. Sometimes I would wake up in the middle of the night, bathed in sweat, tormenting myself with the reminder of my mother's eyes that tragic afternoon. She steadily declined—at least physically. She lost weight to such an extent that a doctor commenced giving her injections to fatten her. He said she was anaemic, recommending red wine, so we bought her a bottle a day and thrust it upon her. He recommended red meat too, so we also forced that on her, but still she did not appear to improve.

I began watching for signs of mental illness and almost gave myself a nervous breakdown in consequence. Was it my uneasy imagination or did she seem ever so slightly neglectful of herself, not caring any more about her appearance, once her main concern? Did I sometimes only feel that one eye drooped just the littlest bit, seemingly half-shut, while the other ranged with every show of normality? Oh, I watched for a thousand signs, and all the while the fear inside of me refused to be stilled.

For days at a time she would be her old self; then, without warning, irritability would break out stormily, moroseness and dissatisfaction cloud her face, and fretfully, like a child, she would complain of headaches.

I took her to a well known nerve specialist who questioned her, set little traps for her, examined her physical health, and then said that there was nothing wrong with her whatever. We came away from his consulting rooms, I conscious of relief that was yet only half-relief. Uneasiness persisted in the face of medical opinion. I could not trust them, but I could not trust my own intuition either. I took her to another specialist with similar results—except that this one ordered a course of injections for her, perhaps so that I should not feel cheated in the face of the large fee asked. I did not know what to do. She *seemed* to be better, and was so pathetically eager to please me, so like a child wanting my approbation, that my heart was wrung with pity.

During the winter of 1937, on a Saturday when I was doing a spell as Duty Officer, my batman telephoned to me in a terrible state and asked me to return home immediately. He said that my mother was ill again and urged me to make haste. He sounded so agitated that I at once asked for permission to leave the airdrome and was even given my senior officer's car to deliver me to my home with all speed.

When I arrived home, there was my mother, sitting up in bed, with a swelling on her neck about the size of an orange. It was a ghastly, horrible thing, a great excrescence of flesh weighing down her neck and face. She was trembling with terror, and I asked my grandmother if anything had been done about it.

"Oh, no," she said, looking surprised. "It came very suddenly, a few hours ago, getting bigger and bigger until we thought it would burst, and then we sent for you!"

"Great God!" I cried, exasperated. "Could you not have immediately sent for a doctor and for me afterward?"

My batman was sent for the doctor and I sat down to wait, unable to hurt my mother by leaving her room yet at the same time unable to look at the great ugly swelling. Within a very short time a doctor arrived, a large bearded fellow, his whole attitude very polished and complete. He examined the neck, prescribed medicine, and directed that my mother should be brought to the hospital on the following Monday.

After he had gone I asked my mother if she was in any pain, but she said No, that it did not hurt at all; that it just felt very heavy and she could not bear to look in a mirror.

There seemed little that I could do, so I left her to return to the airdrome, sternly instructing my careless grandmother to be sure and call a doctor again if anything else seemed likely to go wrong and to telephone me afterward. She meekly agreed that she would, but I felt that her meekness was deceptive.

For the rest of that night I was consumed with worry and by the vagueness of this continued illness that haunted the house. As soon as I was free on the following morning, I rushed home on feet that had to be chided into hurrying, for the message the brain was sending to them was to go slowly lest other, greater troubles be found at home awaiting me.

When I rang the electric bell, which made a star of pattern on the air with its shrill sound, my batman opened the door, a large grin on his moonlike face.

I looked at him inquiringly and he directed my gaze to the garden doors, which opened off the back of the hall in a direct line with the street door. There an amazing sight met my eyes. The mother I had left in bed only the previous evening was calmly watering flowers, her face turned toward the house and the swelling, to all appearances, entirely gone.

I walked quickly out to her and she smiled at me. I caught her two hands in relief; the water hose fell spurting to the ground and the smell of the wet earth came up refreshingly.

"Am I dreaming?" I asked, "Or did you not telephone me yesterday? Did I not come home and find your neck three times its normal size. Did I not get a doctor for you?"

"You are not dreaming," she said happily, her eyes childlike and wide, yet concealing their secrets.

"Well, then!" I said. "What is this? I cannot believe that the medicine cured you so quickly!"

"Oh—the medicine," she said, as though she had forgotten all about it, "No, that did not cure me. In fact, I am afraid that we threw the medicine all away. It was not necessary after all."

"But—" I protested, utterly at a loss, perhaps even thinking a little bit impatiently, These women and their feminine secrets!

"Come," she said, "Let us tell you all about it, my son. You will see: doctors are not always necessary."

I turned to the grinning batman behind me and asked what the devil it all meant; and then I heard a most curious, almost unbelievable story—except that it happened, thereby giving credence to it. But for the fact that there were three witnesses, besides my mother, I should have thought I had been the victim of a hoax.

Now there was in Eskişehir at that time a reputed Wise Woman, an Albanian, as old and wrinkled as a crab apple, and at least one hundred years old. My mother, having been born in Albania of Albanian parents, had a very soft spot for this old woman; and because she lived in appalling poverty, she now and then sent food and other things to her by my batman. Incidentally, they both fondly thought that this was being done behind my back, but in point of fact there was not much that happened in the house without my knowledge—though I did not always make use of that knowledge.

It appeared that after I had gone back to the airdrome the previous evening and the batman had returned with the medicine prescribed by the doctor, a little conference had taken place around my mother's sickbed. My grandmother automatically distrusted all doctors—especially after they had ordered the removal of my mother's teeth and she had, in consequence, nearly bled to death. She eyed and smelled the medicine with great suspicion. The servant made sympathetic noises in her throat to intimate her profoundest suspicions too. The servant then gloomily said that medicine would never cure *that* swelling. This dire prophecy alarmed my already alarmed mother, who was suddenly all for rushing to the nearest hospital to have the offending, painless lumps removed by a surgical operation.

At this the servant snorted and said that that would be useless too, and the conference was temporarily in a state of deadlock. But the servant, resuming authority as the undisputed leader in this affair, slyly reopened negotiations by remarking that in such a case as this the Wise Woman ought to be called in. Seeing no noticeable reaction to this, she followed up by saying that the Wise Woman had already performed a remarkable number of cures in the district, and she pointed out some of them to my mother, who was in no position to argue with her, as many of the cases were already quite well known to her.

The result was that my batman was dispatched to the mud house of the Wise Woman to ask her assistance.

She came to my home with him in a great state of fear, for she half expected that I would return from the airdrome and ruin everything. I might even have her arrested, she confessed to my grandmother.

My grandmother pooh-poohed this idea uneasily, then briskly said a prayer that I would not suddenly take it into my head to come back and bade my batman double-lock all the doors so that in the event of my homecoming I should have to ring the bell, thereby giving them warning. She even thought of a place to conceal the Wise Woman if this happened. When the doors were locked and they felt safe from all outside interference, they set about the serious business of what was to be done with the offending growth on my mother's neck.

The Wise Woman looked at it with one eye half-closed, then heavily pronounced that undoubtedly someone had put the evil eye on my mother. Everyone readily agreed that this indeed might be so, and the servant said with triumph: "There's doctors for you!" or words to that effect.

"Lie back on your pillows," commanded the Wise Woman, having the situation well in hand now that she had so satisfactorily gained the entire confidence of her "patient." She added that my mother would be quite better by the next morning.

She then turned to my batman, that poor, long-suffering soul at the mercy of three determined women, and commanded him to go to the graveyard and bring her back the bone of a dead person.

This terrible, unexpected request almost shook his determined loyalty to my mother, for the thought of scrabbling about in a dark cemetery, with all the white tombstones watching him, made him shiver with fear. His fear of what I might have to say when I heard about it was infinitely more manageable.

Despite his terror he still had sufficient spirit left to argue with the Wise Woman, telling her that he could not be expected to find the bones of any dead people because they were all safely in their coffins, and he absolutely refused to prize any coffins open.

The Wise Woman remained completely unmoved by this state of affairs, saying that she wanted a bone from a dead person and that was all there was to it. She told him, with obvious knowledge, that all he had to do was to go to the old part of the graveyard, where they no longer buried people, and there—just beneath the soft earth—he would be able to find plenty of bones for her. She assured him that she knew there were bones there. Alarmed that if he refused she might turn him into a toad or a frog or something even worse, he set off on his gruesome errand.

His eyes rolled with remembered horror when he told me of the darkness of the night, the tall cypress trees guarding the lonely dead, the sinister sound of the wind in the poplars, the screeching of the owls and their terrible swooping about his head. But he had scrabbled furiously in the earth until at last he had found a bleached, dry human bone. It had been so ghastly looking, so frightful to the touch, and his fevered imagination had been so fearful of ghosts about to lay their clammy fingers on him, that he had perspired until all his clothes were soaked and he had run, terror-stricken, from the cemetery.

Reentering Eskişehir, he had tried to control his shivering, gradually becoming conscious of the odd-shaped, gruesome object in his hands. He had thrust it swiftly into a pocket, where it unpleasantly jabbed his thigh, and sidled past a policeman, anxious only to get home before anything more unpleasant happened to him.

When he arrived home, still in an abject state, instead of receiving thanks that he had gone at all on such an errand, he was severely chided by my grandmother for being so long away. Her whole attitude suggested that had she gone she would have brought back an entire skeleton in that length of time.

The Wise Woman took the bone from him and went out to the

kitchen to cleanse it. She then demanded an egg, which she broke into a bowl, and another bowl, which she filled with cold water. Then she handed the batman a lump of lead, which she instructed him to heat for her. When she had finished her preparations, she went back to my mother's room, the batman following her; for, having done so much for the cause, he could not bear now to be excluded from the rest of the ritual. For quite a long time nothing was done. The Wise Woman sat reading from the Koran, and all the others remained uncomfortable and silent in the face of such holiness. Then the Wise Woman stood up and massaged the swelling with the cleansed human bone and asked that the heated lead be handed to her. She placed a large towel over my mother's head and stood the bowl of cold water over this, balancing it precariously with one hand; but the others were too open-mouthed in amazement by this time to care very much whether the water upset or not. The lead was put into the water, making a sizzling sound, and then the egg was poured in. It was an appalling anticlimax when the Wise Woman said:

"Everything is over. I shall remain here all night, so let us have something to eat now."

The batman, disappointed that nothing more spectacular had occurred, sat down to his meal in a very disgruntled frame of mind, for he rightly felt that after so much effort on his part, something really dramatic should have happened.

After she had eaten, my mother was told to sleep and forget everything. Amazingly, she was able to do this.

When she awakened the following morning, her first thought was to feel for the offending lump, but to her amazement it had entirely disappeared! She rushed to a mirror, only to find her neck back to normal once more, and she commenced to cry with joy, immediately calling all the household to witness her marvelous recovery.

I listened to their combined story with growing horror and indignation, furious that my mother had allowed herself to be persuaded to employ the wiles of an old, half-crazy woman. I gave tongue to my feelings, but when I had finished, my grandmother said, perfectly reasonably:

"But what is there to be cross about? The swelling has gone and your mother is better."

This I could not dispute.

My batman brought the bowl to me so that I could see the aftermath of the wonderful cure for myself. When I looked into the bowl, I saw the queer, twisted shape of the lead; and the egg floating atop it looked, indeed, oddly like a giant eye.

"And what about the bone?" I asked, feeling that they were quite capable of having kept that too.

The batman looked sheepish and hung his head.

"It's back in the graveyard again," he said. "I was told that it had to be put back there before the dawn came, otherwise something would happen to me."

I commenced to laugh, for his face expressed quite clearly his belief that something awful might have happened to him had he disobeyed orders.

He looked reproachfully at me, as if to intimate that this was not a laughing matter.

24

The Beginning of the End

MY MOTHER'S HEALTH CONTINUED TO grow worse. She became more and more morbid and absent-minded, complaining constantly of headaches. Eventually I managed to obtain a transfer to İzmir because the doctor had ordered a change of air for her.

Mehmet, who at that time was stationed in İzmir, managed to find a house for us, and I sent my family on ahead of me while I remained behind to clear up outstanding affairs.

Mehmet and I had not met for over two years, and when we saw each other in İzmir we embraced warmly, each commenting on the apparent ruddy health of the other.

He told me that my mother and my grandmother had already settled down quite well in the house he had discovered in Karşiyaka —a pretty house, he said it was, on the other side of the harbor.

He and I sat in a casino overlooking the water and discussed my mother.

"She is very neurotic of course," said Mehmet, with detachment, as if she were just a patient and not his mother. I envied him his indifference, and then I remembered that he had not lived at home for a very long time. I thought, too, how little we all knew about each other, how, springing from the same root, we had nevertheless divided until now we knew less than nothing about each other's dreams. Mehmet's decisive eyes looked as if he were not interested in dreaming. He was only interested in the physical ailments of humanity and the best way to cure them, anxious to make well the hurt, not studying too deeply the psychological pattern the mind made. He asked me what it was I was thinking about so seriously, and I said it was nothing, unwilling to share with him the intimacy of thought. I suggested that we go home.

The new house stood squarely in a garden full of palm trees and roses, and a large sloping lawn at the back gave on to a patch where lemon and tangerine trees grew stockily. What was it about that house that reminded me of another house that had stood squarely in its gardens and had been burned so long ago?

There was a terrace that overlooked the harbor, and I hoped that this peaceful spot would give my mother back her health. There was a balcony, too, at the front of the house, and my grandmother never tired of sitting here to watch the passers-by; but my mother sat at the back and watched the boats that sailed to far places. She would talk of İstanbul and the Bosporus, and I knew that her heart would remain in her beloved city forever. Far into the nights they would sit together, talking, with the moon riding high in the clear skies, throwing its light upon the water, lavishly gilding a path in the sea, softening the outlines of the houses that by day looked so harsh. My mother appeared to be contented. She had her sons with her once again and she complained less and less of headaches, but she talked about İstanbul with nostalgia, as if she would never return to it again.

I wish I had the words to paint the strange enchantment of İzmir: the little crooked streets with their air of secrecy and squalor; the haphazard shops in the side ways; the open carriages and the noisy trams and the hooting of the boats, overriding all other sounds; the casinos fronting the harbor, with the never ending strains of music issuing from them; the hot sunlight and the blue sky and the golden sands, the tree-lined roads and the wistaria and bougainvillaea that hangs everywhere like a scented purple curtain.

Many times Mehmet and I rode in the open carriages, drowsing under the evening warmth, the steady *clip-clop* of the horse's hoofs beating their rhythmic tattoo. The tall green mountains rose steeply behind the city; the half-tropical vegetation grew rankly and luxuriously among the old sun-warmed stones.

On hot nights we would sometimes visit the swimming pool, which was filled with sea water, and then walk back home together in the moonlight, the houses we passed standing asleep in their tranquil gardens. The smell of tangerine and orange trees hung heavy on the air, the lime trees giving off their own soporific essence. Most of the houses boasted growing vines, fig trees, and exotic palms. Nearer the harbor were new tree-lined boulevards; and always, no matter what the hour, there was the twanging of a guitar or the strains of a Turkish tango from the casinos to break the stillness sweetly.

There was a fishing village just beyond Karşiyaka, and occasionally I dined there alone in a little café where the fish were cooked upon request. The owner of the café showed me the sea pool where the fish swam and invited me to take my choice. I spent many a pleasant hour there, choosing and eating and drinking raki until my belt had to be ignominiously loosened.

Further on lies Güzelyali, where the houses march up the green hills facing the sea. There is a cool hillside café there, with terraces and tropical vegetation in the gardens and good food to make the journey worth while.

And everywhere in İzmir, in crazy profusion, are the flower beds, with their hot splashes of color that hurt the eyes and beat upon the senses. It still looks like a foreign place, a cosmopolitan city, with only the mosques and their slender minarets to remind one that one is still in Turkey.

Life here was a great deal easier than anywhere else I had ever been. Duties at the airdrome were not onerous and the summer passed pleasantly, with my mother seeming to grow stronger and better with each day. She spent most of her time in the garden, eternally planning new borders, new arrangements of flower beds, finding an outlet for energy in the design of growing, living things. Sometimes we found her embroidering—something she had not done for many years. She would sit out on the terrace, a scarf protecting her head from the heat of the sun, with a pile of shining embroidery silks on a small table beside her. Seeing her thus, the years fell away from all of us and we were back again in a gracious house where my father walked and the rafters rang with the shouted laughter of Uncle Ahmet.

My sister arrived on a visit from Ankara with her baby and an Arab nurse. When I looked at the dark face of the nurse the illusion of childhood was complete: it might have been Inci again, or Feride.

Muazzez appeared peeved when told that she and her unnecessary entourage crowded the little house. She flew from my sarcasm to the spoiling of my grandmother, complaining that I was becoming embittered.

She remained with us for a month, her husband joining us for the last week of the visit. Every day my mother appeared better, and we heard her joyous laughter for the first time in many months. Mehmet and I, noticing this, told each other that she was getting better, that she would never slip back into depression again.

On the 10th of October, 1938, Kemal Atatürk died, and great was the sense of bereavement when we heard the news. Turkey wept and wailed for her lost leader; the whole nation was plunged into mourning. I got permission to go to İstanbul, traveling in civilian clothing. I realized my error afterward, when I was caught in the press of frenzied people, while uniformed officers strutted freely where they might. I joined the never ending crowds entering the Dolmabahçe Saray, where Atatürk lay in state and the police tried vainly to keep order. Old women and young women wept for their hero who would never come again. Bareheaded men shuffled silently into the vast hall of the sultans, where the Father of Turkey slept his last long sleep.

They had draped him with the Turkish flag, and four officers stood on guard about him, their swords held upward in their clasped hands. The weeping, desolate people he had liberated filed past him, paying tribute, and I remembered many things about him. I remembered my first close sight of him, on the tenth anniversary of his Republic, almost five years ago. I remembered how the lean fanatic's face could light with a smile so dazzling that even his enemies forgave him much, and how, more frequently, the pressed-in lips smiled when the eyes remained dark and somber, challenging.

On the day they took him to Ankara, I managed, with incredible difficulties and with much unchivalrous jostling, to get a place in one of the boats leaving Galata Bridge. We followed the battleship that was taking him to his capital, the city he had wrested and built out of Anatolia, but we only followed as far as the islands in the Sea of Marmara. There we waved farewell to him, 'for we could go no farther. We watched over the rails as the bleak battleship rode the unquiet sea, and Atatürk, who perhaps one day will become less than a memory, continued his voyage alone. We who had been privileged to know him even a little would look for a long time and in vain for the figure that would never come again, the tall stern leader with the hard eyes that could so suddenly soften, the welcoming hand on the shoulder and the amused, harsh voice that said: "Well, Lieutenant, still running the Air Force?"

The lack of ceremony surrounding him upon formal occasions had not perhaps been in keeping with his impatient, autocratic temperament, yet sometimes he had affected simplicity. We had never known when he would drop into the Officers' Club, what he would next suggest. As I looked back to the battleship, I remembered the person he had been; and I felt the tears rise to my eyes, as if a friend had gone.

It was December, 1938, and winter touched İzmir kindly, with the lightest of fingers, but specialists were once again called for my mother. Injections gave their temporary relief and quietness, but my grandmother's straight shoulders were bowing permanently now under the great weight of my mother's illness.

In the early spring of 1939, when my nerves were reduced to tatters after the long months of tension at home, Mehmet brought home a small, fair girl with babyish blue eyes, telling us he was engaged. Bedia her name was. She looked frail as a doll, and one could not help wondering what sort of doctor's wife she would make. But they were so much in love—she was seventeen, he, twenty-seven—that one could not remain indifferent. My mother received the news calmly, but my grandmother—dear martinet!—loudly demanded to be told where the girl had come from and who her parents were. I think Mehmet must have already warned Bedia, for she showed no surprise, no trace of indignation at the questions, but smiled her gentle angelic smile, moving closer to the dark Mehmet, who gave the information my grandmother required.

For a space my mother came out of her dream world. Dinner parties were arranged, and she bought new clothes to attend other parties. Muazzez, growing more and more like my grandmother in her younger days, wrote peremptorily from Ankara, demanding that the happy couple visit her in order that she might have an excuse for giving parties too.

That incredible, undying beauty came back to haunt my mother, so that one was always caught by the exquisite surprise of it. The years dropped away from her like magic, and she became a young girl again, matching Bedia's innocent youth.

One evening she asked me when I would marry too. Before I had time to make any answer, my grandmother said with a harsh laugh that half the mothers of İzmir wanted the same question answered. I could not help laughing at her sublime, conceited exaggeration, and my mother repeated her question.

I kissed her hand and replied, "When I love."

She answered, "That you will never do. You have no heart. I should know that."

Then she commenced to cry, long tremors running through her body. Impatience swept cruelly upward in me, so that I left the tearful house and spent the evening in a bar, deserting the dinner party where I was to have been host. When I returned, my mother was in bed again, Mehmet pushing injections into her.

Mehmet was ordered to İstanbul in May, and my mother's favorite doctor also left İzmir, to take up residence in Ankara. She brooded alone, worrying more than ever about her health, about Mehmet and Muazzez in far-off Ankara, about Bedia, feeling now that she would not make a suitable wife for my brother. She began to eat alone, sometimes not eating at all. Then again, she grew careful and would only eat if I were at home. So I curtailed my visits to friends' houses or to the casinos and ate at home each evening, trying not to chafe too much under this new restraint. She bound me with chains of love, even taking to waiting up for me at night, watching from the terrace to see me walking up the street.

Even if I did not arrive home until three in the morning, still she would wait in a corner of the terrace, never saying anything, never letting her presence be known; yet I could feel her mournful eyes watching me out of the darkness. I took to coming home earlier so that she could get some sleep. Her gaunt look grew more pronounced, and my grandmother complained that she kept her awake at night. They shared a room now, since my mother did not care for the servant we had engaged in İzmir and grew very grand and regal at the thought of having her in her bedroom.

One night during dinner she looked really ill. Her hair was unkempt and uncombed, and one eye seemed to grow smaller and smaller as I watched her. I asked her why she sat at the table like this. She looked startled for a moment, as though I had rudely interrupted some far-away, private thought, then stammered that she was not well, that her head ached. Suddenly she lay her head down among the dishes, so wearily, so uncaringly that my heart was wrung with pity. My grandmother rang for the maid and she was put to bed, coaxed and petted out of her clothes like a child.

Later, when my grandmother and I sat in the salon drinking Turkish coffee, I said I thought the time had come when my mother needed constant, experienced nursing, and put forward the suggestion that she would be better off in a private institution I had heard of.

I remember that my grandmother looked at me very oddly; then she said:

"Your mother is not bad enough to separate her from her family and everything she has always known. That would be great cruelty, my son. She is only neurotic, and the doctors all say that her headaches are migraine. . . ."

"I suppose they must be right," I said uneasily, unwilling to set myself up as an authority, in the face of medical opinion, on nervous disorders.

"If one day she has to be sent away," continued my grandmother, following her own train of thought, "I pray God that I may not be here to see."

She looked away from me, but I could see old, bitter memories struggling in her face. I knew that though she and my mother had never liked each other, one always resenting the other, still they could not live apart for long. They had been together for too many years now, had shared all the important things that had ever happened to them.

We sat silent for a long time, and then I rang for more coffee. My grandmother came out of her reverie.

"If only there was something more I could do," I said, and my grandmother put out her hand and touched my knee lightly.

"You have done everything that was left in your nature to do."

The odd words startled me and revived the times I had had of impatience, the harsh words I had uttered. My grandmother watched my struggle and said sadly:

"It is too late now to torment yourself. You grew away from us a long time ago, shutting us out, and perhaps the fault was our own. I have seen how you have tried with your mother, how you have forced yourself to do as she wanted, but it was all false, my child. She knows that too; but you could not give more than you had to give, so there is no need to reproach yourself. You have done more for her than many sons who loved her might have done."

"You make me feel ashamed," I said to her, hating my unnaturalness, remembering, too, the restraints that Mehmet had never had.

"I *can't* come closer!" I shouted in desperation. "I can't give her all my thoughts!"

My grandmother's wise old face looked understandingly at me. She nodded her head.

"Hüsnü should not have died," she said, pressing my hand tightly. "She should not have been left alone so young in life."

She shook her head sorrowfully, her eyes bright with tears, but none were falling. I took her old worn hand and kissed it.

I felt her looking down at my bent head, and then she said irrelevantly, "How like Ahmet you are!"

25

Disintegrating Family

MEHMET RETURNED TO İZMIR IN AUGUST, 1939, for his wedding, and Muazzez and Ali arrived from Ankara, adding grandeur to the little house.

I never saw Mehmet married, for the day before his wedding I was ordered to a maneuver and had to leave all the bustle and the excitement behind me. The maneuver lasted ten days, and when I returned home I was unutterably shocked, for my grandmother had left us for good, returning to İstanbul with Mehmet and Bedia. My batman was in the hospital.

It had been previously arranged in the family that when my grandmother went to live with my brother and his wife, my mother would go to Muazzez in Ankara. My grandmother would never have left us at all but for the fact that Mehmet was more often away at sea than he was at home. It was felt to be unwise to leave the youthful Bedia unchaperoned.

Perhaps this chaperonage would be quite unnecessary in other countries; but to leave Bedia at seventeen alone in İstanbul, where scandal, false or true, needs but the slightest flicker to grow into a roaring flame, was unthinkable. There were far too many traps for unwary young wives in İstanbul.

When the arrangement was originally suggested, my mother professed herself pleased, telling me in confidence that she had perhaps lived too long with my grandmother and that living in Ankara would do her good.

It was therefore a surprise for me to return to İzmir to find her still there. That she was alone in the house made it seem far worse. "Where is the servant?" I asked.

"I dismissed her. She was lazy," returned my mother, who had always hitherto extolled her.

My mother herself was in a terrible state. I trembled when I thought of the heartless criminality that had left her alone in that echoing house. She was unwashed, uncombed, and slatternly. Worst of all, she was unaware of this.

I cursed Mehmet for having done such a thing, but I could scarcely blame the flighty Muazzez, who was always much too concerned with her own affairs to have bothered very much when my mother refused to accompany her.

I inquired for my batman and was told that he had gone to hospital. She started to complain in a high, whining voice of the maid she had dismissed, and all the while her hands were twisting, twisting, busily destroying a lacy handkerchief. She looked as if she had not eaten for days, and the house was a shambles. Most of my grandmother's furniture had gone to İstanbul, and the few pieces that remained were pulled out from the walls. Beds were unmade and the kitchen was littered with the remains of meals obviously several days old.

I took her into the stuffy, airless salon and flung wide the windows. Here was a shambles too. It was heartbreaking to see my mother like this, in this dirty, uncared-for house.

"Why did you not go with Muazzez?" I asked her gently.

She stared at me for a moment or two and then she replied, "And who would look after you if I had gone?"

I bit back the searing retort that burned on my lips, and she said fretfully:

"I told your grandmother not to look back when she left the house. I said that if she did it would bring us bad luck. But she ignored me and she stood at the corner, looking back for a long, long time, and I had to shout to her, to go, go, go!"

My mother's voice was high with hysteria, and I stirred uneasily, seeing the scene again through her eyes: the old woman leaning on her stick at the corner, looking back to a place where she had been happy, and my mother on the terrace shouting at her, attracting attention perhaps, my batman trying to pull her back to the silent house. She watched me unwinkingly, trying to find out my reaction to what she was telling me. I said nothing. She had been silent for so long alone that talking was necessary to her now.

"Your grandmother did not want to go. She said that I wanted to be rid of her. That is why she turned back when I told her not to, so that she could leave her curse on this house and everyone in it. I know," she nodded to me: "she hopes I will die!"

"Oh, Mother," I said, wondering when this feud would cease between them.

Still I could see the departing figure of my grandmother, and I wondered if we had done the right thing, we younger ones who had thought only to separate them, to keep them from fighting as they had done all through the years. I thought of my mother, remaining here for me, and could not see her in the alien atmosphere of my sister's house in Ankara. I did not know what I could do with her now, when only I was left with her. I had tried to be good but had failed somewhere, perhaps many years ago. I felt helpless sitting there, watching her. The others had shelved their responsibilities and had gone away, leaving us alone, the one thing I had always dreaded.

When my batman returned after a few days, the house was normal again and I was glad to leave her in his hands each morning when I went to the airdrome, knowing no harm could come to her.

At the end of August I was sent to Kayseri to bring back a new plane for my unit, but on September 3rd I received a telegram from the commanding officer, ordering me to return immediately.

War had come again to Europe: Poland had been invaded, and all the lights of the world were going out again, one by one. When

I arrived at Eskişehir for refueling, I saw that all the planes were out of their hangars in the fields. Tents were out and lorries. I wondered if Turkey would come in and, more importantly, on whose side.

I was told in Eskişehir that all leave had been canceled, that all officers now had to remain in the airdromes day and night. I took off for İzmir, wondering about my mother. Who would look after her now?

At İzmir excited friends crowded about me, but I could not listen to them. I sought out the commanding officer and begged him to relax the new rule for me, just for one night, as I was anxious about my mother. He knew of her illness and gave me permission to go home immediately, saying that if I should be wanted he would send a car for me.

When I got home, my mother appeared quite calm, greeted me affectionately, and said that she had heard that war had been declared over the radio. She also had heard from neighbors that I should no longer be able to come home at night. I was relieved by her normality.

During September everything went all right, for my batman was excellent with my mother, and I spoke to her each day by telephone. A new servant was engaged and at first she spoke highly of her. Then the old dissatisfaction began to creep back into her voice, and she no longer seemed pleased with her.

In October my batman was demobilized, having finished his military service. A new one came to take his place, and my mother hated him, telling me he was too stupid to do anything or to understand half of what she said. I sent another one and another one and then another, but they would not stay. In any event, she disliked all of them on sight. Then she threw the servant out and was at last alone in the house with the dog.

I was half frantic with anxiety and would circle in my plane over the garden each day, to see if she were all right. I wrote to Mehmet, explaining the situation and suggesting that my mother go to his house in İstanbul, where at least she would not be alone.

I managed to get home one day and discuss this with her.

"Your grandmother is there," she said, "and perhaps we have missed each other more than we know. Anyway, I shall be back again in İstanbul."

Mehmet replied promptly, saying that Bedia would be glad to have my mother with her and to send her immediately.

Again I obtained leave, helped my mother to pack her things, and took her to İstanbul.

Bedia welcomed her kindly, showing us the large, airy room she had prepared for her. My grandmother looked thoughtful, as though wondering how this *ménage à trois* would work out.

Alone I returned to İzmir and went to the empty house, wondering what to do with the furniture that was left. The dog, who was also called Fidèle, refused to eat his meals, all the while crying quietly to himself, watching me anxiously, as though he were begging me to tell him what was the matter. Now and then he would pad softly to the door, sniffing the carpets, then would come dispiritedly back to me, flopping down beside my chair.

My batman brought dinner, and the silent room seemed filled with ghosts. Fidèle had followed me to the table, but he would not eat. He lay down, resting his nose on his paws, only moving to cock an ear if he heard a sound. He was waiting for my mother to walk into the room, but she would not come here again.

The house was given over to silence and the remembrance of all the unquiet things that had happened beneath its narrow roof.

26

Goodbye, Şevkiye

M Y MOTHER PROVED TROUBLESOME IN İstanbul.

She soon left Bedia's house, taking a room for herself in a tall old house in Şişli, saying she preferred to be alone. Sometimes she would visit my grandmother, who, with Bedia, soon noticed her rapid deterioration, the carelessness of her dress. She told people that her children did not want her. She started to go without food, giving most of her money to poor people whom she met in the streets. She would talk to all the beggars of İstanbul, inviting them to her room in Şişli, where she would give them quantities of food to take away. She could not bear to see people in tattered clothes, and began to give them her own. At other times she would walk miles in the course of a day, returning home weary and hungry, without money left to buy food for herself. She used to go to the old places where she had lived before, frequently taking taxis, haughtily telling drivers to wait for her. When she could not pay them, she would direct them back to Bedia's house.

She bought quantities of sweets to distribute to the slum children, and once she was discovered sitting in the rank, overgrown garden of our ruined house—the house my father had bought for her before he went to the war. I could not get leave to go to İstanbul; I could only write frantic letters, imploring her to return to Bedia and my grandmother, where she would be well looked after. These letters she completely ignored.

From the time she left İzmir, she never communicated with me, even indirectly through my grandmother's scrappy letters. I grew despairing, wondering what would be the end of this bad business.

On February 2nd, 1940, I received a telegram from Bedia, asking me to come to İstanbul immediately, as my mother was seriously ill. I went to the commanding officer and showed him the telegram. He took one look at my face and gave me permission to leave the airdrome. I left Bedia's address with him and hastily booked a seat by train to Bandırma. From Bandırma I took the boat for Galata, impatient of the slow-seeming journey, my heart continuously in my mouth.

When I finally arrived at Mehmet's house, Bedia's tear-stained, swollen face did nothing to reassure me that all might after all be well.

"Is my mother dead?" I asked her, clutching her arm, and my grandmother came through the narrow hall and drew me into the salon. She seated herself and bade me do the same, but this I was totally incapable of doing.

"Tell me," I said to her quiet face. "Is she dead?"

"No," she said. "Better if she were."

I walked up and down the still room, seeing the familiar furniture that still could remind me of childhood and hunger, though I had nothing to fear on that score nowadays. All the houses we had lived in, even when prosperity had come back to us, were linked with those early insecure years, because the heavy old furniture was always there to remind one. There was never any escape from memories.

"Come, sit down," said my grandmother gently. "There is nothing to be gained by walking up and down the room or by hysteria."

I sat down on a brocaded chair, once beautiful but fraying at the edges now through long usage.

"Where is my mother?" I asked. "What has happened to her?"

But I think I knew the answer before anyone replied. It was Bedia who told me, Bedia who started to cry, irritating me with her persistent tears, yet who had the courage to say what was difficult for my grandmother. "She has lost her mind," said Bedia, with dignity in her voice; and I was glad that she was here, new to the family, able to speak of hurting, hidden things as we others would not have done. She was so new to the family that our horror could not touch her too much.

My grandmother stood up very erect, her face without color and her stern eyes filled with compassion. She put a hand on Bedia's young shoulder and said:

"There, my child! There is no need to cry!"

She went on patting the thin shoulder absently, her eyes looking to something we could not see. I leaned against the window, my body light as air, and waited for them to tell me everything.

It was Bedia who was the storyteller.

"Mother came to visit us two nights ago," she said, "and she looked very ill. She said she was hungry, so I gave her something to eat. Then she asked if she might spend the night with us. She complained that her head ached. Of course I said that I should be glad if she stayed with us, not only for one night but for always. For a while she was all right; then she began to get irritable and would not have the radio on, saying that it made her head worse, so I turned it off. When I had done that, she remarked how obedient I was, asking me if I did not find it difficult living with Grandmother. I said No, I did not. She grew quarrelsome, saying that Grandmother was a most difficult woman, that all mothers-in-law ruined their daughters-in-law's lives and that that was the reason she would not live with me. She said she wanted me to be free of older people's influence and then turned to Grandmother, saying she ought to leave me and take a room by herself somewhere. 'You are foolish to remain here,' she said. 'Bedia does not want you. When one is old, one is useless,' she continued; 'children do not want one any more.'"

Bedia paused uncertainly, and I was aware of my grandmother's still, immobile face from the shadows of her wing chair, of her hands demurely folded in her lap. Bedia went on:

"Mother started to get angry because Grandmother would not answer her. She seemed to direct all her talk to her; she was really only using me as an excuse. I could see that. Then she told me that she hated Grandmother, that she had hated her for many years, and that she was responsible for a house that was burned—a long time ago, I think," added Bedia apologetically, not yet being familiar with family history, not knowing of the square white house that had burned to the night skies.

"Mehmet is in Bandırma. He went there by torpedo boat a few days ago, so he was not here for all this. Mother kept asking for him, forgetting that I had told her where he was. Then she burst out to my face that she could not understand what I was doing in her son's house. 'I know you are his wife,' she said, with an awful contempt in her voice, 'but I do not like your painted mouth. Nobody in this family ever used paint on their mouths.' Then she told Grandmother that she would cure her deafness for her and asked me to fetch her some olive oil. She said she would heat it and pour it into the bad ears. I did not want to do it, but she insisted, so I went to the kitchen and got what she asked for. When I came back, she was looking at a knife that was still on the table and which she had not used when she was eating." Here Bedia shuddered in remembrance, her eyes going dark. "And she said in an odd sort of voice that the knife had a lovely edge, that it was so clean and shining. She looked at Grandmother while she spoke, but Grandmother only watched her, not having heard anything she had said. I took the knife from Mother and put it away, and when I turned back to her, she said, 'But is it wrong of me to admire the way you keep your cutlery, Bedia? Did you think perhaps I was going to injure Grandmother?' I said No, I had not thought that. Then she came over to me, and I screamed. She looked surprised and asked why I did that. I did not know what to say. And all the time Grandmother sat there, not saying a word, not interfering, making Mother more and more angry. I was terrified of what was going to happen." She added naïvely, "Grandmother is very obstinate, you know."

I nodded, remembering that obstinacy from other years.

"Yes, I know," I said to Bedia. "Go on."

"There isn't very much more to tell," she said. "After a while Mother said that she would go to bed, that she could not bear the aching of her head, and she asked me if I had any aspirin. I had not, but she said it didn't matter. When she had gone to her room, Grandmother suggested that we should get a doctor for her. I asked why, and Grandmother said that she knew her daughter-in-law very well, that she had given trouble for years, and that in the mood she was in tonight she was capable of doing a lot of troublesome things. Anyway, I went to get a doctor, and he came straight here with me, wondering what was wrong, for I had been unable to explain very much to him. When he went to her room, she was still awake and asked me who he was. I told her that he was a doctor and that he would give her something for her headache. She seemed very suspicious of him but allowed him to examine her and to leave some tablets. Then he came to the salon with me and commenced to ask Grandmother all sorts of questions about Mother. Finally he said that it would be better if she were put into an institution for a few months, where she could get good nursing and good food. 'She looks as if she has been starving herself,' he said. Then he left us. We did not realize it, but Mother heard everything that was said. You see, the doctor had to shout to make Grandmother understand him, and she had shouted back at him, without knowing that she was shouting. It was terrible. Mother came back into the salon in her nightdress and said: 'Do you think I am mad that you want to put me away where I shall never see my children again?'

"Grandmother tried to pacify her, although Mother was very quiet, but upset too, and she sat down on the divan and looked at me pitifully.

"'Bedia,' she said, 'do you think that I am mad? Is it madness to want to help the poor, to love my children too much, to fear for

my eldest son's death? Is it madness to live alone so that I shall not
be a burden to the married happiness of you and Mehmet or
Muazzez and her husband?' And I said No, I did not think so. She
sounded so terribly sane that I began to think we had done the
wrong thing by calling a doctor to her and by telling him so much
afterward. Mother sat there until suddenly she burst into tears and
ran back to her room, where she locked the door. I ran after her,
but she would not let me in. I could hear her moving about all the
time, crying, and then Grandmother came and banged on the door
and roared out to her to open it for us. Her voice seemed to set
Mother crazy. She suddenly flung open the door. She was already
dressed, and she pushed us out of her way, saying to Grandmother:
'You are responsible for everything that has ever happened to me.'
Then she flew down the stairs and out of the house. I ran after
her immediately, but I could not catch her. She seemed to have the
strength of ten people. We heard afterward that she had run almost
to Sişli and had called a taxi; but when she was getting into the
taxi, she fainted. She was weak, of course, for she had not eaten
anything for days—only the small amount I had given her that
evening. The taxi driver took her straight to Medical Jurisprudence,
and the police came to tell us so this morning. They said she had
screamed at them in the police station and had fought to get away.
They had called a doctor and he had given her injections and then
sent her in an ambulance to Jurisprudence."

Bedia stopped speaking and I looked at her, she who was not yet
eighteen, to have seen so much passion unleashed, to have witnessed the outbreak of the sores that had rankled for twenty-six
years. . . . I thought that she had emerged from it all with the
little touching look of youth gone from her face forever, her little
fragile air vanished like snow before the wind.

"Where is she now?" I asked.

"I do not know," replied Bedia wearily. "The police will tell
you. I would have gone myself to ask but I was waiting for you
to come."

My grandmother laid a hand on my shoulder, and I thought of

the listening, straining face that must have watched my mother, the closed ears that had heard nothing, though she must have been aware of danger. I thought of the indomitable courage that had held her in her chair in the face of the bright, sure blade of the knife, when one unguarded movement might have incited my over-wrought mother to use it on her. My heart turned over and I felt my skin begin to creep. Of the pain and the heartbreak and the jealousy of the long years, of the teeming, crowded brain of my mother, I would not let myself think. Not just yet, I said. Not yet. Time enough to think of that later on. If you think of these things now, you will hate Bedia and your grandmother for not having understood enough. Think of something else.

I went to Medical Jurisprudence, and the doctor who had admitted my mother granted me an interview.

He was an old, white-haired man with kind eyes. When I asked him if I could see my mother, he said gently:

"She is not here any more. You are a young man and an airman, and you have witnessed many tragic things. It would not be right to subject yourself to such torture."

I pleaded with him but he was firm.

"She is not here," he repeated. "We have sent her to Bakırköy. She will be well looked after there."

I remembered the red windowless ambulance that had just driven off as I had arrived at Jurisprudence. Suddenly I knew that it had held my mother. They had boxed her up in that airless place to make sure that the already unstable brain would crack. I felt the cold sweat break out on my forehead. Was there no humanity any-where? Was it necessary to treat her like a possessed, witless creature who had no feelings, who knew nothing? I knew as surely as if she had been speaking to me that she was perfectly aware of what was going on, that she had known why they put her in the windowless ambulance.

How her own heart had always been wrung with pity whenever she had caught sight of these ambulances in the İstanbul streets.

"Poor things," she had said. "They are unwanted by their families. They are being sent to Bakırköy, where they will not be allowed to give anybody any trouble."

I could not rest until I had tried once again to see her, to comfort her if she could still be comforted.

I left Medical Jurisprudence and got a train for Bakırköy, fretting at the long wait at in-between stations, cross because I had not taken a taxi for the whole journey.

I managed to get a phaeton at the station and was driven to the Mental Home, a grim building enclosed in lovely gardens, with high, unscalable walls all about it.

I walked in through the gates, after a porter had sharply inquired my business. He looked at me suspiciously, and except that I was in uniform, I do not think he would have admitted me at all.

A man came toward me, a perfectly normal-looking man, and I asked him where I could find the doctor on duty. He grinned at me, making vague gestures with his hands. I looked at his luminous eyes and passed on. I could not control a little shiver of apprehension.

I went up some steps and inside, in a hall, I saw a door marked "Private Secretary." I went in and stated my business.

"When did she arrive?" the secretary asked fussily, thumbing through a sort of ledger.

"Today," I said, risking the shot in the dark. He looked in a file on his desk and said Yes, she had been admitted that morning. He directed me to a building opposite for further details. He spread his large white hands, indicating that he was only the secretary, that he could not know everything.

I went out into the hall again and found that it was now full of patients, with their sleeves rolled up, all waiting for injections. I passed through their tidy ranks, feeling horror if I had to touch them, perhaps half afraid of them. They looked at me incuriously, but I passed through their lines quickly, my head bent, embarrassment uppermost in my alienation to them.

In the other building I found a doctor who informed me that on no account would I be permitted to see my mother.

"Come back in six weeks' time," he said thoughtlessly. "Perhaps you can see her then."

Beaten by his obduracy, I asked if she could be moved into a private room. He shrugged, intimating that the treatment afforded her there would be no better.

"She will feel more private there," I said. "She will not be all the time aware of the other patients around her."

Coldly his eye raked me.

"Lieutenant," he said with terrible hardness, terrible lack of understanding, "she is not yet in a condition to be aware of anything."

I hated his cold, precise voice, but I insisted nevertheless that she be moved to a private room. He arranged for this while I was there, accepting the check I handed him with a doubtful air, as though suspecting that it might not be valid. As he was writing out a receipt for me, he said:

"It is preferable to pay with money, Lieutenant. I wonder would you be good enough to remember that the next time you come?"

I did not reply and he stood up, indicating that he was a busy man, that the interview was at an end. As he said goodbye, his white hand lay limply in mine, and his eyes seared through me. I realized that here was a man with a mission: given half a chance, he would put me under observation too.

I left Bakırköy, having accomplished very little. During the return in the train I speculated wildly as to what they would do with her. Would there be a window in her room, to give her all the fresh air and sunlight that she loved? Would there be a view over the gardens? Or would they keep her strapped down on her bed, helpless in the face of their sane administrations? The tears were never far from my eyes, and I did not return to Mehmet's house. There was nothing more to say, and I did not want to meet the questions in my grandmother's eyes, the compassion in Bedia's.

I returned to İzmir, threw my energies into work, and waited for news. Mehmet wrote several times, but I did not bother to reply. What was there to say? I hated their continual harping on the subject of my mother. Could they not leave her alone now?

I was glad to be living in the airdrome, where companionship now assumed a precious quality.

In March, 1940, I was given permission to go to İstanbul. From Galata Bridge, when I disembarked, I went straight to Bakırköy, by-passing Mehmet and his family. I was eager to learn about my mother for myself, with no secondhand information to influence the mind.

By great good luck it was a visiting day when I arrived at the Mental Home, and the lovely gardens were crowded with visitors and patients. Sometimes I had great difficulty in distinguishing one from the other.

I stated my errand to a crisp-looking, hard-faced nurse. As she walked away from me, I hoped she did not have the handling of my impatient, impetuous mother, for if she did, her chances of recovery were zero.

I waited in the gardens, feeling unequal to sitting tidily in the bare waiting hall. My heart almost choked me, and my stomach kept turning over and over in the most ignominious way. Suddenly I wished I had waited until Mehmet had been free to accompany me. I felt foolish and insecure as I hesitated on the springy, dry grass. As I looked about me at the patients and the visitors, I thought that one should have nerves of steel and the imagination of a brick wall to come here.

There was a tall old man making an impassioned speech to a dim, elderly lady who might have been his wife. He talked at her without ceasing, scarcely seeming to pause for breath, his bony fingers wagging before her passive face. Occasionally he would thump his chest with a massive, destructive gesture and let out a roar like an angry lion. A doctor halted by me, his distinguishing marks in all this mass of doubtful humanity being a white coat and a stethoscope dangling from his pocket.

"The old man is not really so bad as he looks," he said amusedly to my disbelieving face. "We hope to have him completely well again in another twelve months."

A young girl held court with her father and mother, who watched her with fond, anxious faces.

"So of course I could not marry him," she was saying in a light, scornful voice. "I could only refuse him—"

She looked all around her, so pretty and young and witless with her chestnut hair and large eyes. She caught sight of me and smiled entrancingly, pointing me out to her parents.

"Look," she said. "That is my husband. Do you not think he is very good-looking?"

I pulled the doctor by the arm, hurrying away across the lawns. I asked him about my mother.

"Has she any chance of recovery?" I asked, and he paused for a moment. I paused too, turning to face him.

"Tell me," I said. "I should like to know."

He replied, not looking at me:

"She has very little chance. She became worse suddenly, you know, and we have to keep her quiet with injections."

I saw her in my mind's eye, knowing the place she was in, wanting to get away to freedom, becoming violent because they had thwarted her, kept quiet with the injections that would be ruthlessly, relentlessly shot into her. We must have quietness here, I could hear them all saying. This patient is not quite mad enough yet. She needs disciplining.

The doctor was watching me now, reading perhaps many things from my face. He said gently:

"She will die soon. You would not wish her here for perhaps many years, would you?"

I thought of my grandmother and the words she had spoken that morning in İstanbul, when Bedia had told me the awful truth.

"Is she dead?" I had asked, and she had answered sternly, "Better if she were."

But I could not face the thought of her death like this. She still represented all the things I had looked for in life, even though I had never found them in her.

I found myself telling the doctor all the things I thought I had forgotten, things from childhood that suddenly, for this brief, illuminating second, stood out in high relief. I told him of my father's going away, of the fire, of poverty, of the years in an orphanage in Kadıköy, my mother's working in the sewing depot at Gülhane Parki, of the old, old hatred that persisted and magnified with the years between my mother and my grandmother. I spoke of the love that had tried to chain me, of the restraints imposed; and all the while the doctor listened, nodding now and then, as if he were beginning to understand her better. Presently he left me, and I stood alone on the sunlit grass, trembling, glad to have spoken of these things to another person.

I waited for my mother.

Presently I saw her coming, with two nurses, one on each side of her, supporting her. Her high, querulous voice reached me across the space that separated us as she tried, in vain, to rid herself of the encompassing arms of the sturdy nurses. My heart bled for her, and I thought it would have been better not to have come here, not to have seen her so defenseless.

She stopped in front of me and I said, "Mother." I saw a wary, trapped look come into her eyes. She looked at me as if she did not recognize me.

I said, "Don't you know me?"

Then she said, "Oh, it is you? My eagle, my airman son."

There was no emotion in her voice, nothing but haughtiness, the voice she would have used to a stranger. She pointed to a man and said:

"He is our cook. Not a very good one, I am afraid, but we could not get anyone else."

I looked at the man she pointed to, a visitor, and she saw my look, adding, "He is really far too distinguished to be a cook, but there you are . . ."

Her voice trailed off and she turned away from me, ignoring me,

and began to tremble with such frightful violence that the nurses
had to lead her to a seat.

I followed them, and when she was sitting down I took one cold
hand in mine and kissed it, but she did not pay any attention to
the gesture. She persisted in treating me like a stranger. After that
first flicker of recognition in her eyes, she had withdrawn from me.
She felt me watching her and turned her head to me, saying:

"Once I had a son, too, who was an airman like you. He broke
my heart."

The calmness of her light voice was terrible.

"Oh, Mother!" I said, trying not to weep for her and for myself
too. "Don't you know me?" I asked.

It was cruel to go on knocking at memory like that, but I could
not help myself. She did not answer me, but commenced to hum a
little nameless tune, an odd thin sound, and the shivers still spas-
modically shook her frail body.

I gave her some Turkish delight. She ate it and then asked, with
incredible courtesy, if she could have some more, as her friends
were too poor to buy any for themselves. I handed her the box,
but her hands were too unsteady to hold it, and it fell to the grass,
spilling its contents. The nurses stooped to pick the pieces up
for her.

She turned away pettishly, refusing to speak to me any more,
trembling all the while. Her body was wasted; only skin and bone
remained of her. She persisted in keeping herself turned from
me, and presently one of the nurses said she would have to be
taken back to her room. She was to be put to bed.

She went away with them docilely, never looking at me, never
turning her head backward as she went through the door, not
caring that I stood there looking after her, not knowing who I was.

I stood there watching the dragging, bent, trembling figure of my
mother, and I thought that I should not come here again. Silently
I said my goodbye to her, and then she vanished from my sight. I
felt the tears running unchecked down my cheeks.

I wept for myself and for the young lover who had once

imprinted herself on my memory, the day she bade my father goodbye in the gracious salon of a long-dead house. I wept for the beauty who had flashed jewels and hospitality, who had brought poetry into a house in a back street of Bayazit. I wept for the pale young girl who had drudged untold hours in an army depot, sewing coarse linen for soldiers. I wept for the middle-aged woman of the fugitive, persistent beauty, who had worn a flower in her hair against my return from the airdrome, who had once sparkled and shone like the noonday sun, and who had withered to dust inside the body of this bent, trembling old woman who knew no one. But I wept most of all for my mother.

A light touch on the arm made me turn to see a nurse with a face of great gentleness, of compassion. She said:

"We have put her to bed now. Would you like to see her room?"

"No," I said. "No, thank you. There is no need. I am sure she is very comfortable."

She did not say anything to this, and I asked if there were a window in the room.

Her eyes lit with that rare understanding that comes so seldom in the world.

"Yes," she said. "She likes us to keep it open for her. And we bring her to the garden quite often, too. She loves gardens, you know."

"Yes," I said, seeing the gardens she had made in İstanbul, in Eskişehir, in Kütahya, in İzmir, and I wondered if loving hands still tended them.

"She had green fingers," I said irrelevantly, and the friendly nurse smiled.

"Well, goodbye, Lieutenant," she said. "Come again, won't you?"

"No," I said, "I shall not come again. It is better not."

Suddenly the face of the friendly nurse closed and grew hard, unable to understand.

She said tartly, "But you can help her so much, you know."

I remembered that the doctor had said she would not live for long, that she would never get better; and I wondered at the terrible, ruthless sanity of the sane, of the stupidity that asked me to come back and see my mother, to force awareness of myself upon her when she did not want to be reminded, when her son was dead for her because once he had broken her heart. I had thought that such pitiless cruelty was alien to the friendly nurse, but there was no way of explaining to that closed face that there was nothing more to be said between my mother and me, that both of us were gone from each other.

My mother had traveled farther than we who stood here in the sunlight. She had gone to that world of soft illusions where she was always a young girl, the world she had tried to escape to when her home was burned, when she learned that her husband had died on a far-away road under a blinding sun. She had wanted to go there long ago, but we had always held her back, calling to her to stay with us. Now she no longer cared and could not have been persuaded to stay any more.

I turned away from the gardens. The same man still talked impassionedly, the same young girl haughtily told her parents that she could never marry, all of them living in their illusory world, where hurt could not touch them. Their voices followed me to the high iron gates. The porter opened them for me to pass through, and I went out to the quiet country road.

On the eighteenth day of May of that eventful European year of 1940, my mother died, but for me she had been dead this many a day.
' I received the telegram the morning they were burying her, when it was too late to go to İstanbul and too late for anything else to be done by me.

Alone of all her family, Mehmet saw her lowered into her grave outside the fortress wall of İstanbul. An imam read the Koran for her, and presently Mehmet was left alone with her for a little while. Then he too had gone, leaving her with the sun and the kindly rain and the eternal nights still to come.

Later we erected a tombstone for her, and made a low stone wall about the narrow grave. We put rose trees at her head and at her feet, and her name was carved into the shining marble of the stone. Şevkiye Orga, we wrote, 1895–1940. Ruhuna Fatiha (Pray for her); and the name looked lonely there among all the nameless dead about her.

Then we left her alone, a little outside the İstanbul she had loved.

27

The End of the Story

FIDÈLE GREW MORE AND MORE MISERABLE, finally refusing to eat at all, and one day I came home to find him barely able to wag his tail feebly at me when I called out to him. He missed my mother, and there was nobody now to fuss over him in the old way, so he went off his food and died quietly. With his death I resolved never to keep another dog, and the house seemed strangely, unnaturally still, empty with no Fidèle to bark us welcome.

My grandmother came from İstanbul with Bedia, who was going to spend a holiday with relatives in İzmir. My grandmother stayed with me, and I asked her if she would not like to remain with me always.

"Ah no!" she said. "I am too old now and it would be lonely. And I like to live in İstanbul with Bedia: she is very kind."

It seemed strange to see my grandmother's busy figure in the house, interfering with the batman, who had never known her or my mother either, and who did not take kindly to feminine restrictions. But after a while it seemed as if she had been there always, that at any moment my mother would join her in one of their interminable arguments, that Fidèle would bark for attention, and I thought that I should miss her when she left. She was old now and wrinkled, her thin hair completely white, and her days were mostly spent looking out through the window, watching the people passing by.

Sometimes when I returned from Headquarters, where I was now stationed, she would be looking vacantly out, unable to see very much because her old eyes were fading. I would stand beneath the window, waving to her frantically, but she would ignore me completely until my waving became so insistent that she would peer closer, closer, until the failing eyes would light with recognition and she would hurry to welcome me home. Her movements, too, were slow and indecisive, and she was frequently absentminded. I could not help remembering the days of my childhood, when she was still a young woman, when she had bewailed the loss of her servants, had cried for the eldest son who had been killed, had bargained with a dealer and got the better of him, had made us watery soup from cabbage stalks, had starved for us—but had kept her jewels for her beloved granddaughter. She had forgotten all these things now and only muttered to herself about small, immediate things, like the loss of a needle and cotton, wondering whether it would be found in someone's bed, or sighed for warm weather again, as though already her old bones felt the long chill of the grave.

I suppose I had always been fonder of my grandmother than of my mother, although in earlier years I may not have felt this so clearly, still looking, as I did, for perfection in my mother. And on that last time in İzmir, my heart ached for the things that had vanished forever, the changes that had relentlessly taken place. All the older generations were dead. I looked down the years to the dim figures of my grandfather, my father, and my mother, to Uncle Ahmet and Aunt Ayşe, all the figures who had crowded babyhood, and I thought it sad that they had gone so far, leaving this lonely old woman, this enfeebled, frail grandmother behind them. I wondered how clearly she remembered any of them. Once I spoke to her of Sariyer, but she looked blank, unremembering, as though that gracious rose-red house had never been, as though she herself had never wandered through its gardens. I left the subject and was glad she lived with Bedia, who was strange and new and held no link with the dead past.

Now there was no one who remembered my childhood.

During my grandmother's stay with me, a Government decree bade every householder or tenant dig a trench. One afternoon, when my batman was digging, my grandmother asked me with a puzzled frown what it was he was doing.

"He is making a trench," I told her, knowing that she would not understand.

"It is like a grave," she said thoughtfully. "Why is the Government ordering us to dig our graves, my son?"

I said that if enemy airplanes attacked us, in the event of our entering the war, the people would go to these trenches, where perhaps there would be a measure of safety.

"I shall not go," she declared with a ghost of her old energetic, autocratic self showing through for one fleeting instant. "I intend to die in my bed. I am too old now to care."

Then she forgot what she was saying, speaking of other things, and I kissed her old, withered hand, which still smelled of eau de Cologne, as it had through all the years.

She seemed glad to return with Bedia to İstanbul, saying good-bye to me tranquilly, relieved to be going home again to familiar things.

The house was the emptier for her going, as though her quiet presence had disturbed the atmosphere, and I was filled with restlessness for many days, aching for something I could not name.

At the end of October, 1941, I was unexpectedly ordered to England on duty. I was to escort many young air officers who were to complete their training with the Royal Air Force, and I would be eventually transferred to the Embassy in London.

A part of me was glad to be saying farewell to the old life and old sorrows that had not yet healed, yet a part of me, too, reached back nostalgically, unwilling to relinquish memories.

The little house in İzmir was handed back to the agents, and a new, young, noisy family came to dispel our ghosts. I sold the furniture haphazardly, not making the bargain my grandmother had once made long ago, keeping only a few souvenirs from her time, sending them to Muazzez in Ankara against my return.

In Ankara it was winter, the raw chill winter of Anatolia, and the little hills were covered with snow.

On that last evening, when all the baggage had been sent to the station ahead of us, when the last ticket had been bought and the last traveler's check issued, some friends of mine gave a dinner party for me. We dined in the station restaurant. The place was filled with noisy, excited young officers with their families, but one had not the heart to restrain their high enthusiasm.

Our glasses were raised in the final toast, and the train came in majestically, the train that would carry us from familiar things on the first stage of our long journey.

Ankara station smelled of grease and oil, and the late paper sellers cried their wares lustily in the soft Turkish we would not hear again for a long time.

Last chocolates and sweets were bought from the wheeled trolleys, American magazines with lurid covers, books that would never be read.

I looked over the heads of my friends, and suddenly, for no reason at all, I remembered the words spoken by the general in the İstanbul War Office many years ago:

"The only way I ever got a horse," he had said, "was by becoming a cavalry officer. . . ."

And I had had to become an Air officer before I could go abroad.

Suddenly Ankara became a thing of poignancy, something one would sentimentalize by reason of distance.

I thought of my grandmother in İstanbul, so far from this busy scene, and I wondered if I should see her again, or had we already, unknowingly, said our goodbye?

I thought of my mother lying outside the fortress walls, of my father and my grandfather. Yes, I remember you and you and you. Dead images clothed in flesh and blood who have walked across the pages of this narrative for your brief moment, your terrible silence mocks the puny, noisy wisdom of the living. You keep your own counsel. Beside you, the figures of me, of Mehmet, busy in a ship's hospital, intent and confident, not needing dreams; of Muazzez, who stands before me now, with her family, an older, harder Muazzez—beside you we dim to nothingness.

We are the restless living, our names are not haloed by nostalgia.

When I think of you who are gone, long-dead dreams rise up again to catch me by the throat on this last evening in Ankara. All the graceful life you represented comes back in full measure to haunt this jaundiced eye, to torture this foolish heart for the things that might have been had Time stood still.

The long line of the Bosporus I see, too, in the mind's eye, which discerns everything so clearly this night, and Kuleli lying under the quiet sky. Far away there is a square white house that will for me burn eternally to a disinterested heaven.

Our train is pulling out of the noisy station.

"Goodbye," we shout. "Goodbye. . . ."

Printed in the United States
140494LV00008B/36/A